TIBETANS IN EXILE

ALSO BY ALAN TWIGG

Full-Time: A Soccer Story
Thompson's Highway: British Columbia's Fur Trade, 1800-1850
Understanding Belize: A Historical Guide
Aboriginality
First Invaders
101 Top Historical Sites of Cuba
Intensive Care: A Memoir
Cuba: A Concise History for Travellers
Twigg's Directory of 1001 BC Writers
Strong Voices: Conversations with 50 Canadian Writers
Vander Zalm, From Immigrant to Premier: A Political Biography
Vancouver and Its Writers
Hubert Evans: The First Ninety-Three Years
For Openers: Conversations with 24 Canadian Writers

TIBETANS IN EXILE

THE DALAI LAMA
& THE WOODCOCKS

ALAN TWIGG

RONSDALE PRESS

RONSDALE PRESS
3350 West 21st Avenue
Vancouver, B.C., Canada V6S 1G7
www.ronsdalepress.com

Typesetting: Get to the Point
Front cover photo credit (top): Michael Buckley. Front cover photo (bottom): Teacher
trainees help build the Munsel-Ling School's hostel and new classroom, 1995.
Cover design: Get to the Point
Paper: Ancient Forest Friendly Silva Enviro (FSC)

Ronsdale Press wishes to thank the Canada Council for the Arts, the Government
of Canada through the Book Publishing Industry Development Program (BPIDP),
and the Province of British Columbia through the Book Publishing Tax Credit
Program and the British Columbia Arts Council.

Library and Archives Canada Cataloguing in Publication

Twigg, Alan, 1952-
        Tibetans in exile : the Dalai Lama & the Woodcocks / Alan Twigg.

Includes bibliographical reference.
ISBN 978-1-55380-079-8

        1. Tibetan Refugee Aid Society--History. 2. Refugees--Tibet. 3. Woodcock,
George, 1912-1995. 4. Woodcock, Ingeborg. 5. Bstan-Î"dzin-rgya-mtsho, Dalai
Lama XIV, 1935-. 6. Humanitarian assistance, Canadian. 7. Tibetan Refugee
Aid Society--Biography.

HV640.5.T5T95 2009   362.87'5760899541   C2009-904122-7

The author wishes to state that TRAS holds no political or religious affiliations and
assists communities only on the basis of humanitarian needs. All contents herein are
strictly the work of the author, who is an independent journalist.

At Ronsdale Press we are committed to protecting the environment. We are working
with Markets Initiative (www.oldgrowthfree.com) and printers to phase out our use
of paper produced from ancient forests. This book is one step towards that goal.

Printed in Canada by Marquis Printing, Quebec

ACKNOWLEDGEMENTS

The author gratefully recognizes the support of the British Columbia Arts Council for its assistance in the research and writing of this book. He also thanks David Lester for his integral design and collaboration, the Writers' Trust for permission to quote from George Woodcock's writing, TRAS and CIVA for permission to quote from their newsletters, Martin Twigg for his typing and patience, Ron Hatch for his vigilance, and everyone who generously gave their time to be interviewed.

Photographs in this book not taken by the author are used by permission of TRAS and/or its members. Others have been separately provided by Linda Bassingthwaighte, Michael Buckley, John Conway, Doane Gregory (formal Dalai Lama portrait), Tenzin Lhalungpa, Sarah McAlpine, Suzanne Martin, Sylvia Rickard, Peggy New, Yukiko Onley and Judy Tethong.

This rare portrait of Ingeborg Woodcock was taken by a studio photographer in Mexico City when the Woodcocks were undertaking research for *To the City of the Dead: An Account of Travels in Mexico* (Faber & Faber, 1957).

To Ingeborg
who knocked

DALAI LAMA, c. 1959–61

"The Dalai Lama was standing just inside
the doorway, a tall young man in fine
woollen robes, with an intelligent, sadly
humorous face. His hair was cut en brosse,
and he wore heavy black-rimmed spectacles. He came forward smiling, took the
scarves ceremoniously, and then shook
hands and led us into the chamber."
— George Woodcock

CONTENTS

▲ Aborted Tibetan revolt 1959   Chinese riot police ▼

FOREWORD

Motivated by their first meeting with the Dalai Lama, George and Ingeborg Woodcock created the Tibetan Refugee Aid Society, or TRAS, in 1962. It was followed by a similar non-profit society, Canada India Village Aid society, or CIVA, derived from their friendship with an Indian philanthropist named Patwant Singh, and formed in 1981.

I have chosen to write a small book about the Dalai Lama, the Woodcocks and their humanitarian work to mark the 50th anniversary of the Tibetan uprising against the occupation of Tibet by Chinese Communist troops, and to recognize the importance of small organizations of unselfish people in contributing to world peace on a grass roots level.

Long before the Internet facilitated fundraising for micro-aid projects, TRAS and CIVA were models for organizations dedicated to empowering people to help themselves. Always taking care to be apolitical, TRAS alone has, since 1962, undertaken more than 300 projects, frequently cooperating with the Canadian International

Development Agency (CIDA). Administrative expenditures, as George Woodcock once proudly noted in the early days, amounted to "only a cent out of every two dollars we received."

George Woodcock was Canada's most prolific and remarkable man of letters. Variously described as "Canada's Tolstoy," "quite possibly the most civilized man in Canada," and "a kind of John Stuart Mill of dedication to intellectual excellence and the cause of human liberty," he arrived from England in 1949 to build a cabin in Sooke, British Columbia, with his German-born wife Ingeborg.

The story of how George Woodcock wrote and edited 150 books has been well told in a 1988 biography by George Fetherling but this biography does not investigate Ingeborg's role in the Woodcocks' highly unusual marriage and the couple's inspirational role in creating two charities that have outlived them both.

I knew the Woodcocks—but not well. I was on their periphery towards the end of their lives. Like most of their friends, I "owe" them. They bequeathed me their no-nonsense car (a Toyota Tercel) and all the signed editions in their extensive library including, most significantly, George's rare, signed first edition of George Orwell's *Animal Farm*. I sometimes keep it under my keyboard as I type. The Woodcocks have disappeared but they definitely have not gone away.

George and Ingeborg Woodcock did not have children, ostensibly by choice, so they adopted strays and cultivated friendships. In doing so, they were both extraordinarily generous and uncannily selective. They cemented loyalties by lending their house to people whenever they went away on their many research trips. Nearly everyone who looked after their cats ended up on the board of directors of either TRAS or CIVA.

Neither was an angel or saint. George could hold a grudge. And, in some respects, Inge could be a bully. Both were secretive. Although they operated their voteless meetings on anarchistic principles, it was their way or the highway. They never suffered fools gladly. They were semi-nocturnal. They drank a lot. They believed in ghosts. And they were *really* interesting people.

George never drove a car and voted only once. Both believed in reincarnation and past lives. Ingeborg fed the raccoons by hand and felt fellowship with rats. They never visited Africa because George once had a dream that he would die there. Their two charities pertaining to India have helped millions of people and they donated nearly $2 million to help Canadian writers via the Writers' Development Trust (renamed The Writers' Trust of Canada).

I hope this modest book about the Woodcocks and their friendship with the Dalai Lama convinces the reader that George and Ingeborg Woodcock are worth celebrating—and that organizations such as TRAS and CIVA, which continue to emulate the Woodcocks' convictions, must be encouraged and supported because they epitomize the essence of Margaret Mead's famous saying: "Never doubt that a small group of thoughtful, committed citizens can change the world. Indeed, it is the only thing that ever has."

When asked to explain how he and his wife came to be involved with the Dalai Lama and Tibetan refugees, George Woodcock explained, "Our Tibetan friends insisted that it was not chance at all, but Karma the appropriate working-out of destiny."

This appropriate working-out of destiny began in the 1930s, in London, when George Woodcock was still very unhappily employed as a railway clerk, having rejected a relative's offer to pay his way through university if he would agree to become an Anglican clergyman.

Proud and poverty-stricken, Woodcock, a would-be poet, quarrelled in print with a new writer named George Orwell (Eric Arthur Blair). This spat proved fortuitous. In an interview conducted one year before he died, George Woodcock told me the details of how he met Orwell, the subject of his biography, *The Crystal Spirit*.

"I got into a disagreement with him over something he'd said about my pacifism in the *Partisan Review* in 1942. In response, in

After his spat with George Orwell, George Woodcock (left) participated in a BBC broadcast to listeners in India on September 8, 1942, accompanied by Indian novelist Mulk Raj Anand, George Orwell, critic William Empson, Herbert Read (seated left) and poet Edmund Blunden (seated right). Mulk Raj Anand turned out to be an important connection when the Woodcocks travelled to India.

the *Partisan Review*, I pointed out that after all he was a former police officer in Burma. He himself had been a pacifist one year before. And so I wrote this down and Orwell wrote a furious reply. Then somehow or other, through an Indian writer named Mulk Raj Anand, he invited me to take part on his India program at the BBC. So I did and we were very formal.

"And then I was getting on a double decker bus on the top deck at Hampstead one day and I saw a familiar crest of hair. It was Orwell. He'd seen me come across the street. He turned and patted the seat beside him so I went up. He said, 'Woodcock, Woodcock, we may have differences on paper but that doesn't mean anything derogatory to our relationship as human beings.' And with that our friendship started. It was the most extraordinary kind of thing."

As the two Georges participated in BBC radio programs, they increasingly rubbed shoulders with expatriate writers from India. These literary associations bore fruit for Woodcock decades later when he and Ingeborg Woodcock travelled to India on a research trip for his book *Faces of India, A Travel Narrative* (London: Faber and Faber, 1964).

In 1961, in Delhi, Woodcock accepted an invitation to be interviewed on All India Radio with India's leading novelist of that era, R.K. Narayan (Rasipuram Krishnaswami Narayan). After that interview in the radio station, Ingeborg Woodcock noticed a sign on a door: TIBETAN SECTION.

As a German-born pacifist who had supported her husband's anarchism during World War II, Ingeborg Woodcock had met some Tibetans in Seattle and started to learn their language. "Ingeborg had been fascinated with Tibet ever since she read Sven Hedin at the age of eight," George Woodcock wrote. "Later—seven years

Dekyi and Lobsang Lhalungpa (1926-2008) became the first Tibetans brought to live in Canada by TRAS after a chance meeting with the Woodcocks in Delhi in 1961. That meeting led them to the Dalai Lama.

before we reached India—she had learnt at an American university [University of Washington, in Seattle] to read and—as she thought—to speak Tibetan."

And so there, in the Delhi radio station, Ingeborg knocked.

Behind that door they met scholar-turned-broadcaster Lobsang Lhalungpa, who introduced them to his wife Dekyi. The friendship of these four people started a chain of events that led the Woodcocks to form the Tibetan Refugee Aid Society.

PART ONE

AND SO, TIBET

The Dalai Lama on his throne

A BRIEF HISTORY OF TRAS & DIDI'S STORY

After Chinese Communist troops punished an abortive uprising of Tibetans in 1959, killing 40,000 Tibetans, His Holiness, the Dalai Lama, and some 80,000 Tibetan followers fled over Himalayan mountain passes to the neighbouring countries of India, Nepal, Bhutan and Sikkim.

George and Ingeborg Woodcock of Vancouver visited the Dalai Lama at Dharamsala, India, in the freezing December cold of 1961. Immediately after, the couple cajoled financial support from private donors, chiefly in British Columbia, to alleviate poverty, illness, malnutrition and lack of education among Tibetans in northern India.

The Tibetan Refugee Aid Society was subsequently incorporated in British Columbia as a non-profit society in 1962. All board members were volunteers. The position of chairman was an honorary one, accorded to the president of the University of British Columbia, Norman MacKenzie.

The executive responsibilities were to be chiefly handled by vice-chairman, George Woodcock, who was a literature lecturer at UBC.

The aims of the society were expressed in a report by George Woodcock and W.L. Holland, as follows:

■ to collect funds for the relief of Tibetan refugees

■ to participate, either independently or in co-operation with other organizations, in active relief or rehabilitation measures for Tibetan refugees

■ to collect and disseminate information regarding Tibetan refugees

The first priority for TRAS was to buy winter clothing for approximately one thousand children in Mussoorie and Dharamsala. In its first year $11,436.61 was collected through membership fees, donations, an art show and Christmas card sales. The key contacts for aid were Mrs. Rinchen Dolma Taring, affectionately known as *Amala* (mother), and the Dalai Lama's younger sister, Pema Gyalpo.

George Woodcock's TRAS manifesto noted that relief efforts were hampered by the fact that the United Nations and India did not recognize the independence of Tibet and consequently the Tibetan status of refugees was "ambiguous and did not officially warrant aid."

The Woodcocks returned to Dharamsala in 1963, and were further galvanized in their idealism by visits to Dr. Florence Haslam's Maple Leaf Hospital below Dharamsala at Kangra, where two young CUSO (Canadian University Services Overseas) workers, Judy Pullen and Lois James, were persevering under conditions as daunting as those encountered in 1961.

George Woodcock became hyper-efficient in his dual capacity as fundraiser and chief expediter of funding, no doubt benefiting from his much-loathed training as a railway clerk in London. While he corresponded with aid workers, funding agencies, government organizations and TRAS supporters, Ingeborg Woodcock managed fundraising by instigating art sales, flea market and rummage sales, handicraft sales and sponsorships of individual children.

George and Ingeborg Woodcock worked unpaid, with ceaseless

RINCHEN DOLMA TARING

After meeting the Woodcocks in 1961, Mrs. Rinchen Dolma Taring became a trusted partner of TRAS for four decades.

Her role in Tibetan refugee relief was fundamental ever since she was ordered by the Dalai Lama to leave her teaching job in Kalimpong, in January of 1960, and travel to Mussoorie. She stayed at Kildare House, a few miles from Mussoorie, at a place called Happy Valley, where she converted a two-storey house into a school for refugees. The Dalai Lama was living in Birla House, in Mussoorie. Mrs. Taring and her husband Jigme lived in one room at Kildare House, a small area portioned off by a curtain.

His Holiness opened Kildare House school, administered by the Tarings, for 50 male students, on March 3, 1960. The students were in rags, and there were no toilet facilities. Relief arrived by providence: when the Dalai Lama's mother had to travel to London for medical treatment, the English-speaking Mrs. Taring was selected to accompany her. In England, Mrs. Taring met Lady Alexandra Metcalfe of the Save the Children Fund, giving rise to the Simla homes for Tibetan children.

While feeding and educating 600 children at Mussoorie, the Tarings were told by the Dalai Lama to establish a series of group homes, with 25 children each, in Mussoorie. The Tibetan Homes Foundation was founded in 1962, eventually housing 625 children in the

Happy Valley area. Mrs. Khando Chazotsang, daughter of the founder of the first Tibetan Children's nursery in Dharamsala, took over management of the Tibetan Homes Foundation in 1975. TRAS continuously supported projects overseen by both Mrs. Taring and Mrs. Chazotsang. Mrs. Taring wrote her autobiography, *Daughter of Tibet* (1970), a rare female view of Tibetan life.

determination, from 1962 to 1970, until George's heart attack in 1971 halted their efforts. UBC history professor John Conway, as the organization's second vice-chairman, worked unpaid from 1971 to 1981. Major funding during this period was obtained from CIDA, the Canadian International Development Agency (first brought on-side as a funding partner in 1970), as well as a little-known B.C. government initiative for agricultural aid to developing countries and the Vancouver Miles for Millions charity walks.

Between its formation in 1962 and the visit of the Dalai Lama, at age forty-five, to Canada in 1980, TRAS raised more than $3 million from Canadian sources for distribution to projects throughout India. The majority of this financial aid was arranged and administered by John Conway, who matched the Woodcocks' industriousness and zeal, while exceeding them in diplomacy and finesse, expanding the funding to the large south Indian Tibetan settlements in Bylakuppe, Kollegal, Hunsur and Mundgod.

With the departure of John Conway, TRAS hired a part-time secretary to handle the paper work, but the tradition of minimal expenditures for administration has persisted, and the volunteer board of directors still does much of the work. To recognize its expanded focus to include large, rural projects for Indian and Nepalese communities, the Society changed its name to Trans-Himalayan Aid Society on May 14, 1990, but has retained its acronym TRAS at the request of local partners.

The number of Canadians inspired to work for TRAS has been legion. Senior patron Dorothea Leach, whose first husband, Barry Leach, was a major force in instigating new projects beyond India, has been with TRAS for

Former TRAS president Joan Ford is a medical doctor who worked in Sir Edmund Hillary's clinics in the Himalayas.

46 years. Patron Joan Ford has been on the TRAS board for over 20 years, as have Directors Frank and Lynn Beck, and Daphne Hales. Their collective knowledge is an invaluable resource. It is complemented by the enthusiasm and new ideas brought by more recent additions: Jennifer Hales, Marion Tipple, Videsh Kapoor, each with TRAS for over a decade, as well as Russil Wvong, Rob Asbeek-Brusse, Shirley Howdle and Cheryl Sullivan.

TRAS continues to support small, locally managed and staffed projects in the Himalayan region. TRAS has never sent Westerners abroad, preferring to work with local partners using local expertise. In recent years the focus has been refined to address "the health and education of children and youth in north India, Tibet and Nepal."

In 2008, TRAS supported the following projects:

■ Vocational training, HIV/AIDs education and infirmary maintenance at Buddha Academy Boarding School for destitute children in Kathmandu, Nepal

■ Construction of healthcare centre, toilet block and greenhouse, implementation of health screening, and creation of health curriculum at Munsel-Ling School, Spiti, northern India

■ Lhasa Yuthok Kindergarten for 60 Tibetan children, Lhasa

■ Dekyiling and Little Flower Crèches for children of Tibetan government workers, teachers and weavers, Dehra Dun and Dharamsala, northern India

■ Nurses' training for 11 young Tibetan women at Indian hospitals

■ Assembly hall construction, nutrition education and provision of teaching materials for nuns, and outreach program to local women and girls, Spiti and Zanskar, northern India

■ Library for school at Choephelling Tibetan Settlement, Miao, a remote border region in northeastern India

Even today there are approximately 800 children coming out of Tibet every year into Kathmandu and Dharamsala. In 2009, TRAS members are directly sponsoring 250 Tibetan, Indian and Nepali children. Until CIDA abruptly closed its Volunteer Sector Fund, no proposal submitted by TRAS to CIDA was ever rejected during the thirty-five-year relationship between the two organizations. Now that the fund is open for business again, it is limiting its funding for all NGOs to projects with a minimum budget of $100,000. This does limit TRAS' access to this fund for much of its work, in spite of its record of unquestionable success and efficiency.

Thousands of people who have benefited from TRAS projects have spread the ripples of altruism further.

Didi is one example.

As a girl in the mountains in eastern Tibet, Didi grew up in a place without roads. There were no cars, no machinery of any kind, other than some antiquated rifles. She lived in the area called Kham, at 14,000 feet above sea level, one of the highest inhabited regions of Tibet and the source of the Mekong River. Her family was nomadic, living in yak-hair tents.

Her grandmother was very religious, saying prayers all day long. Her grandfather was a chieftain who liked to tell her about an event that occurred before she was born. He once met two very strange men, tall and lean, with yellow hair and blue eyes. Didi was fascinated to learn their skin was so white that you could see the veins through it, just like mice babies. Both men were ill and exhausted. Her grandfather took care of them until they recovered.

She did not see an airplane until 1958, when she was nearly nine years old. She recalls she was playing with her toy baby—a rock with lamb's fur tied onto it—when suddenly everyone was screaming. The earth trembled. She looked up and saw a magnificent and frightening silver bird. Inexplicably this apparition was dropping thousands of white feathers from its belly.

Her people naturally picked up these white droppings to examine them. These were propaganda leaflets from the Chinese, forewarning her people of the horrors that awaited them if they did not cooperate and allow the Chinese to gain control of her people's

Didi devotes all her time to fundraising for Tibetan children and elders, working long hours in her booth at Lonsdale Quay, North Vancouver.

traditional lands. The leaflets showed them bloodied bodies and the horrible power of bombs.

Her parents decided they should flee. Buddhist pilgrims had told them about Nepal. They would try to go there. But they did not know the way. The family travelled together until her mother and father could not agree on which direction to go. On her final night with her father, Didi and her older brother slept outside with their father under a star-filled sky. Her father spoke to them about the stars, describing the various constellations, until she fell asleep.

When Didi awoke, her father and brother were gone. In fact they had fled directly into the hands of the Chinese. Her father would remain in Chinese detention camps for almost twenty years, gaining a remarkable education from fellow inmates, many of whom were distinguished scholars and intellectuals. Didi saw him only once more, much later in her life, when he was an old man. During this reunion she told him she had sent her love to the stars every night, in remembrance of their final hours together, and he surprised her by telling her how he had done the same thing in order to reach out to her.

The Chinese detained her father in a labour camp until 1978, along with her great uncle, a doctor. The prisoners existed on one bowl of rice and one cup of tea. Each morning they were loaded onto a truck and forced to spread buckets of raw sewage onto the rice fields.

Didi's father told her he was grateful to the Chinese because, having previously lived as a wealthy man, they had taught him about poverty. This knowledge had brought him back to Buddhism. He returned to the family land to live with his son who had not been held in the same camp, but instead lived with a family as their labourer. The son had married and had five children. Didi's father was happy leading a simple life, spinning wool and playing with his grandchildren, but he would never again touch rice.

After Didi's father's flight, her mother, who was pregnant, courageously led Didi, her younger sister, her cousin, her grandmother and other Tibetans towards the remote Mustang region, hoping to find the traditional pilgrim route into Nepal. By a marvellous stroke of good fortune, their group crossed paths with Didi's eleven-year-old brother, who was a monk-in-training at the Sera Monastery. He joined them.

After several weeks, the travellers optimistically decided they had reached Nepal. The youngsters fired the group's old (possibly British) rifles in celebration and shouted with joy. But they were near an army camp, still well inside Tibet. When Chinese troops approached to investigate, Didi's mother grabbed two of the horses, snatched up her four-year-old child, and they all fled on horseback, leaving behind most of their possessions. In their haste, they lost their way.

Didi's mother, who was seven months pregnant, became very ill and the baby died inside her. Didi and the others were somehow able to carry her mother into Mustang territory, a forbidding geographical buffer zone between Lhasa and Khatmandu. But Didi's problems were far from over.

The older brother of Didi's grandmother had already reached Mustang. He was an important lama, the Sapchu Rimpoche, so the King of Mustang permitted the Sapchu Rimpoche to stay in his castle near the border of Tibet and Mustang. The rest of the family were given tents to live in the castle grounds. The Sapchu Rimpoche instructed Didi to become a nun, so her head was shaved.

The following morning, after her head was shaved, Didi was taken to her grandmother. They went to a big tent where two rows of monks were chanting. There were about twenty monks and her lama uncle was seated on a throne. Usually monks smiled at her and some gave her candies, but on this day some of the monks were crying. In front of the throne was a large pile of mud.

Didi understood. Her mother had died. She was buried under the mud. Didi ran from the tent. She wandered all day in the forest, crying and screaming. Daphne Hales has described what happened next in the TRAS newsletter:

"In Tibet, the soul of the deceased is thought to stay in limbo for three days, then it goes into a state called 'bardo,' a kind of purgatory. If the soul can find its way within 48 days, it is reborn. During the bardo, the lamas and family call to the departed not to be afraid, but to follow the light. The lamas and family pray to help the departed on her way to rebirth and they burn barley powder and butter. It is therefore very important to have close family members present from the third day onward, to help the departed."

Didi went to the barley and butter fires to talk to her mother. By a stroke of good fortune, her powerful grandfather arrived at the outset of the bardo. He was a great soldier who had recently gone to Lhasa to help plan the Dalai Lama's escape, then he had left Tibet himself, first going to Assam before coming to Mustang—only to discover his daughter had just died.

Didi's grandfather took charge of Didi, her brother and her sister. Didi's brother was sent to further his training as a monk in Dalhousie, at the "British Cabin," with other young monks. To finance this education, Didi's grandfather sold his wife's jewelry, including a silver belt with turquoise and coral ornaments. Didi's four-year-old sister was sent to live in Dehra Dun, in northern India, with an aunt.

Didi remained in Mustang for a year with her grandparents. Her grandfather bought some donkeys and became a trader, assisted by a young man who had accompanied him from Tibet. He purchased trinkets and other trade items in Nepal, then sold them to herdsmen and villagers in Mustang, bringing back wool and butter. Didi was mainly occupied with caring for her grief-stricken grandmother who was grieving the death of Didi's mother.

Didi remembers the first time she earned any money. Having received permission to go on a picnic with a friend, Didi followed her friend's example and spent the day picking some leaves. These leaves were rolled and sold to some men. When Didi received a five-rupee note, she was delighted. But when she proudly displayed her money to her grandfather, he was and angry and tore up the five-rupee note. Unknowingly, she had been harvesting marijuana.

After a year in Mustang, Didi and her maternal grandmother were told they were moving to Kathmandu. There the Sapchu Rimpoche would accept a position at the nearby monkey temple and her grandfather could more effectively work as a trader. She carefully led the horse that carried her frail grandmother along the rough trails but her grandmother fell and broke a rib. Eventually they reached Kathmandu, where Didi became seriously ill with chicken pox. She willed herself to get better because she knew she must look after her grandmother.

"Reaching Nepal," she says, "was like entering a totally other planet. We had never read about or seen pictures of the rest of the world. If it hadn't been for groups like TRAS, I would have died. The western helpers brought medications as well as food and shelter for us, and now I see how they did it—through selling beads and garage sales."

In exile in Nepal, Didi learned that the government in India was creating wonderful settlements for Tibetan refugees, but that it would not be easy to get there. She and her grandmother ended up at a train station in India, where everyone was segregated into three groups: the children, the middle-aged and the elderly, before being taken to refugee camps. In order not to be separated like the rest, Didi managed to hide beneath her grandmother's skirts. Her grandmother hobbled strangely, with Didi concealed under her. Vultures were flying constantly overhead and many people died. Didi cannot forget the day a vulture dropped a piece of flesh nearby her. She went to look at it. It was a baby's hand.

Traumatized, Didi lived in India for more than ten years before she eventually made her way to Canada, first to Toronto, then to Vancouver, where she has raised three children. She attended the 40th anniversary gathering to celebrate TRAS in 2002.

"When I saw a slide show of TRAS's history," she wrote afterwards, "I was filled with joy. The story of the early days of TRAS gives me courage. Since that evening I have had the confidence to start working to help the elderly people in my home town [in Tibet]. That slide show was my life. That was me, especially crossing the border. To see those slides of the crossing, the refugee camps, the early schools and then nurses training—that was exactly my life—and then seeing myself here in Canada now!—brought back a lot of emotions.

"I learned there is a history of how one or two people can help. Hearing about Inge making beads and running garage sales showed me that a few people doing little things can help so many needy people.

"There is still a lot of pain to work out. The pain is still happening to those coming out of Tibet now. They are lucky in a way, because there are Tibetans to greet them, but there is a lot of poverty and they need help.

"The slide show completed the circle for me because I learned the story of my life from the other point of view, that of the many westerners who reached out to help us. I am the fruit of that help. My joy, my gratitude, is immense for all who helped my people. At the dinner, I wanted to hug everyone. We were desperate, emotionally as well as financially, coming to a strange land with nothing, meeting new diseases. I would have died—I was in a coma—if it hadn't been for groups like TRAS. And it wasn't just me. You have helped thousands of us. Your generosity wasn't wasted!

"I have rented a stall in a Chinatown market and have created Christmas cards with Tibetan pictures and photos of the old people and they are selling well. This has led to another healing experience. People have asked me how I, a Tibetan, can go to Chinatown, but being in close proximity to the Chinese at the market has made me realize that they are ordinary, caring human beings, just like me. They are compassionate and supportive."

Initially, after she rented her stall in Chinatown—the only place she could afford—Didi could not bring herself to go there. After some difficult procrastination, she went and sat with her cards. A beautiful Chinese woman, obviously well-to-do, "with purple hair," came to examine her cards. Didi began to tell her story to this woman, whose curiosity was genuine. Soon the Chinese matron had tears flowing down her cheeks. She asked Didi, "How much money are you trying to raise?" Didi replied that her goal was to raise twenty thousand dollars. The Chinese woman wrote Didi a cheque for $20,000.

Didi now lives in Vancouver and spends long hours, seven days a week, minding her new stall of Tibetan products at the Lonsdale Quay in North Vancouver. TRAS has allocated funding to "Didi-la's Old People" project to provide much-needed stoves with chimneys to an impoverished old people's home. She also arranges for individual sponsorship of children in the region.

TIBET

LADAKH

Dharamsala • • Tashi Jong

NEPAL

BHUTAN

Simla •

SIKKIM

Puruwala • • Mussoorie

• Delhi

• Tezu

Darjeeling • • Kalimpong

INDIA

BANGLADESH

• Bhandara

Chandragiri •

• Mundgod

Bangalore

Bylakuppe • • Hunsur

Cauvery
Valley   Kollegal

Locations of some of the
early TRAS projects*

*Up to 1980

A DETOUR TO DESTINY

The story of how the Woodcocks met the Dalai Lama in 1961 has been told by George Woodcock in his somewhat misleadingly titled *Faces of India*. The title of this travelogue refers to the three faces of Siva at Elephanta, representing creation, preservation and destruction.

Published in 1964, George Woodcock's memoir of India specifically states that they set off for India with every intention of finding Tibetan refugees. It also makes clear it was Ingeborg's interest in Tibet, and her facility with languages, that chiefly propelled them to meet the Dalai Lama. At considerable length, he vividly describes how their visit to Mussoorie, one of the hill stations nearest to Delhi, resulted in their detour to Dharamsala in the winter of 1961–62.

When the Woodcocks first came upon some Tibetan refugees in the streets of Delhi, Ingeborg's attempts to communicate with them proved incomprehensible and frustrating. But at All India Radio, after George Woodcock participated in a radio broadcast, they met a man "with a Mongol face and a slightly ruddy complexion," dressed in Western clothes. This was Lobsang Lhalungpa, a former member of the Dalai Lama's secretariat in the high towers of the Potala, in Lhasa. He had left Tibet on a diplomatic mission thirteen years earlier, having correctly foreseen the oppression of the Chinese upon their early incursions in 1949.

Lobsang Lhalungpa spoke English with only a slight accent. In India, he was dedicating his life to preserving the ancient wisdom and culture of his people. Having lived in the Indian border towns of Darjeeling and Kalimpong, Lobsang Lhalungpa had associated with Western scholars and published several books. He invited the Woodcocks to meet his wife Dekyi who, according to George Woodcock, "had the kind of ivory beauty, set off by jet-black hair, which characterizes the aristocratic women of Tibet." Always keen to return hospitality, the Woodcocks would soon afterwards sponsor the Lhalungpas to immigrate to Canada.

The two couples socialized in Delhi where Lobsang played his recordings of Tibetan music; he also found Ingeborg a Tibetan language tutor, a thin young man named Nyawang Lungtok, whose name means Castle of Meditation. "He had a bony, wizened face that in repose looked sorrowful and old," George wrote, "but when he smiled [it] became suddenly radiant and young." Much impressed by the translator's elaborate Tibetan courtesies, the Woodcocks mirrored his displays of bowing and salaaming whenever they met. Although he was obviously very poor, Nyawang refused to accept any payments for Ingeborg's two-hour sessions beyond "his meticulously calculated taxi fare to the other side of Delhi" from their hotel.

This man, who would later become headmaster of a refugee school in northern India, had attended one of the monastic schools in Lhasa. Trained in calligraphy, learned in classics and religion, Nyawang had been one of the Dalai Lama's personal attendants when His Holiness took flight in March 1959 on his secret trek over the mountains to Assam. He was anxiously awaiting some news of his wife and children who had been imprisoned by the Communists.

THE FOUR SECTS OF BUDDHISM

There are four sects of Tibetan Buddhism. In theory, these sects do not challenge one another. The current Dalai Lama and the majority of Tibetans belong to *Gelukpa*, a sect derived from a great religious reformer named Tsongkhapa, whose disciple Gedum Drup became the first Dalai Lama. *Nyingmapa* ("old") follows the teachings of Padmasambhawa. *Kargyupa* is derived from the sect of Marpa, a great teacher and translator. *Sakyapa*, or *Sakya*, is derived from the "gracious teacher" of Tibet, the translator Sakya Panchen. The Dalai Lama studies the texts of all four sects, and all sects maintain the belief that the Dalai Lama is the reincarnation of Chenrezig, Lord of Compassion, "the karmic deity of the Land of Snow," but the Dalai Lama's *Gelukpa* sect is generally considered to represent the state religion. The conjunction of institutions generally known in the West as church and state have been in place in Tibet since the fifth Dalai Lama became the official head of the Tibetan government in 1642.

"Until we met Nyawang," George Woodcock wrote, "we had seen the tragedy of Tibet as something distant, a stylised pattern of events taking places on a remote tableland where the world's last mediaeval civilization foundered under the onslaught of modern politics in its most ruthless form. Like everything connected with the Tibet of the past, even its fall took on in the imagination the emblematic form of a faraway legend."

This connection with Nyawang, and the dignified sorrow he felt for his missing family, stirred the Woodcocks' sympathies. He spoke nostalgically of springtime picnics, Buddhist festivals, yak meat, buttered tea and "great coloured processions."

The Woodcocks' affinity for the oppressed minority, the persecuted underdog as prisoner of the state, was clear in George's prose. "Tibet had once been a land without famine where even the poor never starved; now food was scarce, consumed by the locusts of invasion."

Sensing the sincerity of the Woodcocks' curiosity in his people, Nyawang Lungtok arranged for the Woodcocks to have an appointment for tea with the Dalai Lama's representatives in Delhi. After an interminable taxi ride, the Woodcocks found themselves in a suburban house in the far south of Delhi, invited into a semi-monastic enclave where Tibetans dressed in Hawaiian shirts and turtleneck sweaters, and had English high tea.

They met the Dalai Lama's head of foreign affairs and the education minister, who was a tall, rugged-faced man named Kundeling, who urged them to visit the nearest of the residential schools for Tibetan refugee children, at Mussoorie, in Uttar Pradesh. He also suggested they might like to visit a remote mountain village above the Kangra Valley, the place where the Dalai Lama lived, called Dharamsala. But George Woodcock was reluctant to go there.

"We had already decided to visit Mussoorie," he wrote, "but I had firmly made up my mind that from there we must go on to Chandigarh, the city Le Corbusier designed as the new capital of the Punjab, and also to Amritsar, the sacred city of the Sikhs, with

Funding for Mussoorie Central Home has been provided by TRAS since 1963.

its golden temple. I was reluctant to abandon them for a trip to a
distant village in the mountains on the uncertain chance that the
Dalai Lama might be willing to see us. Inge was eager to take the
chance; even the slightest possibility of meeting and talking to the
Dalai Lama seemed to her worth the effort."

Ingeborg Woodcock persuaded her husband to take the uncertain chance. She succeeded, as he recalled, in "melting my obsti-
nacy."

The story of their journey to Mussoorie and then on to Kangra
and Dharamsala is best told in George's own words, enabling us to
view the situation of the Tibetans at an early stage in their exile and
also how it was that the Woodcocks came to found TRAS, the first
of their altruistic offspring.

Soon we saw houses of Mussoorie, strung out along the highest ridge, six thousand feet above the valley, like the fragments of a broken ivory necklace scattered on the blue-green velvet of the distance. There were still twenty miles to travel, and the road toiled in loops into the hills, every curve seeming sharper than the last. . . .

Like most Himalayan hill stations, Mussoorie has remained obstinately pre-mechanical in its transport; its streets and lanes are closed not only to automobiles, but even to riding horses. The buses and trucks stopped at a depot below the town, from which the goods were taken by porters who carried immense piles of trunks and boxes supported by headbands.

As we got down from the bus the rickshaw men crowded round us, and before we were fully aware of it we had hired a massive, carriage-built vehicle with brass lamps and a monstrous black hood in which four men proposed to push us up and down the hilly road to the hotel, which we learnt with some perturbation was four miles away, almost at the western end of the Mussoorie ridge. No sooner was the deal concluded than our repugnance at the thought of being pushed around by human labour rose up again, and we stood there in hesitation.

"There's nothing else. You'll have to take a rickshaw." A horsefaced Englishwoman in tweeds stood imperiously before us. "Don't worry about them," she shouted. "They don't care. Glad to get a meal out of season."

We looked at the four skinny little men in their flower-pot shaped Nepali caps, waiting barefooted before us in thin pyjama trousers. We did not have the heart to disappoint them by walking off with a single porter. So I signed to them to load the baggage into the rickshaw; we would tramp behind.

The Englishwoman raised her eyebrows, turned away, and whinnied to her friends. An Indian clerk smirked. We were obviously being most eccentric. But in fact we had made the more comfortable choice, for the sunlight had already abandoned many stretches of the road to the hotel and the chill of a November Himalayan night was settling in; except that the change in altitude at first made us a little breathless, we enjoyed tramping along at the sharp pace of the trotting rickshaw coolies. . . .

The narrow road ran through bazaars of open-fronted Indian booths, and down sloping streets of shops that looked as English as those of a town in Surrey except that the proprietors standing in the doorways were jovial, black-bearded Sikhs. Sometimes the mountainside steepened so that the road hung between the bluff above and the precipice beneath, and in some places the rocks were splashed golden with marigold, pink with wild cosmos, or over-hung with the mauve blossoms of tree dahlias that clustered on the ledges wherever a little earth gave them sustenance. On the slopes above and below the road, among deodars and giant rhododen-drons, lay the boarding-houses and villas and Norman-towered churches left from the British past.

The hotel was one of the town's most gallant monuments to that era. A turreted Balmoral in white stucco, it stood on its own flat-tened hilltop, with a great double view, to the south of the plains and to the north of the dark shadowy valleys. Our arrival created a small stir, for the season in Mussoorie ends in October, and visitors are rare in November.

The manager, a square-built Sikh in an orange turban, came out to welcome us personally, and we set off in a little procession, with the Anglo-Indian clerk and the Gurkha bearer, all wrapped to the ears in scarves, followed by the four rickshaw men humping our luggage on their shoulders. Only an annex was open. "We have a mere three guests," remarked the manager apologetically.

The view was magnificent, straight out to Nanda Devi and its attendant range, already turning peach pink in the evening glow, but the two rooms of the little suite into which the manager showed us were grimy and dank. "Have you nothing better?" Inge asked.

"You shall have the suite for princes," declared the Sikh in his rich, plumcake voice. "It is in the main part of the hotel, which is now closed, but we shall open it in your honour. The hotel is yours." He bowed like a hidalgo, and off we marched, across the tennis court, into the hall that sprouted with antlers and up the stairs decorated with "The Stag at Bay" and "The Monarch of the Glen."

"It is a historic suite that I offer you," said the manager as we filed through the three enormous rooms, each large enough for a modest banquet, with their high coffered ceilings and deep-cut window embrasures which revealed the fortress-thickness of the walls. The bed was a vast carved structure of a bog oak; above it hung "The Soldier's Return."

"It is a historic suite," repeated the Sikh, gently patting his well-coiled beard. "In these very rooms stayed His Holiness the Dalai Lama when he came to Mussoorie for the first time in 1954."

He waited to see the effect of his statement; Inge's eyes lit up, and I suspected that she regarded it as an omen. "At the same time," the manager continued, "came the Panchen Lama. He was in the suite on the other side of the landing. A grave responsibility was laid upon me."

He went on to describe, with many flourishes and embellishments, how he had been responsible for seeing that the two dignitaries were treated with scrupulous equality so that there was no suggestion of precedence being granted to either of them. He energetically mimed out the whole procedure, how he had stationed men at each door, so that they could knock simultaneously at his signal, and how he led the two Holinesses down the stairs in such a way that neither entered the dining-room an inch before the other. "I flatter myself that I gave general satisfaction. Tomorrow I bring you newspaper cuttings." And, filled with the emotion of his recollections, he bowed himself out and departed.

That first night at Mussoorie we learnt how cold, even at the beginning of winter, the Himalayan foothills can be. . . . Yet despite the cold and the hard bed and the monotonous diet, with mutton curry for every lunch and tough chicken for every dinner,

I liked the hotel. It had the melancholy charm that descends on holiday places when the end of the season leaves them deserted, when a deliquescent autumnal silence pervades the courtyards and the leaf-dank gardens where late tea roses bloom, and when the coming of the new guest who arrives after oneself is an event fraught with romantic curiosity.

The Tibetan school lay three or four miles back in the foothills from Mussoorie. . . . Eventually we left the main road and turned westward along a rocky track that dipped down past a tall balconied house from which a fat, goitred man in purple brocade trousers looked down silently at us. A Tibetan girl in a long-skirted dress came along a path through the bushes with a red-cheeked child on her back and a flowered milk jug in her hand. In answer to Inge's question she nodded shyly that we should follow her, and we went on to another hillside on which stood two large wooden houses.

The voices of children sounded from the field below as we climbed to the second house, on the top of the hill. Long prayer flags blew out in the wind from tall poles that had been erected beside it, and on the verandah waited a middle-aged Tibetan woman with a sad, benevolent face. She spoke to us in slow, precise English, and introduced herself as Mrs. Taring, the wife of the principal.

We handed her Kundeling's letter of introduction, and she led us upstairs to a room where a group of people were sitting around a table laden with teacups—a Tibetan in a Harris tweed jacket, a hearty-looking American woman missionary, and a slender, talkative girl in a long dress of purple silk and a white cambric blouse that set off her dark, amused eyes and rosy freshness of complexion.

The girl with the amused eyes was introduced to us as Khando Yapshi. The man in the tweed jacket was Jigme Taring, the principal of the school. As a young man, full of fresh vitality, Jigme Taring figures in more than one book on travels in the Tibet of the late 'thirties, for, when he was a high official in the Dalai Lama's court and a general of the bodyguard, he was noted for his hospitality to the rare English who visited Lhasa. Now he had become a careworn exile, with a lined sallow face and a quiet, melancholy voice.

We sat and talked of the problem of the four hundred Tibetan refugee children whom the Tarings were trying, with a minimum of money and help, to bring up in a world so different from the mediaeval land they had left behind them—left behind in time as well as in space, for it is no longer on the map of the real world. The girl in purple silk entered animatedly into the conversation, and finally she said to us, "You must come to Dharamsala! You must absolutely come and see Uncle! He will be happy to meet people who are so interested in Tibet."

"But who is your uncle?" asked Inge, somewhat perplexed.

They all looked at us in surprise.

"But of course," said the woman missionary. "How could you be expected to know? Khando is the Dalai Lama's niece."

Khando went on talking persuasively. "We will send Uncle's car to meet you in Pathankot. That is the end of the railway, and we are seventy miles away. Please do come! The car will be there. I shall not forget."

Now it was the noon mealtime at the school, and Mrs. Taring led us up to the trodden hilltop under the prayer flags where the children were sitting with their hands together and chanting in shrill voices one of the monotonous Buddhist prayers. As they sang I watched them. They were

Refugees from Bhutan, at Dekyiling

"You absolutely must come and see Uncle," said Khando Yapshi,
who turned out to be the Dalai Lama's 17-year-old niece.
This photo of her was taken by Ingeborg Woodcock.

of all ages, from eight to eighteen, girls and boys, with black, straight hair and complexions that varied from ivory to copper-brown. Some of them wore Tibetan cloth gowns, and others cast-off Western clothes, but all of them were shabby and ragged, and many had no shoes. They were sturdy children, for the Tibetans are generally a rather big-boned mountain people, but they did not look well fed. And indeed they were not, for when the prayer was over servant women began to walk among the children with buckets—first of all buckets of soup which they ladled into the children's bowls. We went and looked at it; a few bits of vegetable floated in the almost clear water. The next series of buckets were filled with what the Tibetans called *momos*, a kind of steamed dumpling of mixed wheat and corn flour; there was nothing to accompany the *momos* or to give them flavour, but each child wolfed down hungrily the two that were given to him. The meal ended with weak tea. There was no meat, no milk, no fat, no fruit. The wonder was that the children still seemed to possess such stoical good-humour; their open and usually smiling faces made one understand the almost extravagant liking that every traveller who goes among the Tibetans seems to conceive for them.

On our other days in Mussoorie, Jigme Taring and his wife, whose Tibetan name was Rinchen Dolma, showed us the other activities of their school, which the Dalai Lama had founded in 1960 when he became concerned with the problem of homeless refugee children. We would go in the middle of the morning when the children were taking their lessons, squatting in groups among the ragged old gardens where the volunteer teachers did their best to instruct with a few old schoolbooks that were carefully preserved and passed from hand to hand. For the children themselves there were no books at all, and they wrote on wooden boards, shaped like mediaeval hornbooks, using bamboo pens and an ink made from charred wheat grains. The teachers were as untrained as their materials were makeshift; they consisted of an American missionary, two young English pacifists, and a handful of older Tibetan boys who had gone to the Literary Institute in Lucknow for a few months' training. The tall young son of a former Prime Minister of Tibet was leading the younger children in a monotonous repetition of English vowel sounds. A round-faced grinning lama was showing a group of boys how to write the Tibetan cursive script. And the missionary's wife was instructing a class of girls in hygiene; as she drew fleas, bugs and lice on the blackboard the girls scratched themselves and giggled, and a monitor standing behind the class tapped their heads in the traditional Tibetan schoolroom manner with a long bamboo switch.

The mornings were warm and sunny, and the whole scene of the great neglected garden with the groups of children sitting under the trees and the voices of teachers and students lecturing and chanting was charming and, at least in appearance, idyllic. But the open-air classes took place mostly because there was no room to teach the children under cover. Mrs. Taring led us into the two houses and showed us the rough wooden bunks stacked twenty and thirty in a room, with bags of straw on the floor for those who could not sleep above. She took us behind the building and showed us the taps which the cooks had to share with the three hundred boys who washed at them every day. She looked anxiously at the scene on the hillside. "What it will be like next month when the snows come, and the children still have nowhere to take their classes, we do not know. . . ."

On the day we left Mussoorie the clouds moved down over the long ridge, and autumn was suddenly transformed into winter, for within their crepuscular folds the temperature failed to rise very far above its nocturnal level, except on the rare occasions when a gap of light was suddenly torn in the fabric of the clouds and the sun illumined, never for longer than a few minutes, a small patch of the mountainside. . . . The manager of the hotel, who had become extremely attentive as soon as he learnt that I was intending to write a book on my impressions of India, insisted on accompanying us. "You will find His Holiness an A-one gentleman," he re-

An advanced class in Mussoorie. Photo by Ingeborg Woodcock

marked as we walked down. "God bless you. I value your friendship!" he said, shaking hands and bowing at the step of the bus.

And then, having satisfied the claims of Western politeness, he paid tribute to his own double world by raising his hands before his face in the namaste gesture, and saying, in his richest baritone, "Come back to Mussoorie! My hotel is your home!" He still stood there, waving, as the bus started down the sharp quick curves into the warmth of lower lands and into the twilight through which the lights of Dehra Dun began to glitter in the plain below like the gold in a Benares sari. . . .

By the time we reached the junction of Jullundar, we were already three hours late; when the train finally emerged from the low scrubby hills before Pathankot and we saw the white snowfields of the mountains bordering on Kashmir, we were almost four hours late. We hardly expected the car which Khando had promised would still be waiting, and as we walked along the platform behind our coolie we were wondering where we would be able to stay in in this rough little frontier town.

But then we saw a young Tibetan monk trotting along the platform, stopping the two or three European passengers who were walking in front of us. He finally came to us and opened a little slip of paper. "Woodkuk?" he said. "Woodkuk?"

We followed him into the station yard and found that the car was still there, with the Dalai Lama's flag of state discreetly covered. The Indian chauffeur smiled gently at us and salaamed, unconcerned with his long wait; in this remote region time was evidently even less of a commodity than it had appeared to be in Bombay or Delhi. . . .

Our route lay along the Kangra valley, running up into the western hills, and here the links with the modern world became even more tenuous. We drove through villages of wooden-fronted Himalayan houses, and past massive Rajput forts perched on the mountain bluffs.

The pale-skinned women of the valley were barbarically magnificent; they wore full crimson skirts and shining necklaces of silver coins, massive gold earrings and large jewelled nose-rings like those in the old Kangra paintings. Heavily moustached shepherds tended their flocks in the meadows by the road, like Byronic bandits in their thick white tunics which were belted at the waist and jutted out beneath in a kind of short pleated kilt. The season, it turned out, was locally regarded as auspicious for weddings, and we met several parties of men bearing red-curtained palanquins that carried the brides back to their husband to the shrill music of clarinet-mouthed marriage flutes. In the flatter parts of the valley the dark banks of rice paddies lay like a black net over the green fields, but soon we entered a country of moraines, spattered with great mossy boulders and broken by little romantic valleys down which the white, turbulent streams flowed from the wooded hills.

It was seventy miles to Dharamsala, which is an old military cantonment, dating from the 1840s when the British took over this region from the Sikhs, who in their turn had seized it from the Rajput chieftains. Later, Dharamsala became a minor hill station where the families of British officials in the Punjab would move during the summer. The lower town, five thousand feet up, is now a settlement of Punjabis inhabiting the shell of the old British community, with its bungalows, churches and administrative buildings still intact. Upper Dharamsala, where the Dalai Lama and many of the Tibetan exiles live, is almost another two thousand feet higher.

At the end of the long serpentine road through the rain forests of conifers and rhododendron we entered a setting that in the falling twilight seemed magically different from the prosaic little town in the valley. The place at the end of the mountain road was incongruously named McLeod Bazaar; it was a settlement of brown wooden houses which had been entirely taken over by Tibetan refugees. The driver stopped the car under one of the great old deodars that overshadowed the bazaar and went off to find where he should take us.

We sat there, inside the car, as the darkness fell like a curtain from the branches overhead and enclosed us from the scene before our eyes. The house opposite to us bore a roughly painted sign— Tibetan Restaurant—in both English and in the bold beautiful characters of Tibetan; from its door hung a yak-wool curtain, stiff with grease, which men with strange winged hats lifted up as they went into the dim, candle-lit interior. The letters of the sign faded out as women in the stalls began to light their hanging oil lamps to illuminate piles of vegetables and black lumps of brick tea. And in the growing darkness the long-gowned people padded about softly in their felt boots, and came to peer into the car and touch the doors with gentle cat-taps, so that we felt like caged beasts that some hunter brought into a remote mountain market.

After a wait that seemed interminable the driver came back with two young men in black Tibetan coats and high leather boots. They looked at us, at the car, at our luggage, and then went away. A quarter of an hour later a young Tibetan in sports coat and flannels looked in through the window. "A messenger has been sent," he said in perfect English, and then vanished along a path up the mountainside.

It was now completely dark, and as we sat waiting for these incomprehensible Tibetan arrangements to work themselves out we wondered whether it would not be wiser even now to return to the bungalow in the valley. At last the driver came back again. We were to stay in the Nursery which Khando's mother—the Dalai Lama's sister, Mrs. Tsering Dolma—had established in a group of old bungalows called Egerton Hall.

The driver edged the car for a short distance along a rough, narrow track that hugged the mountain; on one side the lights revealed rocks and on the other only darkness. Then we got out of the car and began to scramble in the pitch darkness over wet mossy stones, forming a chain of hands with the driver as leader. In our light sandals we tripped and floundered up the steep, slippery mountainside, until we saw a faint light jogging down the path towards us. It was one of the Tibetan servants from the Nursery, carrying a storm lantern. When he reached us we realised that we had been stumbling on the very edge of a precipitous cliffside. . . .

The next morning we were awakened at dawn by the monotonous chanting of prayers from the rooms of the Nursery, followed by the noise of the children gathering to eat their breakfast on the ground beneath our window. I looked out and watched them. It was *momos* and tea once again. And the general routine at the Nursery was not very much different from that at the refugee school in Mussoorie. There were the three young English volunteers—Valerie, the handsome pacifist nurse, Diana, the sharp-tongued teacher who had come back nostalgically to the India of her birth, and Michael, the young journalist who had come for a day to write a story and had been so moved that he had stayed for two months to work with the Tibetans. There were the Tibetan monks monotonously chanting words and sentences which their classes repeated by rote.

And once again everything took place out of doors because there was no room inside the crowded buildings. Yet there was a feeling here of being much closer to Tibet than we had experienced in Mussoorie. Partly this was because the land was wilder and the most distant peaks that we saw through the gaps of the nearer ranges were in Tibet itself, while the mountains we had seen from Mussoorie were in Nepal. And partly it was because the children still wore Tibetan dress, as did most of the teachers. But what made one most conscious of the nearness of Tibet and of its tragedy was the presence of the suppliants, the peasants in long dirty coats and high felt boots who came in the middle of the morning to plead with Mrs. Tsering Dolma on behalf of their children.

Mrs. Tsering Dolma arrived with Khando just after we had finished our breakfast with the Tibetan teachers and the English volunteers. She was a grave, proud woman, with a broad, rosy-cheeked face and thick black hair which she wore in long plaits; she retained the Tibetan costume, the woman's dress with its skirts sweeping the ground and the striped apron, but she had abandoned, as all the Tibetan women in exile have done, the elaborate headdresses, encrusted with coral and turquoises, which all the noblewomen had worn in Lhasa.

But Mrs. Tsering Dolma was a woman of compassion as well as pride. We realised this when we walked around the Nursery with her and watched her receiving the people who had come with their children. There was one man with a deeply lined face and almost white hair, who looked sixty, though he was only forty; he had four children with him, and as he bowed low before Mrs. Tsering Dolma and pleaded with her to take his children into the Nursery, the tears ran down his cheeks and hung glistening in the wrinkles. His wife was one of those who had died on the way out over the high passes. A man and a woman, in stained, ragged clothes, came with two children; they were working on the roads of the Punjab at a rupee a day each and they could not look after their children properly in the road camps where dysentery was rife. A thin, ragged Khamba man in a wolfskin cap had come a thousand miles from Darjeeling with a tiny girl a year old whom he carried on his back; her mother was dead, and he feared that he too would die and the child would be left without care.

All these people had come recently over the border from Tibet into India, for there was still a steady stream of refugees fleeing from the Chinese terror. Mrs. Tsering Dolma listened silently to their stories, quietly asked a few questions, and never refused to take their children. On that day alone she added eight to her already overcrowded Nursery. It was not only the children on whom she took pity. A tall, thin old man in polished boots and a coat that had obviously been splendid in its day, bowed and put out his tongue to us. "I remember him from Lhasa," Khando said. "He was a servant of the Thirteenth Dalai Lama, and now he has nothing. Mother is going to let him stay here and do what he can for his keep."

"Uncle would like to see you this afternoon," said Khando when she came to the Nursery after breakfast the next morning; it was in this almost casual way that our meeting with the last Buddhist ruler of Tibet, the Fourteenth Dalai Lama, was arranged. After lunch an elderly man in a corduroy robe with long sleeves hanging below his hands, and with a woolen cap framing his long, sensitive, aristocratic face, came to our room, accompanied by the young man who had looked so fleetingly into the car on our first evening at the McLeod Bazaar. The young man introduced himself as Thondop Kyibuk, otherwise known, even to the Tibetans, by the less Swiftian name of Ben. He told us he would be our interpreter that afternoon, and introduced the older man as Phala Thubten Wonden, a member of the formerly powerful Tibetan council of ministers called the Kashag. Phala intended to accompany us to the Dalai Lama's residence.

The polite formalities were exchanged and translated, and then we set off with Khando and our new acquaintances through the woods of deodar and glossy-leaved evergreens. The smell of resin was thick and fragrant in the afternoon sunlight, and small white rhododendrons were already in bloom.

Here and there among the trees we began to see the roofs of scattered bungalows. Khando identified them one by one, and we realised that the whole mountainside had become a kind of shadow capital for a ruler whom no government recognised. At last we saw the green lines of prayer flags fluttering among the trees, and then the red roofs of the Palace and, on the other side of the valley, those of the house inhabited by the Kashag.

The Palace was merely the largest of the bungalows on the mountain. A Sikh sentry stood on guard outside the compound, and an Indian secret service man came out of a little hut to examine and register our passports. The Indians clearly had no intention of allowing the Dalai Lama to share the fate of Trotsky. Khando and her mother had their own apartment in the Palace, for customs had changed since the days of Lhasa, when no woman was allowed within the Potala, and there we waited until Ben came to tell us that His Holiness was ready to receive us. We walked on to the wide verandah in front of the bungalow, with its great view plunging down over the forests to the white river in the valley. Lamas in maroon robes and noblemen in silk gowns waited outside the audience chamber. They bowed in greeting. By the door stood a gigantic monk, almost seven feet high; he was the Dalai Lama's personal bodyguard.

Well-schooled beforehand, we flicked open our rolled scarves as we went into the chamber, and offered them on our extended palms, with the fringed ends hanging on each side. The Dalai Lama was standing just inside the doorway, a tall young man in fine woollen robes, with an intelligent, sadly humorous face. His hair was cut en brosse, and he wore heavy black-rimmed spectacles. He came forward smiling, took the scarves ceremoniously, and then shook hands and led us into the chamber. There was a throne at one end, quilted in yellow silk, with a brocade canopy above it and a series of brilliant Tibetan thankas hanging on the wall behind. But in front of the throne, settees and easy chairs were arranged on a thick-pile Tibetan carpet; they also were in the yellow sacred to Buddhists.

The Dalai Lama sat on one of the settees and we on another. The only other people present were Ben and a lama secretary, who spoke in the curious sucked-in whisper which Tibetans use when addressing their social or spiritual superiors. But there were other, invisible presences, for two doorways led out of the audience chamber to the rest of the house, and occasionally, as the wind moved the curtains, we would see shadowy figures standing behind them like listeners in a mediaeval drama. Every now and then, from an inner room, a cuckoo clock would call.

The Dalai Lama understood English almost perfectly, and would often answer in Tibetan before Ben could begin putting our questions, but except for a few interjected phrases like "For example" or "You see," he spoke only Tibetan. He answered deliberately, sometimes slowly, seeking to frame an idea precisely, but never hesitantly. He listened with a slight smile, and occasionally would throw back his head and laugh unrestrainedly.

Our conversation, which originally had been planned for a quarter of an hour, went on for almost two hours, and we covered many subjects, from Buddhism to the future of Tibet, the plight of the refugees, and our own plans, which had been growing up in our minds ever since we visited Mussoorie, to found some kind of organisation for aiding the Tibetans as soon as we returned to Canada.

It was Inge, puzzled by the intricacies of lamaist doctrine, who asked most of the questions on religion; I noted the Dalai Lama's replies in my diary immediately after the audience.

"Discussion of Tibetan Buddhism. The Dalai Lama insists that there is no specifically Tibetan element in the religion he professes. All comes from India, except that Tantrism, secret in India, became open in Tibet. The Gods of Lamaist Buddhism are in some senses real, in others not. Real as objects of contemplation on the way to Buddhahood, or as projections of our own passions (in anger, for example, we may give substance to angry gods), but ultimately non-existent, sheddable by those who have gone far enough along the path of enlightenment. Asceticism. The Dalai Lama declares this is not necessary except for those who need its help in a stage on the way to truth. For the truly wise it is possible to do all things, since for them all things have ceased to be objects of desire. "It is possible," he says, smiling gently at us, "to achieve enlightenment even if you are married." To George's question on the possibility of advancing towards Buddhahood by contemplating gods of other religions, the Dalai Lama replies, with seeming inconsistency, that such contemplation will merely lead to a man's becoming the god he contemplates. The Dalai Lama says that Hinayanist Buddhism (the Lesser Vehicle of the Ceylonese) is limited by its concentration on personal salvation. Hinayana may lead to the lower Nirvana, the release from rebirth. Yes, there are two Nirvanas. The higher Nirvana is Buddhahood, total enlightenment; to this only Mahayana Buddhism, with its insistence on the need for the salvation of all living beings, can lead. Hence the Tibetan Buddhists, even when they follow Hinayanist practices, combine them with the Mahayanist philosophy of universal compassion. But in the end each man must find his own path, the path that is proper to him. That is what the Buddha taught."

When we talked of the future of Tibet, it was clear that His Holiness had no illusions about the strength of the present Chinese hold on his country; he remarked that it might be a very long time before he and his exiled subjects would be able to return. But he was convinced—partly because of his reading of ancient prophecies and partly from his knowledge of the Tibetan people—that the Buddhist religion would survive. Yet he realised—perhaps more than most of his followers—that the old, mediaeval Tibet was gone for good. Even if the Chinese departed, it could never be resurrected in its old form.

Throughout our conversation we were impressed by the apparent contrast between the broadness of the Dalai Lama's views and the circumscribed and ceremonial life his office demands. His days are bound by the timetable of prayer and meditation, and are lived according to the strict ceremonial of a royal household, where chamberlains and food-tasters still have their place; on formal occasions the protocol is at least as elaborate as that of the Vatican. Yet within this pattern His Holiness clearly maintains live links with the modern world. He reads the newspaper carefully each day, and he is passionately interested in the developments of modern science and mechanical invention; he has the reputation of being an excellent amateur photographer. Furthermore, he and his family show a liberalism of attitude which I suspect, from certain remarks I heard at Dharamsala and in Delhi, is not welcomed by all his advisers. One product of his attitude has been a plan for a "constitutional democracy based on the tenets of Buddhism" which the Dalai Lama insisted should be discussed by the refugees in their various camps before he promulgated it. The constitution includes all the democratic features that are familiar to us but strange to Tibetans, such as independent courts of law and an elected legislature. It even allows for the deposition of the Dalai Lama himself by due process of law, and in Tibetan terms this is a positively revolutionary change, since it means that the Dalai Lama has quietly dropped the assumption of infallibility that traditionally goes with his office.

All this, the Dalai Lama insisted, could only apply if he went back to Tibet. But, whether or not that return took place, the Tibetans in exile would have to come to terms with the modern world if they were to survive. The problem that seemed to concern him most—even more than the present well-being of the refugees— was the education of the young people who have come suddenly from the Middle Ages into the twentieth century. For this reason he told us that he wished to see something new in the history of Lamaist Tibet—an end to traditional isolation by sending as many young Tibetans as possible abroad, to take their pick of modern knowledge and then return and use it in the service of their people. There are no Tibetan doctors or dentists, no Tibetan engineers or agricultural scientists, and only a minute handful of Tibetan trained nurses and teachers. All these skills have to be learnt, in addition to the basic training being given to a minority of Tibetan children in residential schools like that in Mussoorie. In the long run, he thought, the best contribution that people of democratic countries could make to the cause of Tibet might be their assistance in creating an efficient educational system for refugees.

Late in the afternoon the interview ended. The Dalai Lama came with us to the door of the audience chamber, and there he gave us his blessing and handed back the white scarves we had presented. It was the ancient Tibetan courtesy to those who go on journeys.

At the Nursery Mrs. Tsering Dolma and the minister Phala had come to talk with us before we left. I sat with Phala, discussing the problems of the eighty thousand Tibetan refugees who were his peculiar responsibility—of those imprisoned by the snows and starving in the high valleys of Nepal, of those who had found such a

Jigme Taring (right) was a prince before he became principal of the Mussoorie school for refugees, working alongside Mrs. Rinchen Dolma Taring (left).

hostile welcome in the primitive mountain Kingdom of Bhutan that they had fled a second time into India, and of the few who had gained some promise of a settled life in the land schemes of Mysore and Uttar Pradesh. . . .

We all walked down the slippery path to the road where the Dalai Lama's car was once again waiting. The servants loaded our luggage into the car, and Mrs. Tsering Dolma presented us with two magnificent scarves of fine silk. Khando rode with us a little way down the hill, to start us on the journey.

"Our Karma has brought us together," she said, as she left us. And then the car went speeding down the mountain roads on the long drive into the Kangra valley, where the villages sprang out of the darkness like little fountains of light as we drove through them towards Pathankot and the Delhi train.

[From *Faces of India: A Travel Narrative* by George Woodcock, illustrated with photographs by Ingeborg Woodcock (London: Faber and Faber, 1964)]

It looks like a frolic-filled moment down at the swimming hole, but Judy Pullen (crouching) had to be vigilant to keep her Lower Transit School children from drinking the river water at Kangra for fear of typhoid. "It was a losing battle because the kids have to walk one-half mile to get drinking water in a pail from the nearest well. And that's no joke when there are over 200 people to drink it."

"I CAN'T NOT DO IT"

Nobody has been involved with TRAS longer, as effectively, or as bravely, as Judy Tethong. Having arrived in Kangra (near Dharamsala) for a one-year stint with CUSO (Canadian University Services Overseas) in September of 1963, as Judy Pullen, she stayed for two, two-year stints, teaching and caring for refugee children in the Kangra transit school, as well as teaching Tibetan monks how to become schoolteachers at the Dharamsala Tibetan Teaching Training College where the Dalai Lama made an impromptu visit to her classroom.

After a two-hour parting audience with His Holiness in 1967, she returned to her hometown of Oakville, Ontario, where she married the Tibetan nobleman Tsewang Choegyal (T.C.) Tethong in 1968, having met him in Dharamsala in 1965. After their wedding in Canada, the Tethongs spent seven more gruelling but exciting years building and administering the Tibetan resettlement project in Mundgod, India, south of Bombay, enabling 7,500 Tibetans to forge a viable community out of the wilderness. While her husband served as the Dalai Lama's official representative at Mundgod and the other south Indian Tibetan settlements, Judy Tethong administered the hospital.

At Mundgod, she maintained a steady flow of funding from TRAS, corresponding with both George Woodcock and his successor, John Conway, while giving birth to two of their three children, as well as raising numerous foster children. Dervla Murphy wrote in *On a Shoestring to Coorg*:

"Throughout a middle-aged lifetime I have felt for few people the whole-hearted admiration and respect I feel for this couple. To administer funds wisely, to organize practical affairs efficiently, to treat people kindly—all that is accomplished often (though not often enough) in the refugee world. But to have settled a group of people as culturally fragile as the Tibetans, without destroying their spirituality, is a rare and very wonderful achievement."

The Tethongs moved to Victoria, British Columbia, in 1975, where their children became Canada's first Tibetan Canadians. T.C. Tethong orchestrated the Dalai Lama's first visit to western Canada in 1980.

T.C. Tethong was born in 1934 in Chamdo, in eastern Tibet, near the Chinese border when his father was posted there from Lhasa as the governor of eastern Tibet. But not long after, the family moved back to Lhasa where T.C. went to school until he was sent to India to attend St. Joseph's school, North Point, in Darjeeling. He graduated from college there and was planning to go to medical school in Calcutta. But after the 1959 uprising in Tibet he went instead to help in the refugee camps in Assam as thousands of Tibetans fled over the mountains. From there he was called to Mussoorie to work as a junior interpreter for His Holiness.

At the behest of the Dalai Lama, T.C. studied in Germany for three years, working towards a political science degree. But in 1964 he was called back to India to help out at the Bureau of His Holiness in New Delhi and then in Dharamsala. After nine years in

T.C. Tethong (right) was the young Dalai Lama's junior English interpreter after His Holiness fled from Tibet in 1959. Members of the Tethong family have served the Dalai Lamas for over 400 years.

Mundgod and 21 years in Canada he was again summoned back to India in 1996 to become the Dalai Lama's personal representative in New Delhi. Subsequently he accepted the post of Minister of Information and International Relations in the cabinet of the Tibetan Government-in-Exile. He served in that capacity until the end of 2001. Among his many other responsibilities, T.C. Tethong was instrumental in the reestablishment in south India of several of Tibet's great monasteries.

Emulating their parents, the Tethong children have become activists on behalf of Tibet, the exiled Tibetans and the Dalai Lama, who named their son, Losel. Their daughter Deyden Tethong helped to organize a series of Free Tibet rock concerts in the 1990s, sponsored by the Milarepa fund and supported by the Beastie Boys.

Their other daughter, Lhadon Tethong, is the Executive Director of Students for a Free Tibet, a New York–based organization with 650 chapters around the world.

In the summer of 2007, at age thirty-one, Lhadon Tethong was arrested in Beijing for organizing and publicizing a pre-Olympics protest during which demonstrators rappelled down the Great Wall of China to hang a huge banner in English and Chinese declaring ONE WORLD. ONE DREAM. ONE TIBET.

The following year Lhadon Tethong helped to organize demonstrations and rallies along the route of the pre-Olympic torch relay run in Europe and in San Francisco, the only North American city in which the Beijing Olympic torch touched down.

"Hitler held those Olympics [in Berlin] to glorify Nazism and racism," T.C. Tethong told *Monday* magazine journalist Sid Tafler, "to show German might and superiority. We see the same kind of self-promotion in China with all the shortcomings and contradictions hidden in the background."

KANGRA & DHARAMSALA

Once upon a very different time—in 1961—Judy Pullen was a young woman, from a well-to-do family, engaged to marry a handsome lawyer. A comfortable future was hers for the taking.

"I was completing an undergraduate degree in health education with the aim of becoming a doctor," she says, "when I realized that by the time I got through med school, got married and had kids, I would never get abroad. I wanted to go and save the world."

At age twenty-one, she joined the Canadian Voluntary Commonwealth Service in order to spend one summer with the Jamaica Youth Club Council. This was the beginning of her practical awareness that the world can only be changed one child at a time.

She returned to Canada and enrolled in the Ontario College of Education in September 1962, training to be a teacher instead of a doctor. But matrimony still beckoned. "It was during that winter at OCE that I had to wrestle with 'Am I going to marry Bruce or am

A portrait of the young Dalai Lama overlooks Judy Pullen (Tethong) teaching
English to 24 monks and two nuns in her makeshift classroom in Dharamsala.
The room is actually on a verandah. After a freezing winter, monks built the
wall on the right by hammering together old packing cases; the rest of that wall
is cheesecloth. During summer months, the monks stayed at their desks from
5:30 a.m. (after getting up at 5) until 11:30 p.m., for six days of the week. In
the winter they were allowed to sleep in. Their first class did not commence
until 6 a.m. Judy Pullen's first class to teach didn't start until 7:15 a.m. "Of all
the classes I teach," she said, "English is the least important."

I going to give it another shot abroad?'"

CVCS had just merged its operations to form the basis of CUSO. For its first year only, the new organization was willing to accept volunteers for one-year stints overseas, so Pullen prepared for a CUSO posting near Calcutta. At the proverbial eleventh hour, she was told she would be sent to a transit camp for Tibetan refugee children instead. "I knew absolutely nothing about Tibet or Tibetans," she says.

Her public library in Oakville, Ontario, had four books on Tibet. She read them all. That was her orientation. "On the way, when we stopped in London, England, I bought a book on Tibetan grammar which to this day I can't figure out."

As part of a 13-member CUSO contingent, she attended orientation classes at Delhi University for a month, staying at a Buddhist ashram where she learned a few words of Tibetan from refugees on their way to Switzerland. Then she was sent to the town of Kangra, situated below the former British hill station of Dharamsala where the Dalai Lama had newly taken up residence.

She and her fellow volunteer, Lois James, a nurse, were astonished by the contrasting beauty and squalor of their new home. "Kangra is on the valley floor at 2,000 feet," she says. "But the mountains are right there, so we'd look out our window of the school at the snow-capped, 19,000-foot-high mountains." But beneath this splendour, the Kangra Tibetan Transit School was an under-financed, rat-infested and dilapidated outpost.

The guardian angel of Kangra was Dr. Florence Haslam who ran the Maple Leaf Hospital at the top of the hill, up which the town of Kangra climbed. Her mother, a Canadian-born doctor, had worked in northern India since the early part of the twentieth century. Dr. Florence Haslam, who had been born in Kangra, received her medical training in Canada and returned to India to run the hospital for forty years. When the Woodcocks sent money from Vancouver, it went directly to Dr. Haslam.

"Dr. Haslam, who spoke five languages fluently, and was well-known and beloved in the area, would go down to the bazaar and haggle and get the best prices for the cloth for me when we needed to make clothes for the kids," says Tethong, "She hired four or five Indian tailors who would sit on the back porch of her mission bungalow. We would march our kids up the hill and they'd be measured by the tailors. We'd have a shirt and pants for the boys, and a skirt and blouse made for the girls."

In 1963, a twenty-seven-year-old Swiss Red Cross doctor named Oliver Senn worked at the Tibetan Nursery in upper Dharamsala. He and Dr. Haslam were responsible for providing medical care for almost one thousand children, along with the help of the Maple Leaf Hospital and Lois James and Judy Pullen. At the transit school, the basic rations of bulgar wheat were donated through Catholic relief services or the American aid organizations. "The food was appalling," says Tethong. "I'd never been so hungry in my life. The Tibetan Government-in-Exile would send down lots of donated grains and our cooks, who weren't really cooks, boiled up this inedible slop that we had several times a day."

The neophyte aid workers were assigned to live in an old, two-storey building that served as a boys' school "with nothing in it," according to Tethong, "except for several hundred kids." Dr. Haslam initially offered the two women refuge in her mission bungalow at the hospital until furniture was made for their small room on the top floor of the school. After a week at the mission bungalow, Lois and Judy moved in with their young charges and were soon on duty, day and night.

Interviewed in Victoria in 2009, Judy Tethong (née Pullen) still vividly recalls meeting the Woodcocks during their second visit to the Dalai Lama in 1963. In one of her letters she wrote: "It rained all day Wednesday and we had a terrific hail storm that night. Rinpoche said he would pray for the rain to stop for the Woodcocks' visit the next day. Sure enough, it stopped! Mr. Kundeling and the Assistant Minister of Education came in the morning. Lois came and got me from lama school and we went up to the Mission for tea. The Woodcocks stayed up there. We were delighted to see them and had a long talk.

"They came to us after spending a few days in Dharamsala. They showed us the most beautiful old Tibetan *tanka* [a cloth embroidered painting] depicting the life of Buddha that His Holiness had presented to them. They were astounded when he did—it's a priceless old treasure. After tea, they walked down to the school with us. We entered the school yard unobtrusively and then they toured the building."

She still speaks fondly of the occasion: "When the Woodcocks came and saw the conditions, they gave money directly to Dr. Haslam for food. Dr. Haslam would deal directly with the vegetable dealers in the market. For years after that, TRAS contributed directly to the school, which was run by the Tibetan Government-in-Exile."

In one of her letters, she notes that the Woodcocks were planning to return the following Christmas and live for a while in Dharamsala, but obviously those plans never materialized.

"After their visit, I remember riding with the Woodcocks in the jeep back up to Dharamsala. It was like a 14-mile drive across the valley floor and up into the mountains. I think it was Inge who kept asking me questions about the trees and the bushes and I didn't know any of the answers! [laughter] She really must have thought I was an ignorant person. That was the only time that I met them in the north. Of course I got to know them later. They have done more for our children than anyone else and they arrived with the least fanfare."

Freezing temperatures in the Himalayas during winter made the plight of the children abundantly obvious. On January 22, 1964, Judy Pullen wrote, "We nearly froze as the temperature dropped below freezing. I wish you could see the outfits we wear to bed to

Judy Pullen with two of her classes:
"The pupils are all Tibetan monks & lamas ranging in age from early 20s to late 40s and 50s. There are nineteen altogether and they were not supposed to have anything at all to do with women except for their mothers & sisters!"

try to get warm! When not shivering in bed we wrap ourselves in blankets to keep out the cold. The kids have half the amount of clothes on that we wear and yet they rarely complain. I am forever whacking little boys on the bottom and telling them to go and put on their long trousers or long-sleeved shirts."

Another literary visitor was the self-educated Dervla Murphy who had ridden her bicycle—alone—from Ireland to India to write her first travel memoir, *Full Tilt*. It was followed by *Tibetan Foothold* (1966) in which she described her arrival at Kangra where she stayed with Judy Pullen and Lois James at the boys' school. Sleeping in blankets on a rotten wood floor, she was forewarned "not to register alarm and despondency if the mammoth rats who share this accommodation should chance to scuttle across my face during the small hours."

Urged to stay for Christmas, Murphy declined the offer. She had had enough. Back in July, when she had arrived for her first day of work in a Dharamsala dispensary at 5:30 a.m., she had been given the job of placing the bodies of two four-year-olds into cardboard boxes. Malnutrition had the two four-year-olds as small as an average two-year-old. They had died overnight. She recalled: "It's quite impossible to cure such miserable scraps once they get measles, bronchitis or dysentery. To make matters worse there is no possibility of notifying their parents, though the majority of the children have at least one parent living; so one often finds a mother or father wandering around the compound searching for their child, who has died perhaps several months ago, clutching the pathetic little bag of cheap sweets that was to have been the reunion present. Most of the parents are working on the roads in the Chumba or Kulu valleys, and they save up until they can pay the bus fare to Dharamsala and provide a few 'extras' for their children."

This was Judy Tethong's world when she was Judy Pullen—a perilous and heart-wrenching world, fraught with disease and despair, and yet buoyed by the inspirational children who depended upon her for their well-being. Dervla Murphy was a very hardy woman, staunchly independent, but even she admitted the mixture of heroes and villains in northern India made her feel as though she was observing a Victorian melodrama.

"These twenty-two-year-old CUSO volunteers—Lois James, a nurse, and Judy Pullen, a teacher—could each be earning high salaries in Canada if they had not chosen to come here for two years and live in unimaginable squalor on an allowance of one and sixpence *per diem*. Since their arrival in October they've visited us occasionally at Dharamsala, and from our first meeting I admired them enormously, both for their rapid adaptation to the complexities of life here and for the courage, resourcefulness and humour with which they were tackling their jobs.

"But now, having seen the conditions under which they live, the food on which they subsist and the incredible improvements they have made during two brief months no words seem adequate to praise them. When I think of the comparative luxury of Dharamsala, where the S.C.F. bungalow almost attains Western standards of comfort and where we lived royally on our S.C.F. food bonus, I feel deeply ashamed of the fact that some people regard me as having endured a martyr's existence for the sake of the Tiblets [Tibetan children].

"Judy and Lois seem to be tough young women—Lois has already spent eighteen months living with the Esquimaux in the Canadian Arctic—but Kangra is a far less healthy spot than Dharamsala and on their present regime of too much work and too little food it is almost inevitable that they will succumb to one—or several—of the virulent local bugs. . . . It is sometimes remarked to me that Canadians are in general more adaptable than Americans, and certainly these two girls fit effortlessly into the Indian scene. Rarely have I seen Westerners display, in their dealings with Indians, such an unselfconscious and total acceptance of the equality of man."

Upper Dharamsala, in the early 1960s, was a conglomeration of mostly ugly cement buildings, at 6,000-feet altitude. It had been a popular British hill station in the nineteenth century until it was mostly destroyed by an earthquake in 1905. It became known as "Little Lhasa" after a local storekeeper learned that the government of India was seeking a permanent sanctuary for the Dalai Lama. He notified the government that Dharamsala had a plethora of unused buildings.

While Upper Dharamsala served as the headquarters of the Tibetan Government-in-Exile, the sister town of Lower Dharamsala, at 4,500-feet altitude, served as the headquarters of the Kangra District. It was either a 50-minute walk via a rocky path between the two enclaves, or an eight-mile journey via a new roadway. Either place was far from Shangri-la.

Back down in Kangra, Tethong wrote in January of 1964, "It has been raining solidly for the past 4 days and nights. The yard is a sea of mud. My two junior classes have had to be recombined on the front verandah since the kids can't sit in the yard. Now I have the fun of trying to discipline a class of 80 squirming boys from age 5 to age 12! All the prayers (an hour every a.m. and p.m.) are held in the classroom outside our bedroom door now instead of outside. I love their Buddhist chants even though we can't hear ourselves think!"

In Upper Dharamsala, the Upper Nursery housed 380 children, aged eight to sixteen, overseen by a highly capable Quaker volunteer named Doris Murray. During monsoon season, umbrellas were required inside the Lower Nursery that housed 600 children, aged one to eight, packed into five rooms, and overseen by one of the Dalai Lama's sisters, Pema Gyalpo, who became another mainstay for deliverance of aid from TRAS. An hour's walk from the Lower Nursery was Kashmir Cottage, a dilapidated bungalow that housed 120 children, aged six to eight.

Judy Tethong and Lois James received an important morale boost early in 1964 when the Dalai Lama made his first unscheduled visit to Kangra one morning at 8 a.m. All the children were quickly instructed to form two lines from the entrance of the school. After

Tethong and Lois James had "dashed around combing hair, washing dirty faces, tucking in shirts, tying shoelaces," they hurriedly prepared themselves. Tethong wrote to her parents, "We were out in the bazaar anxiously waiting when Lois said I still had scotch tape marks on the side of my face. I dashed up to our room and was just reaching for my wash cloth when I heard horns honking and Lois screaming my name."

Tethong hurried downstairs as far as the verandah outside the kitchen door. There she saw the Dalai Lama's entourage entering the yard. It was veneration at first sight. "I stopped dead and saw His Holiness for the first time. It was all like a dream. After waiting for such an event for so long and reading so much about this wonderful person I sort of expected great claps of thunder and flashes of lighting and a shining image in splendid raiment to come out of the heavens. Instead there was a lama in maroon, woollen lama robes—looking like any one of my lama students—walking very normally and behaving like any other human being.

"He never spoke a single word to us. But I felt as though he had spoken volumes. I simply cannot describe how I felt in his presence. It would become trite and commonplace if I tried to capture it in words. Whether he is divine or not isn't up to us to decide. All I know is that he is one of the most unusual men I have ever met. We have become so involved in the life of these people, their customs, their intriguing history and religion that I doubt if I will ever be so affected by any other great leader's presence.

"He turned and waved a friendly good-bye as the car and jeeps of police and officials moved off up the narrow cobblestone street. I was holding up a little boy so he could see over the heads of the Indians. His Holiness gave us a special little wave which thrilled little Karma to pieces—to say nothing of my reaction. What a morning! He is so full of life and vigor. His keen mind and sharp eyes don't seem to miss a thing. The whole episode seemed like a wonderful dream."

After that, the Dalai Lama sometimes arrived unannounced in

Tethong's classroom in Dharamsala where she prepared monks to be teachers. About a month after her arrival in Kangra, the Minister of Education asked Tethong if she would also teach part-time at a Tibetan Teacher Training College, which was located about five or ten minutes climb up the hill from the children's Transit School. She began teaching there in the afternoons until the Teacher Training College was moved up to Dharamsala in the spring of 1964.

"Dr. Haslam said I was fluent in Tibetan after three months," she recalls, "but that's not really true. The head lama was teaching all of the monks the Tibetan poetry, grammar, religion, religious history, all of the stuff they were going to teach the kids. Initially I was asked to give the monks some idea of the western subjects the kids were going to be learning, so with the help of an interpreter I taught some basic science and geography, history, and English. But then I was asked to design, set up and teach the teacher training component of the course. I knew if I didn't do it, nobody was going to do it. At the same time, I wondered why the heck I was doing it. So I went down to Delhi and used TRAS money to buy some of the books I needed."

The challenges of teaching monks how to teach were not merely linguistic or monetary. Her classes were exclusively composed of young men who were unaccustomed to any female company beyond their mothers or sisters. And they were trained to be inquisitive, to be mentally alert, to such an unusual degree that it proved to be intimidating.

"They are so bright," she wrote, "and so well trained in logic and debate that if I tell them that the world is round, I have to prove it. Well, you prove to me that the world is round. I couldn't do it! When they'd ask me questions like that, and I'd try to prove it from their point of view, they would come up with all kinds of other diagrams of how it would work. If they asked me a question about something and I just BS'd my way through the answer, it might be a few months later, approaching something from a different angle, that they would catch me. So I learned pretty early on that if I didn't know the answer, I'd just tell them that I didn't know but that I would find the answer for them."

When their one-year term in northern India was about to expire, Pullen and James wrote to CUSO asking to stay longer. This request was granted but soon thereafter by the Christmas of 1964, Lois James was forced to leave, due to ill-health. Tethong recalls, "I stayed until my two years was up and CUSO said I had to return home for a health check-up, mainly because Lois was in such bad shape. It was during the '65 war with Pakistan. I could barely get out."

During her brief return to Canada, Tethong undertook numerous speaking engagements for both TRAS and for CUSO, appearing on television, raising money and awareness, until she returned to India just before the Christmas of 1965.

Despite her onerous teaching regimen at the Tibetan Teacher Training College in Dharamsala, Judy Tethong retained her ties with the Tibetan children. "At the transit school we'd handle 400 kids at a time. We were constantly getting one group of kids healthy and doing some teaching and then they were gone to the big Tibetan residential schools in the far-flung hill stations of India. So that was frustrating. I ended up going to the transit camps and bringing back sick children to the Teacher Training College. I started out with a couple of kids in the other bed in my tiny room nursing them back to health. Eventually I had about 50 really sick, dying children in my care at the Tibetan Teacher Training College.

"Teaching the monks, training teachers who were going to be out in the schools for the next 20 or 30 years, that part was really satisfying, professionally. So at first I was devastated when they told me they were going to move the college up to Dharamsala. The school had to be moved because those monks worked so hard. They were up at five a.m. and they worked until ten, seven days a week, and in Kangra, by April, the weather was really hot. We're talking about 117 degrees on the old Fahrenheit scale and the monks were all getting sick. That's why the school had to be moved."

Having moved up to Dharamsala in April of 1964, she had expected to conclude her assignment in September, but she and the head lama at the training college were asked by the Dalai Lama to travel throughout the Himalayas to select monks for a second training course. This entailed her commitment to another two-year program.

"So basically I did two two-year terms with CUSO, the first nine months in Kangra and then after that in Dharamsala. All that time I was in India I was writing to TRAS, getting money for various things."

ROMANCE & MUNDGOD

Judy Pullen first met her husband-to-be in New Delhi in 1964 and then again in December of 1965, when they were both getting off the same train in Pathankot. T.C. Tethong offered her a ride to Dharamsala in a government jeep. He explained that he was bringing something for the Dalai Lama. She thanked him but declined his offer because two monks had arrived at the station to meet her. A few days later he came to her room at the college and invited her to a Christmas party in Upper Dharamsala. She accepted.

"During that previous year," she recalls, "there were a lot of young Tibetans who had been educated abroad or who had gone to the good schools in India. We all used to get together to go on picnics or to climb up the mountain, or to socialize at the Swiss doctor's place. That's how I got to know the young man who later became my husband. We went to those same gatherings.

"I had already written to Bruce at the end of my first year, telling him I had decided to stay. It was hard because I did like the guy. It was just at the wrong time in my life. So I broke that up. I knew I'd done the right thing, but I still had feelings about it."

Soon after she became engaged to T.C. Tethong, the Dalai Lama asked them to go to southern India to report on the viability of the Tibetan resettlement project at Bylakuppe. T.C. was so inspired after that trip that he volunteered to start a new settlement for

The Dalai Lama invited Judy Pullen for a private audience to thank her for almost four years of service in Kangra and Dharamsala. After a trip to Canada, she returned to India as Judy Tethong, having married one of the Dalai Lama's translators at a ceremony in her hometown of Oakville, Ontario.

Tibetans on unused land at a place called Mundgod. In November of 1966 T.C. headed off in a Jeep, with four other Tibetans, to the south Indian state of Mysore—now called Karnataka. He was able to return to Dharamsala to see his betrothed only once, in February of 1967, when her mother and father visited northern India during their world tour.

In July of 1967, after the second group of monks had graduated from the Teacher Training College, Judy boarded a train with eleven Tibetans and travelled to Mundgod where she spent a couple of months living in a tent in the middle of a swamp in the monsoon season. "By the time I got engaged to T.C.," she says. "I already had six adopted kids. Then we adopted number seven after our marriage when we were still living in bamboo huts and tents."

In 1966, $4,500,000 from the proceeds of European Refugee Year was allocated to help Tibetan refugees. Specifically, the Government of India persuaded the south Indian government of Mysore to make available some large tracts of undeveloped scrub jungle on the eastern slopes of the Western Ghats. The first small pilot group of Tibetans went there in the early 1960s to found the initial settlement of Bylakuppe in the southern part of the state. Assisted by agricultural experts and machinery provided by Switzerland, they adapted so well that by 1967 the Tibetans were self-supporting.

Non-governmental relief organizations were invited to take part. TRAS immediately agreed to help with this resettlement scheme. In 1968, the Common Project, in agreement with the Indian and Mysore governments, created a counterpart organization in India to implement the proposed settlements, called the Mysore Resettlement and Development Agency (MYRADA), to be staffed entirely by Indians.

TRAS established contact with MYRADA and, by 1969, was providing funds. The Canadian International Development Agency (CIDA) decided to support TRAS projects in 1970, matching the funds raised from private sources. Eventually there would be four main Tibetan settlements in Mysore state—at Bylakuppe, Hunsur,

Mundgod and Kollegal. T.C. Tethong was the Dalai Lama's representative—living in Mundgod and directing its developments—but in overall charge of all four settlements. TRAS also contributed funds to settlement projects outside Karnataka, such as Bhandara in Maharashtra and Tezu in Arunachal Pradesh in the northeastern corner of India. These new settlements provided land and homes to nearly 35,000 people in the 1970s.

The staff of MYRADA and Tibetan community representatives, in consultation with Indian government resettlement officials, would estimate needs and plan the settlements. The various contributing agencies would select projects within the general plan for which they would assume financial responsibility.

The jigsaw of interlocking commitments usually fitted together very well, particularly as it meant that TRAS (as well as other agencies) was able to spread its aid over a number of settlements and thus maintain contact with the development of the entire resettlement program in the scattered areas of land given to the Tibetan refugees.

In Mundgod, up to 1976, with CIDA's partnerships, TRAS was able to contribute $42,500 on buildings for a school, teachers' quarters and a small hospital; $32,500 on rat-proof grain warehouses; $20,000 on trucks; $17,000 on roads and bridges; $5,000 on irrigation; $8,000 on houses; $5,000 on agricultural training; approximately $30,000 on hospital maintenance, $8,500 on a TB control program; $1,250 on an open-air stage; plus small amounts for tree planting, erosion control and maintaining old people.

"In considering these figures," wrote Vice-Chairman John Conway, "one must bear in mind that costs in southern India during the early 1970s were still low in world terms, so that we got a great deal for the money we spent, while very often the refugees were able to help by contributing part of the labour for the various projects."

So even though Mundgod represented only one TRAS project, that project entailed a myriad of funding endeavours, including the fifty-bed hospital managed by Judy Tethong. During one year alone (1979–80), TRAS sponsored ten projects. These entailed $43,000 to assist five different handicrafts centres, $50,000 to help five agricultural settlements with cattle, tube wells and land reclamation, $20,000 on school building and vocational training, and $193,000 on community development (i.e. housing, clean water supplies, irrigation, provision of latrines, tailoring classes and the training of rural workers).

Mundgod became a funding priority for TRAS largely as a result of the determination and correspondence of Judy Tethong who was writing at length to George Woodcock from 1965 onwards. The correspondence that emerged between George and Judy was multi-faceted. On the one hand, they were securing their TRAS relationship, helping Tibetans, and, on the other, Judy was a vulnerable, would-be author seeking support from an esteemed mentor.

"By the time I came back to Oakville to prepare for our wedding on June 22, 1968," she says, "McGraw-Hill had asked me to write a book about my first four years in the north of India. The idea was this was going to be a bestseller and get a Julia Roberts type to play me in a movie. We thought this book was going to fund all our work for the next 50 years."

When she wasn't planning for her wedding in Canada or undertaking fundraising talks for TRAS and CUSO, Tethong was writing her memoirs in the family attic. Mundgod had to take precedence, so McGraw-Hill agreed she could finish her manuscript back in India.

T.C. arrived from India one week before their wedding in Oakville, Ontario, in June 1968. After their wedding, the newlyweds detoured to a family cottage in Georgian Bay, then stopped in Switzerland to visit T.C.'s brother and sister in charge of two Tibetan homes at the Pestalozzi International Children's Village in Trogen.

Judy and T.C. Tethong returned to Mundgod in August of '68. "In Mundgod T.C. had built a little brick washhouse with a little window opening and a rickety bamboo door. I put a table and chair in there. That's where I wrote the rest of my book in long-hand over that first winter. There were thirty-one chapters. It was going to be a bestseller, of course, and then I would write the next book about Mundgod. But I never got the first book published."

At their Mundgod headquarters, the Tethongs had the additional responsibility of transplanting Tibetan religious practices and monks from the northern border areas to the south Indian Tibetan settlements. Judy Tethong still vividly recalls visiting a disease-ridden refugee camp for monks in north India on the border of Bhutan in the mid-1960s. Having been sent by the Dalai Lama to find potential candidates for the teacher training college, she was one of the few westerners who witnessed the plight of the exiled Tibetan monks first hand.

"There was a former prison camp that the British had for the likes of Gandhi and the Indian freedom fighters. I think it was built for about 300 people. When the principal of the training college and I went looking for students for a second training course that was one of the places we were supposed to visit. Well, we couldn't get passes to get in there because it was in a restricted area, so we just went. We took a train from Delhi to Assam, and then rode in the back of a gravel truck until the road ended. From there, we went on foot up to this camp. We arrived the night before Tibetan New Year's Day. There I was, with three thousand Tibetan monks. There was no electricity, just little shacks and dimly lit shelters. It was extraordinary, like arriving in Tibet.

"The next day was New Year's Day. To be there in this great open space on this hill top, with 3,000 monks chanting was unbelievable. But because the camp was so crowded, many of the brightest and best scholars of Tibet were dying like flies from tuberculosis. They were so isolated. T.C. was able to work with the Indian government and the Tibetan Government-in-Exile. He volunteered to have monks come to the settlements in the south to re-establish their monasteries. So those monks came to the south where they became farmers. They tilled the land and built their bamboo huts. Then they built their first little bamboo temples. It was extraordinary."

The Tethongs remained continuously at Mundgod until 1975. During their first year of marriage they had lived in a one-room bamboo hut with a grass roof. Eventually little cottages were made for the staff, but T.C. Tethong had refused to move into houses until the first 1,000 settlers were also in houses. He had arrived on the land with five Tibetan helpers. The Dalai Lama subsequently placed him in charge of all the major resettlement sites in Mysore.

"By the time we left Mundgod there were eight villages and 7,500 Tibetan refugees resettled," Judy says. "There were nutrition programs for malnourished kids. We had a fleet of tractors and a workshop. We had a Tibetan Cooperative Society. We had a bank. We had shops, a big central school, and several primary schools. I was running the hospital and a TB program. We had 500 patients on active TB treatment at any one time."

The challenges were endless. In 1974, when TRAS and CIDA became involved in supporting the resettlement efforts at Kollegal, Judy Tethong was faced with vaccinating 5,000 settlers at Mundgod during an outbreak of smallpox. In April of '74 she wrote: "We are in the midst of a dreaded measles epidemic. Two children died last week of pneumonia complications, and we expect an increase in the number of children with TB as they are left so thin and sickly that they are wide open for TB infection. I've not seen so many miserable and sickly children since the early days in Dharamsala.

"Measles is considered to be a relatively mild childhood disorder in Canada. Here the virus is so virulent that the children run temperatures of 104 degrees to 105 degrees for many days in a row and then they develop pneumonia at the drop of a hat. At this same time of year in 1969 we had a similar epidemic in which 56 children died in the space of six weeks, and at that time there were only about 1,500 people in the whole camp. It is becoming increasingly difficult to obtain the TB drugs required for the resistant cases—and our funds are now nil."

Upon receiving this letter, TRAS immediately allocated funding for the purchase of drugs to combat tuberculosis.

Since moving to Victoria, Judy Tethong's struggle to support Tibetan refugees has been ceaseless. She maintains the Victoria chapter of the Canada Tibet Committee (CTC), organizing and participating in events such as the protest against seven Canadian mining companies cooperating with the Chinese to exploit resources in Tibet. The rally in Vancouver on June 20, 2009, focused on the activities in central Tibet of Continental Minerals, a subsidiary of Hunter Dickinson.

Of the thousands of shoppers who streamed past the modest gathering of people and placards on Robson Street, precious few bothered to stop and listen, as fifty protesters sang "Oh Canada" and presented an agit-prop theatre piece depicting the complicity of Canadian mining in the brutal repression of Tibetans inside Tibet. "The Canadian mining industry has a horrific record when it goes overseas," said CTC vice-president Mati Bernabei, a school teacher. "The Canadian mining industry is behaving in a way that I would not allow my students to behave in my classroom."

As outlined in Michael Buckley's 2009 documentary *Meltdown in Tibet*, the severe changes in the fragile ecology of Tibet wrought by mining have been exacerbated by the onset of severe global warming, the intensive program of Chinese dam building and the large scale exportation of fresh water. It is possible that environmental degradation of the Himalayas—as the "rooftop of the world" and the source of some of Asia's major rivers—will become an issue akin to the decimation of the Brazilian rainforest, re-focusing world attention on Tibet. As noted by 2007 Nobel Peace Prize recipient Rajendra K. Pachauri, chairman of the UN Intergovernmental Panel on Climate Change in 2008, "At least 500 million people in Asia and 250 million in China are at risk from declining glacial flows on the Tibetan Plateau."

Judy and T.C. Tethong with their son Losel, who was named by the Dalai Lama. The Irish travel writer Dervla Murphy saw the Tethongs in action at Mundgod in November of 1973 and observed "holidays are not part of the Tethong life-style."

Asked to speak off-the-cuff on the steps of the Vancouver Art Gallery, Tethong, also a high school teacher, sadly acknowledged Tibet is rarely accorded front page attention anymore and that she was essentially preaching to the converted. Wearing her Team Tibet jacket and travelling to Vancouver with a homemade sign, Tethong delivered an articulate and sober assessment of a deteriorating situation, reminding her friends that China sends students to countries around the globe as part of its campaign to spread negative views of the Dalai Lama. "For decades, His Holiness, the Dalai Lama, has consistently refused to call a spade a spade," she said, but in the aftermath of the Beijing Olympics he has resorted to outright condemnation of China. For Judy Tethong, this level of candour from the Dalai Lama—someone she has known since 1963—illustrates how desperate the plight of Tibetans has become.

Inducted into the Order of Canada for her compassion as a relief worker and educator, Judy Tethong has supported Tibetans in exile since 1963, at which time she met the Woodcocks in Kangra. Here she attends a rally against Canadian mining companies, wearing her Team Tibet jacket, in June of 2009 at the Vancouver Art Gallery. The featured speaker was Tenzin Lobsang Wangkhang of Toronto, Canadian Director of Students for a Free Tibet.

As a former cabinet minister in the provisional Tibetan government, T.C. Tethong remains active in Tibetan affairs, flying all over the world to represent the interests of the Tibetan people. And Judy Tethong retains her fierce and steadfast loyalties. "I've been a member of the Victoria chapter of TRAS ever since we came to Victoria in '75," she says. "For a while T.C. and I were also directors of TRAS Vancouver. So TRAS has been an integral part of my life for forty-six years.

"The people in the Tibetan refugee community in India and Nepal and Tibetans inside Tibet most especially are still suffering, so I can't not do it."

VICTIMS OF INNOCENCE

During her twelve years in India, Judy Tethong became adept at writing long letters, first to her family, and later to George Woodcock and TRAS. Some of her letters can be viewed at UBC Special Collections. They are strikingly clear reports, confessional yet informative. It easy to see from them why she was encouraged to pursue a book project that would encapsulate her experiences. One of her earliest letters to her parents describes her first meeting with the Tibetan Minister of Education, Mr. Kundeling, who had contacted CUSO and requested a nurse and a teacher for the Kangra transit school. She also wrote to the travel writer Dervla Murphy, describing her move from Kangra to Dharamsala. Subsequent letters describe her struggles at Mundgod and her doomed book project. The Canadian publishing company wanted her to call it *I Married a Tibetan*. Her family suggested the title *Victims of Innocence*.

Here Judy describes her early day at Kangra and her meeting with the man who hired her, the Tibetan Minister of Education.

Kangra,
October 1963
Dear Mum & Dad,

I must have been a dreamer to think I could write regularly once I settled down here at the school. There are no screens on our windows so we live with nature. There are three birds' nests in our room and never less than three or four birds hopping about the floor, table and beds. The whole building is overrun with bed bugs so we didn't escape long even though our beds are new. Lois has been eaten alive but I've been lucky. I don't think they like my blood. Every time I think I'll have a few minutes to myself some crisis arises. On Monday I went down to the school and found a boy lying on the floor in the corner, just covered with flies. We carried him up to the bed in our room.

Two hours ago I sat down and got the letter forms out but one of the boys had a coughing spasm outside my door. I dashed out to find him doubled over at the top of the stairs with blood and mucous all over the place. He is the poor little tyke who woke us up the other night with whooping cough. We grabbed our flashlights & dressing gowns & dashed downstairs to see where the horrible sounds were coming from. The poor kid was gagging for breath so we picked him up off the floor and brought him upstairs to the two beds outside our door which are used for sick beds. We pushed over 2 boys who were already on one bed (3 sick kids on the other bed) to make room for him. Lois was up 2 more times that night and an average of 3 times a night ever since to try to control his spasms. He has had this cough on & off for the last 4 months. One doctor said he had TB and another said no. Meanwhile the poor thing is wasting away. He's 12 years old and is a very sensitive looking child with large luminous eyes. When he smiles it's enough to break your heart!

I came down to the school Tues. afternoon to meet Mr. Kundeling, the Tibetan Minister of Education for all the refugee schools in India. He is in his 40s, a large, handsome man with a gruff but kindly manner. Both Lois & I are terrifically impressed with him. He knows exactly what is going on and what needs to be done. He doesn't speak English so he had a young Tibetan girl, who was brought up in north India, with him to translate. She is lovely, Dikki Norbu. He outlined what our duties would be and said he was expecting great things from us. I nearly died when he told me I am to teach at the Tibetan Teacher Training School (which is just up the hill from us here at the boys' school) for an hour every day. The pupils in that school are all Tibetan monks & lamas.

We eat the same food as the kids do—it's pretty monotonous. But we get one egg each for breakfast as we don't get the bits of meat that are given to the children. Our breakfast consists of white Tibetan bread, American Kraft Cheese (all the kids get it, too), one egg (hard-boiled). And tea. Lunch is a bowl of soup-like dhal (like pea soup without any taste!), a small plate of greasy cauliflower or cucumber in Tibetan sauce, and great hunks of Tibetan brown bread. I can stomach the latter but poor Lois can't even look at it! It is very tough and pasty. Supper is a bowl of greasy noodles and a glass of water. Lois manages the noodles but I can't face them after the first few nights! We get rice with our dhal twice a week as a treat. Our supper treat last night was sliced potatoes boiled in the Tibetan sauce & onions instead of the noodles. Breakfast is the best meal of the day!!!

CUSO is giving us 30 rupees (approx. $6) a month each because our salaries are so low. We put our extra 30 in a common pot and use it to buy fresh fruit & cookies—so we have fresh fruit every day. We splurged & bought a can of jam, too, so we put that on our toasted Tibetan bread for breakfast. Now I'm really living high! Butter is something we've forgotten all about. Everyone keeps apologizing for the food and the cook hangs around anxiously after every meal to see if we are satisfied. He's a fabulous cook when you see what he has to work with! We are terribly pampered by everyone here.

Not one child has any personal belongings of any type. The only clothes they have are those on their backs — the khaki outfits that Dr. Haslam had made for them. School supplies are nil. The kids sit on

Judy Tethong (née Pullen) was commissioned by McGraw-Hill to write
a book about her experiences but it was never published.

the floor. No beds. With the cold weather coming we will be desperate for warm sweaters, long pants, underwear (none of the boys have underpants & only about 5 of the girls). More blankets, jackets, pyjamas. We just can't have these kids sleeping in the nude all winter. Already, everyone has bad coughs, runny noses & colds. Lois & I have miserable colds, too. Two new cases of pneumonia today and 4 malaria. I have one little tyke on my bed here with a temp. of 105—probably another malaria. Terrible epidemic of pink eye now amongst the boys. These kids never complain so we catch them only when they drop."

Love,
Judy

In the following letter, Judy recounts to Dervla Murphy her transition to working in Dharamsala where she taught English classes to Tibetan monks, and trained them to become school teachers.

Kangra Boys' School
3 July 1964
Dear Dervla,
Lois was really sick for two months in Delhi with amoebic hepatitis, giardia and another virus infection. The poor kid went through hell—at one time it looked as though she'd have to be sent home to

Canada. However, she recovered and returned to us—we have yet to see how wise that was because she's not in top health yet.

At first we cooked all our own food but I'm afraid she didn't keep that up for long. The weather was as hot as heck and there was no water supply at the school except for an hour morning and night. We walked one-and-a-half miles to the river every day and made the kids wash themselves and their clothes.

Then Mr. Kundeling asked me to move to Dharmasala to continue teaching the Lamas. You can't imagine how torn my loyalties were! My teaching with the children was getting pretty frustrating with the rapid turnover and I was finding it harder and harder to keep my patience in class. 'This is *my* nose, that is *your* nose.' Lois was terrific—she was really firm about me going if I wanted to make any real contribution with my teaching. I felt miserable as I said good-bye to the kids and cried the whole way up in the bus as I looked back over those seven crazy, wonderful months in that old building.

The work here has surpassed all expectations. In addition to two English classes, I'm giving lectures in geography, general science, hygiene, current events, world history, etc. It all sounds very grand but I'm just trying to give some grounding in each subject. A special translator was brought from Delhi so I lecture in English and he translates as I go. The atmosphere became charged with excitement as they learned about the solar system, changes of season, etc. Late into the evening monks could be seen clustered around the globe with flashlights and little balls trying to work out lunar and solar eclipses. They're just lapping everything up and it's such a joy to teach such interested pupils.

Zimey Rimpoche, the head Lama and principal, is young, charming and brilliant. He keeps me running to my books, with intelligent questions on satellites, sound-waves, splitting the atom, etc. Who said Tibetans were resistant to Western science and learning? I spend hours curled up on a rug in his room—speaking Tibetan and English and teaching him but, best of all, learning from one of the most learned Tibetan scholars in India!

On Saturday mornings I climb up to the Dance-Drama School where I'm teaching modern dance exercises to the girls. I don't know who was stiffer after the first lesson—them or me! The girls have improved a lot—they really had no idea how to exercise and develop flexibility and strong backs. Anyway, it's a wonderful chance for me to learn their dances and songs.

I go home to Kangra once or twice a week to spend the night and help Lois. I really look forward to those visits because I miss the children dreadfully. Those Kangra nights are usually sleepless ones—if we aren't battling bed-bugs or rats, it's the heat or a storm that keeps us awake. But it's well worth it.

My first night at the Lama School was a bit of a nightmare. I didn't get to bed till about 1 a.m. after the streams of visitors finally left. Then I started having terrible dysentery pains that got worse and worse. The climax came when something dropped off the shelf onto my head—a large, ugly rat! Soon I had five huge monsters rushing about my room—I had to leave the light on all night and keep kicking them off the bed. I've never seen such bold monsters!

At 5 a.m. a Lama came to sweep my room. I remember wondering if they thought they were going to sweep at that unearthly hour every day—but I've never been so happy to see a human face after that nightmare with the rats! The rest of the day passed in a haze of pain as monks rushed to and fro to nurse me. Then a jeep came in the later afternoon and took me up to Juliet's little bungalow where I stayed for four days to recover.

Then, five weeks ago now, I got sick again but stayed home at the Lama School where I was smothered with loving attention. At one point, when I had a fever, there were five monks standing in a circle around my bed fanning me with newspapers. The head Lama and two other Rimpoches were amongst them. They practically blew me off the bed in their enthusiasm but we had a good laugh over it. When I seemed to be getting sicker after five days, Rimpoche insisted on calling Juliet. I was vomiting all my meals by this time and feeling very dizzy. Mr. Kundeling came with his jeep and I felt a fool as they took me back to Juliet's. And so began a dandy bout of jaundice and infectious hepatitis. You can't imagine how frustrated and fed-up I am at losing so much precious time.

Lois is now living in Upper Dharamsala in what used to be the Education Department. The house was quickly vacated three weeks ago and Lois went there to receive 120 kids who arrived nearly dead. She, Oliver, Claudia, Juliet and Doris battled long into the night to save their lives. Those kids had camped four months on the border without shelter, food or help. They buried two of their number there and then permission came to enter India—on grounds of compassion. Seventeen were left in a nearby hospital—nearly dead—and the others came on here on a nightmare of a train ride in the most blistering heat. You wouldn't believe it unless you saw it—they're still skeletons of children. Two more have died—one in Lois' arms on a frantic jeep-ride to Kangra—of worm-convulsions. Lois had to cremate the body herself.

Life is a bit of a nightmare now. But I'm still madly in love with my Tibetans and don't see how I'll leave in September.

Love, Judy

In the following letter to George Woodcock, Judy Pullen, now Judy Tethong, is writing from her new assignment in Mundgod, in southern India. She confides her own health problems as well as her struggles to finish writing her book. Her contract to write a memoir of Kangra lingered as a challenge for years.

Mundgod
Dec. 12/68
Dear Prof Woodcock,
Your letter of December 3/68 was just handed to me by our barefoot postman from a neighbouring jungle village. . . .
Since my last letter, about four or five more people have died—

I haven't the latest figure. One mother leaves three children orphans—a girl at Kalimpong, one small girl here and a teenage son at Kalakshatra in Madras. The day after the mother died I got a letter from the son saying he wants to come here for his Xmas holidays and could I please send the money for the train ticket. Poor boy doesn't know yet. I wrote to the principal and asked him to break the news just before Ngodup leaves to come here. . . .

Perhaps it would be best if you don't send any money for meds this month—I have enough to last till end of January—we must be very careful—I don't think Mr. Brewster could risk accepting funds for this purpose but he will let you know that. Unfortunately, our "friend" wields a terrific amount of political power (even more than before and would love nothing better than an excuse to get Brewster and all of us out. Since Mr. B. is on the committee in Delhi he would have to put away money through the regular channels and that would be stopped by our friend saying there is no need for meds here etc., etc. This present way it is a direct emergency measure from someone on the spot. I hate to think of all the complications and dangers—only comfort is that we are alleviating a good deal of suffering by taking these risks.

Please keep all the "skullduggery" part confidential. My position here is *very* delicate—T.C. had to sign a letter for me to be allowed to stay here in the camp—promising that I wouldn't do any missionary work and that I will not get involved in politics etc., etc. He was also told outright that he himself would be watched very carefully since he is now married to a foreigner. So the publicity angle in Canada must *always* point out just how much the GOI is doing for the Tibetans (and it is, so that isn't a lie) and how little foreigners have helped, etc. That way the Tibs. [Tibetan children] will be helped, too.

Forgive me for this—you know perfectly well all about it—but I occasionally get cold feet.

I am still plugging away at my book for McGraw-Hill. The deadline is the end of this month and I still have five more chapters to

The Dalai Lama visited the Tethongs' settlement at Mundgod
in southern India in 1967.

write. I seem to have run out of steam lately, what with diversions in
the camp and not feeling too well myself—more kidney trouble.
These past few days I have been at the hospital in Hubli for tests.

The more I write of the book, the worse it sounds on rereading.
Every now and then I pick up your *Faces of India* and wish like heck
my command of the language was even a quarter as good as yours.

I would like your comments on suggested titles—the ones
McGraw-Hill came up with were terrible, ie "I Adopted Tibet" or
"I Married a Tibetan" variety. Apart from the fact that they are
pompous, they have nothing to do with the story. T.C. suggested
"Victims of Innocence" when we were still in Canada and the fam-
ily was most enthusiastic. Since then, I have thought of another:
"Barefoot Down the Mountain" or we could vary it: "Barefoot
Through the Mountains" or "Barefoot in the Snow."

Could you try these out on a few people and then let me know
what their reactions are? I would really appreciate your advice.

Sincerely,

Judy

December 27, 1968
Mrs. T. C. Tethong, Tibetan Settlement,
Mundgod, District North Kanara, India.
Dear Judy:

We were very interested to hear that your book is nearing completion. I certainly know the throes of finishing a book all too well, but I hope very much that you will be able to complete it in time. One always has to bear in mind that publishers, if they really want a book, are not likely to be worried over a few weeks' delay. With regard to the titles, I agree that the "I Married a Tibetan" variety is hopeless. We both very much liked T.C.'s title, "Victims of Innocence." The other suggestion that Inge had was "The Forgotten People."

With warmest regards from us all to both of you for this New Year,

Yours Sincerely,
George Woodcock,
Vice-Chairman

April 26/69
Mundgod
Dear Prof. Woodcock,

Since January 1st this year 13% of our children here at Mundgod have died. What this figure means in terms of human suffering and misery for the families who have already suffered so many losses can scarcely be imagined. On January 1st there were 574 children here of age 10 and under. Of these 44 died between Jan. 1st and April 14th. While measles was the main killer the doctor says malnutrition was mainly responsible—the children had no strength to fight off the infection.

Just now, as I was working on these accounts some men from the camp went by our little hut with a stretcher and a sheet-wrapped body—a woman (in her 20's) has apparently died from acute pulmonary edema. Poor doctor was just here—he worked over her for 2 hours this morning but she was brought to the hospital much too late. We have quite a problem now getting the really sick people to come to the hospital—after a year with the hopeless doctor they have lost faith in the place. . . .

The other day I was doing some camp statistics for Mr. Brewster. Here are a few:

    1967 Total deaths = 9
        of these, one was seven yr. old child
    1968 Total deaths = 76
        of these, 35 were children under age 10
    1969 Total deaths = 54 up to April 26th
        of these 44 were children under 10

Sincerely,
Judy

Mundgod,
August 19/69
Dear Prof. Woodcock,

I had some disappointing news re my book. The whole thing with McGraw-Hill is off. It's a long story but in a way I'm relieved because I was never very comfortable with their editors. I got almost no help or direction—then suddenly, after the book was finished, they asked me to have another go at it to give it more of an Indian slant. All along I'd thought they were interested in the Tib. Story.

I know you are terribly busy but I would be eternally grateful if you would just read the manuscript, see if you feel it is worthwhile for me to put some time into tidying it up and approaching another publisher. Needless to say I was shattered to have this fall apart especially when I'd not wanted to write a book in the first place and McGraw-Hill had pressed me into it!

Judy

TRAS built the Old People's Home at Mundgod for these elderly Tibetans,
who could no longer return to an ancestral village.

TIBETAN REFUGEES IN A DECADE OF EXILE

As a writer, George Woodcock consciously strove for versatility and he took much pride in having different types of arrows in his quiver. He believed writers should develop their skills in a variety of genres, from being a polemicist to being a poet—and few could match his range. In the following excerpts from an essay he wrote for the academic journal *Pacific Affairs*, in 1970, Woodcock shows his predilection for being an historian. He avoids mentioning his personal relationship with the Dalai Lama in favour of providing a strikingly non-personal account, even though the subject moved him deeply.

Tibetans began to leave their country in small numbers immediately after the Chinese army reached Lhasa in 1951. At first these expatriates tended to be relatively well-to-do people who foresaw that their possessions might soon be threatened. A number of noblemen and their families made their way—with their portable property—to Calcutta, where some of them still live, and some of the wealthier Lhasa merchants transferred the scene of their business activities to the Darjeeling-Kalimpong region. In numbers these exiles who came between 1951 and 1959 were very few, and since they did not require assistance they passed almost unnoticed in the polyglot and polycultural society of West Bengal, which contains many native-born people of the Tibetan race.

It was after the Dalai Lama's flight from Lhasa in March 1959, with the concurrent uprisings in Lhasa and in Kham, that large numbers of Tibetans of all classes began to cross the mountainous frontier not only into India, but also into the smaller Himalayan states of Nepal, Sikkim and Bhutan. They fled for a variety of reasons: some because they feared religious persecution, some (particularly the nomads who came into the frontier areas of Ladakh and Nepal) because they feared collectivization of their herds, and some (particularly among the Khambas) because they had fought unsuccessfully as guerrillas against the Chinese army. Especially in the west, towards Ladakh, the flow of refugees continued quite strongly until 1962; since then, there has been a slight but steady trickle of individuals and small groups (Peter Aufschnaiter told me of meeting a family of newly arrived nomads in northern Nepal in the summer of 1969), but not enough to make an appreciable difference to the refugee situation as a whole.

Since many, particularly women and children, died in crossing the 16,000-foot passes in the spring of 1959, or were killed in guerrilla actions against the Chinese, it is hard to estimate how many Tibetans fled their own country. It is even difficult at this date to say just how many reached their host countries in the early months of the exodus.

In 1962 Tony Hagen, who was then in charge of International Red Cross operations in Nepal and whose knowledge of the country is considerable, told me that there were 30,000 Tibetan refugees in that country alone. When I went there in December 1969, it seemed certain from the information I was able to gather that no

These Chinese army trucks appeared outside the Potala palace in 1951.
"The Potala is said to be one of the largest buildings in the world. Even after
living in it for years, one could never know all its secrets. It entirely covers the
top of the hill; it is a city in itself. It was begun by a king of Tibet 1,300 years
ago as a pavilion for meditation, and it was greatly enlarged by the Fifth Dalai
Lama in the seventeenth century of the Christian era."
— Tenzin Gyatso, the 14th Dalai Lama

more than 12,000 remained. Certainly the death rate in Nepal,
where the government has never helped the refugees in any way,
was extremely high up to about 1966, and many of the Tibetans
who originally went there later found their way into India either
directly or through Sikkim, so that Hagen's figure may indeed have
been true for 1962 but not for 1969. However, there are now no
reliable means of checking it, and the same applies to the early
estimates of Tibetan refugees even in India. . . .

I am not concerned directly with the political situation of the
Tibetan refugees, a whole essay could be written on the political
structure of the refugee community, its tensions and intrigues. Here
I am dealing primarily with the resettlement of the refugees in their
host countries. . . .

The most important development in terms of financial aid to Tibetan refugees since the exodus in 1959 was the dedication in 1966 of $3,500,000 in funds from European Refugee Year to the final solution of the problem by means of large-scale resettlement. On the basis of this fund, Prince Bernhard of the Netherlands was instrumental in creating a Common Project to which the United States, Canadian and some European governments as well as voluntary relief agencies are contributing. Their financial grants are expected to bring the total funds for resettlement to about $9,000,000. The magnitude of these funds, in comparison to anything previously raised for the Tibetan refugees, has meant that the Common Project and its Indian counterpart, the Mysore Resettlement and Development Agency (established in 1968) have become the most important factors, outside the Indian government, in the effort to integrate the Tibetan refugees into the general Indian community. Not all the organizations that aided the Tibetans in the

▼ The Dalai Lama escaping from Tibet to India in 1959

This is a second rare image of the Dalai Lama in the Himalayas, fleeing his homeland in 1959, with (seldom-mentioned) assistance of the CIA.

early days have welcomed the Juggernaut approach of the Common Project, and some at least (certainly Schweizer Tibethilfe and the Tibet Society) are likely to remain aloof and to pursue independently projects which they regard as suited to the interests and needs of particular groups of refugees.

The Tibetans themselves are—at least overtly— represented by the shadow government which the Dalai Lama maintains at Dharamsala, where he has given his residence a look of permanence by moving from the old tin-roofed bungalow he inhabited in the early years of exile to a new palace (built in the dreariest of Indian PWD styles) which looks across from its heavily guarded hillside to a large new temple built from the contributions of the devout. Officially, the Indian government does not recognize the Dalai Lama as an exiled head of state, but in practice he occupies that position and retains the traditional Kashag, or cabinet, whose three members deal respectively with education, religious affairs, and resettlement. He also maintains offices in Delhi, Geneva, New York (for the United Nations) and Khatmandu, though there his representative is not recognized even de facto by the Nepal government for fear of offending the Chinese. There is now an elected assembly of the Tibetan refugees in India, which appears to represent all classes, but in the unreal circumstances of an expatriate life it is hard to determine how far this marks a genuine turn in the direction of democracy.

In practice, the Indian government and the foreign agencies deal partly with the Dalai Lama and his officials, and partly with more obscure leaders who range from the "grey eminences" at Dharamsala (powerful among them the Dalai Lama's elder brother, Gyalo Thondup) to the gurus of minority groups. For the Tibetan community is fissured—how deeply an outsider cannot estimate with complete accuracy—by sectarian differences. At Dharamsala, and generally in the exile administration, the members of the Gelukpa sect (Tibet's equivalent of the Church of England) are in control, but many of the refugees belong to the smaller but older Sakya, Nyingmapa and Kargyupa sects; some even adhere to Bon, the pre-Buddhist shamanistic cult of Tibet. These sectarians like to live in the physical locality of their gurus, some of whom are immensely venerated incarnations like the Sakya Lama near Dehra Dun or the Karmapa Lama at Gangtok, or were formerly leaders of prestigious monastic communities in Tibet. The consequence is that a number of small groups have formed themselves in the Himalayan foothills, each sharing a certain sectarian stance, and all resistant to incorporation in large resettlement projects under Gelukpa control.

These groups, which are likely to include both monks and laymen, and which usually follow some important exiled abbot or tulku, maintain that they are worse off physically because the Gelukpas discriminate against them. I am not convinced that a disparity actually exists, since I have seen many completely destitute Gelukpas and some sectarian communities which were

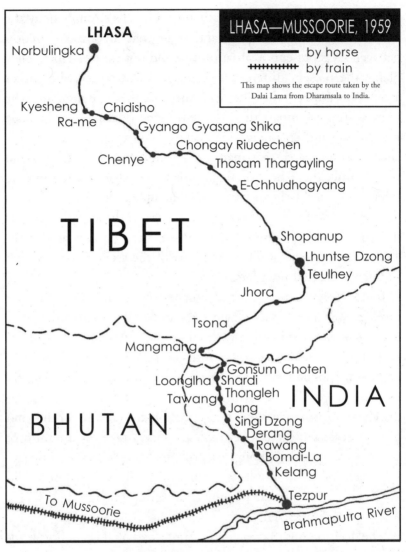

LHASA

Norbulingka

Kyesheng
Ra-me   Chidisho
          Gyango Gyasang Shika
          Chongay Riudechen
Chenye   Thosam Thargayling
                    E-Chhudhogyang

TIBET
                    Shopanup
                    Lhuntse Dzong
                    Teulhey
          Jhora
     Tsona
Mangmang
               Gonsum Choten
Loonglha Shardi
          Thongleh   INDIA
Tawang   Jang
          Singi Dzong
BHUTAN   Derang
          Rawang
          Bomdi-La
          Kelang
                    Tezpur
To Mussoorie
               Brahmaputra River

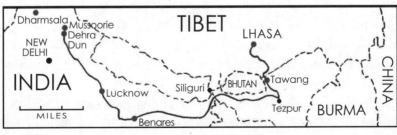

Dharmsala Mussoorie
          Dehra   TIBET
NEW   Dun   LHASA
DELHI

INDIA
          Lucknow   Siliguri BHUTAN Tawang
                                        CHINA
MILES   Tezpur   BURMA
          Benares

relatively prosperous. The Dalai Lama's officials strongly deny the accusations of discrimination and argue that the present friction between sects presents a situation that did not exist in Tibet. They blame the present differences on foreign dilettantes who gather around the gurus of the older sects (because these are thought to be more willing to impart the so-called "secret doctrines" of Lamaist Buddhism) and encourage the sectarians in their sense of griev ance. I would agree that many of the numerous westerners who seek to milk the Tibetan refugees for knowledge or sensation are often irresponsible in the way they encourage divisive tendencies between sectarian groups. In practical terms, the situation means that the Tibetan refugees cannot be treated as a homogenous mass. The desire for separation on the part of the sectarian groups has inevitably affected resettlement plans.

In 1959, when the Tibetan refugees arrived in India, the first problem was to save them from starvation. Many individual exiles brought with them jewels and religious objects, which they sold to keep them alive for the early months of expatriation, and for some years, until about 1963, the bazaars of Darjeeling, Kalimpong and even Delhi were flooded with low-priced Tibetan artifacts. The Indian government avoided as far as possible the creation of the kind of large-scale refugee centres that so quickly take on the form of concentration camps (though one tuberculosis-ridden "temporary" settlement of 1,200 monks at Buxa near the Bhutanese border did acquire a justly unsavoury reputation during the decade before it was dispersed in 1969).

The decision not to create large camps had obvious political reasons. Internationally, in 1959, Nehru's government was inclined to underplay the whole Tibetan situation in the interests of peace with China, while nationally there was the possibility of discontent among Bengali refugees if they had any reason to believe the Tibetans were better treated than they.

The price of avoiding the camps was that thousands of refugees joined the existing mendicant population of India, many living for

SAKYA LAMA

Other religious leaders fled Tibet at the same time as the Dalai Lama, including the Sakya Lama, who had established himself with a thousand followers at the foot of the Himalayas. In 1970, George Woodcock wrote: "There was no road in; we had to travel by jeep, along narrow jungle paths where the branches lashed our faces. The Sakya Lama came out to meet us, a figure out of the Tibetan Middle Ages: a tall and portly man clad in a gown of gold brocade, his hair coiled in plaits above his round face and secured by a jewel of ruby and gold, big turquoise rings hanging from his long, distended earlobes. Head of the oldest Tibetan Buddhist sect, the Sakyas, he

was not a monk like our friend the Dalai Lama. He was a layman, a kind of sacred king revered for the traditions he embodied. He had even, he said rather ruefully, to marry shortly in order to ensure the hereditary succession of the Sakyas. We would eventually be able to help him through the Tibetan Refugee Aid Society. I complimented him on the excellent English he had acquired since he fled from Tibet in 1959. He brightened greatly at this. He enjoyed English, he said. He enjoyed reading English books. What books did he particularly like? I asked. "*Alice in Wonderland*," he answered, and for the moment it seemed hilariously incongruous, to be sitting here in sight of the snow peaks of the Himalayas, talking with this man who seemed to have stepped out of a distant Central Asian past about the March Hare and the Mad Hatter. But there was an odd rightness to the situation, as there is to much about Lewis Carroll. I asked him about the nonsense verses. No problem there, he assured me; they had their own mantras which the monks chanted, and these were so old that nobody really understood their meaning, but perhaps for that reason everyone believed they were very potent. But best of all, he said, with a great smile irradiating his round face, framed by its huge earrings, he liked the Cheshire Cat; it was such a splendid image for the Buddhist belief in the transitory, illusory nature of the physical world."

periods of months or years by begging and by small distributions of food arranged by missionaries or relief organizations. Two examples, from a report I wrote on a visit to northeastern India in January 1962, will give an idea of the number of people in this situation. "In Kalimpong 3,390 refugees queued up on the day [I] visited the town, for a distribution of powdered milk—the only food available—by a Christian organization. In Darjeeling the Dalai Lama's representative in charge of relief said that 1,200 destitute people came regularly for the twice-weekly distribution of powdered milk and a little rice."

In the years between 1959 and 1964, aid to the Tibetan refugees was haphazard and dominated by a sense of emergency. The only agency that even attempted general co-ordination, the Central Relief Committee, had no field staff to make its role effective, and in practice foreign relief agencies co-operated on an ad hoc basis, exchanging information to spread the available aid as widely as possible. Yet despite the absence during this early period of an effective co-ordination, three basic and complementary approaches to the refugee problem quickly became evident.

The foreign agencies were at first primarily oriented to child welfare, and the result was the establishment in the former British hill stations of the Himalayas (from Dalhousie and Dharamsala in the west through Simla, Kasauli and Mussoorie, to Darjeeling and Kalimpong in the east) of a number of residential schools, first supported by voluntary contributions and later taken over by the Indian government. In 1969 there were approximately 4,000 children in these schools, which consciously attempt, with the tacit approval of the Indian authorities, to inculcate and preserve a sense of Tibetan nationalism.

In addition to the residential schools, there are a number of more specialized institutions for child care and education, supported mainly by the foreign relief agencies. These include the Tibetan Children's Nursery at Dharamsala, founded and directed by the Dalai Lama's sisters; the Tibetan Homes Foundation for 600 chil-

When Tibetans first arrived in India, many men and women were forced to become subsistence labourers on road gangs, such as these labourers at Manali in the Kullu Valley. Unaccustomed to India's high temperatures and diseases, many workers died. It became an urgent priority for relief agencies such as TRAS to provide health services, schooling and housing for orphans.

dren at Mussoorie, operated on the Pestalozzi village system by Mrs. R.D. Taring, a Lhasa noblewoman of exemplary devotion; and a number of institutions devised to provide vocational training, such as the Foundation Training Centre at Dehra Dun (established with American, Swiss, English and Canadian funds) and the misleadingly named Indo-Tibetan Buddhist Cultural Institute at Kalimpong where a great monastic scholar, Dhardo Tulku, pioneered in introducing Tibetan children to the kind of training in trades and crafts for which the old-fashioned and academically oriented Indian school curriculum makes little provision.

These institutions for the care of children were intended not merely for the many orphans and semi-orphans. They were also planned to give at least temporary homes for children whose parents were alive but unable to provide for their families. A small number of refugees had salvaged enough capital out of the ruin of exile to set up as petty traders in the largely Tibetan communities

KARMIC RELATIONSHIPS

In 2006, Chung Tsering had the opportunity to study English in Vancouver. There he met TRAS directors Jennifer and Daphne Hales and discovered he had briefly met Daphne Hales and her husband when they had visited his classroom in Dharamsala. "We only discovered this in 2006 when Daphne showed me one of her photos," he says, "and there I am in my 1994 classroom. Sometimes life is hard to explain. I think this is Karma." Chung Tsering now works as a Research Officer for the Tibetan Government-in-Exile's Department of Education (DOE) in Dharamsala.

He recalls: "In 1991, I arrived in north India from Tibet and studied at the Tibetan School in Bir Suja where TRAS has sponsored many projects. I think my relationship with TRAS started at that time. After that I joined the Tibetan teacher-training program at the Institute of Buddhist Dialectics in Dharamsala. Again, TRAS was the sponsor of this program.

"After this program started, many of its trainees got Indian government-recognized teaching certificates and the Tibetan government was able to implement its policy of 'teaching all subjects through Tibetan language' until Grade 5. Ninety-five percent of those trainees, including my wife, are now still working as teachers at schools in India and Nepal. From these teacher training programs, many writers, researchers and editors have emerged. The famous exile Tibetan magazine *TSAMPA* and many others were started by those trainees.

Chung Tsering in 2008 in Dharamsala with his niece (left) and two children

"After I finished my teacher training, I joined the DOE. We have organized many projects, with, of course, support from TRAS. You may think my relationship with TRAS ended here, but it continued, and is even deeper than before. My wife and I needed someone to look after our two children because we both needed to work.

In this 1994 photo of the TRAS-supported Tibetan teacher-training program in Dharamsala, student Chung Tsering is seated in the second row on the right), alongside the teacher, Mogchog Rinpoche.

We have no family in India to care for them and could not afford to hire someone. Again thanks to TRAS, our children have been cared for. TRAS sponsors Little Flowers Creche so we could send both of our 'little flowers' to this 'little flowers garden.'

"I met Jennifer Hales one month after I arrived in Vancouver in 2006. I thought this was just the start of my personal relationship with TRAS. I never imagined that actually it dated back more than ten years. One day, Jennifer invited me for dinner at her parents' house where her mother, Daphne, showed me photos of TRAS projects. That's when I discovered my real relationship with TRAS. I was deeply moved and amazed.

"After discovering my relationship with TRAS, I feel grateful from the bottom of my heart, not only because TRAS helped me and my family many times, but also because TRAS supported and helped many other poor people when they needed it. Thank you, TRAS, for changing my life."

of Sikkim, Darjeeling and Kalimpong, or among the concentrations of refugees at Dharamsala and Mussoorie.

But for many thousands, a means to keep alive on a bare survival level was provided by work on the roads which the Indian government was building in the frontier regions and which were greatly extended for strategic reasons after the Chinese invasion in the autumn of 1962. The majority of the Tibetan road workers were concentrated in Himachal Pradesh, where they lived in makeshift camps; wages were so low that both men and women had to work, and the camps were so unhealthy that children had to be taken away to live in the residential schools or children's homes until some means of re-uniting the families in settled circumstances could be found.

[*Pacific Affairs*, Vol. 43, No. 3 (Autumn 1970), pp. 410–20]

Refugees continue to flee from Tibet, as evidenced by the film *Murder in the Snow*. It had its Canadian premiere at Langara College in Vancouver, March 20, 2009, introduced by Dr. Tsering Shakya, professor, Institute of Asian Research, UBC, who received TRAS support as a youngster in Mussoorie. The Australian-made documentary *Murder in the Snow* includes footage of a fleeing Tibetan teenager, Kalsang Namtso, who was shot to death by Chinese border guards at Nangpa Pass. More fortunate are these earlier refugees (above) in Dharamsala, with their volunteer English teacher Lesley Thomson.

PART TWO

THE INTERVIEWS

MEETING HIS HOLINESS

John Conway first met the Dalai Lama in 1972. Accompanied by his wife Ann (pictured above), they met a second time, at Dharamsala, on March 17, 1977. Conway wrote: "It was one of those fine spring mornings with all the first blossoms ablaze in the garden of the Dalai Lama's residence, and the mountain peaks glistening with snow in the background. His Holiness was kind enough to give us nearly an hour of His time, when we were able to discuss with Him the work of our Society and to bring Him the greetings of our supporters in Canada. The Dalai Lama was particularly pleased by the continuing evidence of our concern for the Tibetan people. He stressed the importance of our remembering not only the 100,000 Tibetan refugees but also the 6 million Tibetans still in the homeland. Their human rights are still trampled on, their freedom to conduct their own affairs denied, their national identity suppressed. The new emphasis placed by President Carter on human rights has been most welcomed." During a subsequent visit with Mrs Gyalpo, the Dalai Lama's sister, Conway was summoned for another meeting with the Dalai Lama in 1995, but he declined: he didn't wish to waste the Dalai Lama's time.

JOHN CONWAY

John Conway, the unsung administrative hero during the first 20 years of TRAS, was one of several people invited by Ingeborg and George Woodcock to serve on the first TRAS board of directors after he had arrived to teach International Relations at UBC in 1957. When George had a heart attack in 1971 and the Woodcocks were thinking they would have to dismantle the organization, Conway volunteered to replace George at the helm as vice-chairman. During visits to India, Conway, a UBC history professor, became increasingly aware that job training for Tibetan refugees should become his top priority.

Born in London in 1929, Conway was sent to public school in northern England at Sedbergh because his father knew the headmaster there. In 1948, as an eighteen-year-old, conscripted private in the British army, he was sent to Austria where his daily job on the Russian frontier was to interview refugees rounded up by the Austrian police.

"These were mainly Hungarians fleeing Soviet collectivization," he says. "There were some families, but mostly it was single men, peasants really. Some of them were in a very sorry state."

With a Ph.D. from Cambridge in International Relations and History, specializing in Germany, Conway accepted a posting at the University of Manitoba in Winnipeg in 1955. There he became active in organizations such as the World University Service and the Student Christian Movement. In the following year, when Hungarian refugees began arriving in Canada after the failed Hungarian Revolution, history repeated itself.

"I was drawn into helping all over again," he says. "By the time I came to UBC, I had joined the Canadian Institute of International Affairs and the United Nations Associations. So my NGO pedigree was firmly established. And I'm still at it."

During the 1970s, John Conway's successful grantsmanship and his highly efficient management style were in strong contrast to Ingeborg Woodcock's persuasive benevolence. In a 1975 essay Conway noted, "Not only have the agencies been able to undertake a more meaningful involvement in overseas schemes, but they have also been encouraged, even prodded, into thinking in developmental terms, rather than in terms of charitable 'do-goodism.'"

In the early 1970s, Conway also differed from the Woodcocks in his assessment of the need for continuing Tibetan refugee aid. In 1970 George Woodcock published an article stating that the influx of Tibetans to India had essentially lessened to a trickle, making refugee-oriented aid far less warranted. Conway at this period remained convinced that there was an ongoing crisis of poverty that required developmental aid and that TRAS should continue its role.

Conway also differed from the outgoing couple on TRAS administrative issues. He does not supply specifics but relates the following incident: "Once, after we had already fixed the budget for the year, George and Inge had some other interests. So they drove over to my house. Basically, I said no. And they departed in high dudgeon." It was a bitter divide. The Woodcocks were irate that Conway would turn down their specific request to TRAS for a generator needed for a new hospital built by a close friend of theirs in India, but Conway was firm that TRAS continue with its agreed-upon plan and budget for the coming year.

On another occasion, Conway and Ingeborg disagreed about the composition of the TRAS board of directors. "Inge was very protective about who was on the board," he says. "I thought the board was in danger of becoming geriatric, so I had invited a younger person to contribute. There was a bit of a scene and Ingeborg was extremely rude." In fact, according to their friend Tony Phillips, the Woodcocks wanted to place their own representatives onto the TRAS board of directors to regain influence.

Managing TRAS with a tenacity that mirrored Ingeborg's dominance, Conway could be a bit of a one-man show at times, but he produced results in the second era of TRAS that arguably outstripped the initial era of the organization's founders. Conway cemented the society's ongoing partnerships with CIDA and accessed grants from a little-known capital fund of $5 million set aside by the government of British Columbia in 1970 called the Fund for Agricultural Aid to Developing Countries and World Disaster Areas.

Conway was also solely responsible for the deposit of TRAS archives in the Special Collections section of the University of British Columbia, a massive undertaking in itself, comprising 43 boxes of carefully organized materials, chronologically pre-arranged by Conway. In addition to his detailed reports for inspection visits to India (1971, 1972, 1974, 1977), he was a skilled political activist who contributed editorials and reports to newspapers and periodicals.

In 1981 Conway gave way to a new chairman, Peter Jones, having arrived at a viewpoint similar to George Woodcock's perspective at the outset of the preceding decade. "At what point should we tell the Tibetans to start looking after themselves?" Conway argued. New programs and new ideas were required. Ultimately the organization kept its acronym TRAS but re-named itself the Trans-Himalayan Aid Society nine years after Conway stepped aside.

Still married after more than 50 years, John Conway remains active in international aid work. For seven years he was the chairman of the Refugee Committee of the Anglican Diocese of New Westminster (Vancouver), which has sponsored refugees to resettle in B.C.

The following interview with John Conway by Alan Twigg took place at the University of British Columbia. John Conway lives in Vancouver, near Jericho Beach.

TWIGG: Who do you think was mostly behind the formation of TRAS: Ingeborg or George?
CONWAY: When it came to organizing help for the Tibetan refugees, it was Inge who was the spark. She accomplished a considerable amount. But George handled nearly all of the correspondence.

TWIGG: How did you become involved?
CONWAY: I taught International Relations. I became the secretary. The minutes were circulated but certainly they were kept, institutionally, by the Woodcocks. George was the vice-chairman, and Larry MacKenzie, the university president, was the purely honorary chair. It was probably George who went after Larry MacKenzie. Larry was a sucker for all this sort of thing. He was a founding member of the Student Christian Movement at Dalhousie when he was an undergraduate, when he had just come back from the war.

TWIGG: So all this was sanctioned from the top. It wasn't done under the radar?
CONWAY: Oh, yes. It was sanctioned from the top. Larry MacKenzie was quite prepared to make use of the university's facilities. One of the first things that Larry did was to say, "Well, if you need a treasurer, I'll put my finger on somebody in the finance department." That happened to be John Lomax, a hard-working

John Conway first visited with his foster child Samten Wangmo in Mussoorie in December of 1974. He met her eighteen years later when she was happily married, with two small children, living in Dharamsala. The Conways now help to support Samten's two children, one of whom is studying to become a dentist.

bureaucrat in the finance office. He was told to keep the books for TRAS. Lomax had no connection with Tibet. Larry said, "You do it." And a very good job he did, too, for many years.

TWIGG: What was the TRAS organization?
CONWAY: Somehow we must have got a constitution, or at least some appointment of officers, and we held regular meetings as to how to raise funds. The key contact was Mrs. Taring. She had acquired these homes in Mussoorie, part of the hill station where the British had gone for their summer holidays.

TWIGG: Mussoorie had also been a hill station for missionaries.
CONWAY: Yes. So there were must have been about 25 to 28 abandoned mansions that were suitable for conversion for the purposes of housing these children. Some of the missionaries are still

there, at the other end of town. The last time I went there I was surprised to see a Canadian flag. The Swedes were some of the first to support these Tibetan refugees. And the most assiduous and active foreigner was the Swiss named Dr. Wiederkehr from Geneva. When I first knew him, he must have been in his sixties. He was devoting himself to raising money on behalf of these children. He had been a banker or something. Each year he spent a good deal of time visiting the individual children he had sponsored, trying to ensure they were put in the right schools, taking the right courses, and so on. Anyway, this was a very obvious model that the Woodcocks wanted to support.

TWIGG: Sponsorships for individuals.

CONWAY: Yes. Inge came back and would rush around to all her friends, and to every possible audience, with the photographs, and say, "I need money to sponsor these children." That was very much the Wiederkehr model. Individual sponsors got a name and a photograph. She did it, of course, entirely out of her back pocket. She had, I think, a card index on which the donations from X, Y and Z were entered by pencil. How the money got into the bank, I'm not sure, but anyway, it did. The principle of operation was there must be no overheads. No overheads! So consequently she paid for the stamps, she paid for the envelopes, and so on. I'm sure she took it out of her own pocket. Nothing would be deducted from the donations. It would go directly to the children.

TWIGG: The original idea for TRAS was that it was people helping people, was it not?

CONWAY: Not only did they know a lot of the literati in Vancouver, but they knew a lot of the artists. Jack Shadbolt, B.C. Binning, all these people. And so, in her good and persistent manner, she would organize an art auction and these people were expected to give a particular picture or whatever. You could get a Jack Shadbolt for much less than its true value. [Chuckling] That was the way she raised the money in the 1960s. Along with the rummage sales.

TWIGG: It was a semi-coercive system that worked until George had his first heart attack.

CONWAY: Yes. That was in 1971. He announced to the committee that, since he wasn't able to carry on, we might as well fold up. We'd done a good job, supporting all these children, and enough was enough. Well, I remember that meeting very well. I said, "Look, it's too bad that George isn't able to carry on. But the fact of the matter is the Tibetan problem is far from finished." The Dalai Lama was still being overwhelmed by the numbers of refugees.

TWIGG: And that didn't sit well with the government in India.

CONWAY: Exactly. The Indian government had accepted the Dalai Lama, somewhat reluctantly. Support for him had grown because of the clash with the Chinese. But when there was a flood of refugees that followed him, the Indian government was becoming much more hostile.

TWIGG: Do you think that the idea to fold up the TRAS tent came from both of them? Or do you think it was mainly Inge being protective of George and his heart? And he was just delivering the message?

CONWAY: Well, I would think it was probably the latter.

TWIGG: How did your ascendancy in the TRAS hierarchy go down with George at the time?

CONWAY: Well, at the time, he sort of said, "Well, if you feel that way, why don't you carry on?" The committee took my side. Basically they said, "Well, if Conway is ready to do this, let's go on." I soon discovered how much work George had been doing. I would spend every afternoon, from four o'clock 'til seven, typing letters. I remember I used to come up to the campus and John Lomax and I would Xerox all these typewritten letters.

TWIGG: How did the partnerships with CIDA come about?

CONWAY: This was around the time that CIDA began to develop under the auspices of a very fine fellow named Lewis Perinbam.

When I first knew him, he was the General Secretary of the World University Service of Canada (WUS). It's a splendid group, still going strong. They came into being after the Second World War. The principal object was to help students around the world with assistance programs. It's a student-run organization but I was enrolled as faculty representative in 1957. There's a student Chair, but the faculty is rather necessary to keep it going from one generation to another. For the past 25 years, from the 1980s, the World University Service at UBC has sponsored refugee students to come to UBC. Every year we have three or sometimes four students who appear from refugee camps, mainly from Africa. As part of their student fees, each UBC student now pays $3.50 to support this program. And we have 35,000 UBC students.

TWIGG: Were you involved in drafting this levy?
CONWAY: Absolutely. Initially it was fifty cents. So every year we have this guaranteed income.

TWIGG: So you don't have to reinvent the wheel to manage this aid program.
CONWAY: Yes.

TWIGG: Do you agree you can only wash so many cars at a charity car wash before the enthusiasm drains away?
CONWAY: Exactly.

TWIGG: George's anarchist approach and your institutionalized approach were necessarily at odds.
CONWAY: Certainly the Woodcocks were leery of governments and institutions. Ingeborg didn't want to have anything to do with the government. I tried to encourage a model based more on the program of the World University Service. When I became Chair of TRAS, I wanted to encourage a model that could be self-sustaining. At the time, in the spring of 1971, Lewis Perinbam had been promoted to vice-president, external, of CIDA, with the responsibility of liaising with all the NGOs of which, of course, WUS was one and

TRAS was another. Having been the president of WUS, Lewis believed that the great disadvantage of the voluntary sector was there was plenty of enthusiasm, but no money. The NGOs had all the inspiration but what they could actually achieve was very limited. On the other hand, a government-run program had no inspiration, there were far too many bureaucratic hurdles, etc., but they had the money. Lewis' view was the best thing would be "public support and private enthusiasm." That was his motto.

TWIGG: And you knew Perinbam from before 1971.
CONWAY: I did. When I immigrated to Canada, in the autumn of 1955, at the University of Manitoba, the campus was visited by the general secretary of the World University Service, one Lewis Perinbam. He was speaking across the country about the program. I went to hear him and I was greatly offended. His view was that the British Empire was the worst possible thing that ever happened. The exploitation, the racism and goodness knows what else. Being himself a coloured person, from East Asia, he didn't have a good word to say. I'm not quite certain, but I think Lewis might have been Malaysian. As a young man he had been educated in Scotland, then he immigrated to Canada. Anyway, he and I had a strong argument about the virtues of the British Empire [laughter]. Perhaps I was somewhat naïve, having just arrived three months ago from Britain.

TWIGG: And this discussion took place in public?
CONWAY: Oh, yes. But he was so nice about it, we became good friends. After that, I went to meetings for the World University Service in Toronto, where Lewis was in charge. I had already joined WUS in Winnipeg, before I came to UBC.

TWIGG: So the role of Lewis Perinbam in the development of Canadian foreign aid was crucial, not just in terms of TRAS.
CONWAY: Precisely. Along the way Lewis Perinbam became the executive director for the Canadian Committee for UNESCO. In

that capacity he was in charge of a very important meeting at the Redpath Library at McGill that led to the formation of CUSO. He was the one who persuaded Diefenbaker, and certainly Pearson thereafter, that CUSO should be given money. After that, I think Lewis took the job with CIDA around 1969. By the time I came along to run the show for TRAS in 1971, Lewis had got this program going for matching grants for small NGOs. He was prepared to offer $3 for every $1 raised. And so, of course, our efforts were enormously assisted.

TWIGG: Had TRAS already applied to CIDA before this?
CONWAY: I am really not sure about that.

TWIGG: Going from rummage sales to CIDA was a major leap.
CONWAY: Well, certainly Lewis Perinbam was the character who saw the vehicle by which things could happen, and he made it happen. In fact, in many cases, Lewis took the initiative to encourage people to apply. Whether this was true in our case, I can't remember but certainly, as soon as I was put in charge, the door was open in Ottawa.

At the same time, it was made quite clear that TRAS would have to expand its horizons. CIDA wasn't interested in the individual sponsorship of individual children. CIDA had already reached the conclusion, and I think I personally had reached this decision along with others on the committee, that what was needed was to provide opportunities for Tibetan refugees, especially those in the north, in the Himalayas, to find some small gainful employment. The Dalai Lama himself stressed that gainful employment was needed.

TWIGG: Because initially the Tibetans had been transferred from squalid refugee camps to road building.
CONWAY: Yes. And that road-building program was absolutely killing. Child labour. Awful conditions. No health facilities. No education. This was why Mrs. Chazotsang wanted to get them out of there. Anyway, the point was that individual relief for children

wasn't going to solve the larger problems. So the Indian government was prepared to allocate unused land in the south, mainly in Karnataka State, for development by the Tibetans. It was scrub land. There was nobody there.

TWIGG: And if it's unused land in India, you have to figure it's not that good.

CONWAY: Of course. So four or five thousand Tibetans would be sent to each of these four settlement areas to clear the land. And the foreign relief agencies would pay for the infrastructure and the machinery. So this is where TRAS came in. In the early seventies, TRAS was able to put together substantial applications to CIDA. In one year we managed to raise $500,000, an enormous amount for such a tiny private agency. This was largely due to CIDA, the B.C. Government's Funds for Agricultural Assistance, and contributions from the private side, through such activities as the Miles for Millions Walk. At the same time, the Dalai Lama handpicked CUSO volunteer Judy Tethong, who had married the aristocrat T.C. Tethong, to go down to Mundgod, one of these four settlements, and look after things on his behalf.

TWIGG: Formerly Judy Pullen, the CUSO volunteer who worked in Dharamsala? And who received the order of Canada in 1976?

CONWAY: Yes. By the time I first went to Mundgod, I think it was '72, they already had a small child. She and T.C. Tethong were in charge of Mundgod. Each settlement had a representative sent by the Dalai Lama. Every Tibetan refugee was to be given one acre per adult. And if they had children, maybe they had half an acre extra. Well, of course, as soon as these four thousand people arrived at Mundgod and were able to subsist, they all started having families. So almost as soon as these settlements were set up, one could see that the land was going to be insufficient.

TWIGG: To say nothing of the facilities.

CONWAY: Exactly. Judy recognized that no provision had been

made for medical care. And it didn't help that the Tibetans were not used to washing often, having few facilities. So Judy found herself called upon to organize a hospital. She turned to TRAS to support this. Although CIDA didn't have ongoing support for a hospital in its mandate, they would help with buildings. And the Pullen family was well-connected in Oakville, Ontario. So Judy and T.C. Tethong took on an enormous challenge. She was a splendid organizer, but it was an uphill struggle because many of the Tibetans were far more eager to put money into building temples than a hospital. When I went to Mundgod, I found they had built a fantastic temple. Judy and T.C. stuck it out for several years before eventually she had to bring her young children to Victoria.

ERIC BRETT

Related by marriage to the Hollywood actress Joan Fontaine, lifelong bachelor Eric Brett was from a wealthy family but lived as a chicken farmer on 32 acres, for five decades, in a two-room shack with a hand pump, near the border of Surrey and Langley. When he sold his property, he decided to give most of his money away to help children. Having heard of the Save the Children Fund and TRAS, he met TRAS president John Conway at the White Rock home of Dorothea and Barry Leach. It was Barry Leach who was able to put the socially awkward World War I veteran at ease. John Conway was expecting to receive a donation of perhaps twenty dollars, at most, Eric Brett wrote a cheque for $100,000. Later Barry helped

arrange for the philanthropist to re-settle in a Fraser Valley care facility—where he lived for only a few weeks until he died. As the executor of his will, Barry Leach was astonished to discover that Brett had bequeathed an additional $300,000 to TRAS as well as $300,000 to the Save the Children Fund. Brett's funds were allocated to teaching job training skills, as he requested.

DOROTHEA LEACH

The Dalai Lama took an active interest in the welfare of TRAS members. As mentioned earlier, he sent medicine to the Woodcocks when Ingeborg Woodcock was ill. He also sent medicine for TRAS director Barry Leach, who died of cancer in July of 1995, shortly after George Woodcock had died in January of the same year. Their widows, both German-raised, remained friends until Ingeborg's death in 2003. Dorothea and Barry Leach were easily one of the most influential and integral couples within TRAS, along with the Woodcocks and the Tethongs.

With Beth Whittaker, Dorothea Leach also trekked for ten days from Pokhara, Nepal, into the remote, harsh area of Mustang (average elevation 13,200 ft.) to reach its capital Lo Manthang, in October of 1996, to further facilitate TRAS sponsorship of 90 girls—a quarter of the girl population of Mustang. Dorothea Leach retired from active service to TRAS in 1999 but has since remained as the society's official patron.

Just as Ingeborg Woodcock went to England prior to World

War II to improve her English, Dorothea Leach, born in Bremen in northern Germany, travelled to the Outer Hebrides in Scotland, after World War II, to improve her English. Hence their pre-war and post-war experiences provided a special bond of understanding when they met in Canada.

"After the war," says Dorothea Leach, "they wanted 10,000 German girls to work in Britain in homes and factories and hospitals. I had worked for the German Red Cross, and because my English was quite good, the English lady who interviewed me said I should work in a hospital. People are still surprised to learn that English was taught in Germany during the war. Well, I never thought of that. English was taught in every high school, six days a week, an hour a day. In northern Germany, we started learning English when we were age ten, and French when we were twelve. In south Germany, it was French first when they were ten, then English at twelve. My mother taught us children always to remember the people 'on the other side' who were suffering as we did. I never grew up to hate the English, although they bombed us all the time."

The following interview with Dorothea Leach was conducted by Alan Twigg in her home in White Rock.

TWIGG: Why have you remained involved with TRAS for so long?
LEACH: Well, let me tell you a story. Once we were giving a talk in Langley and only 21 people came. Barry and I talked about people who were living near a monastery in Tibet. The ground was very rocky so they wanted to buy an orchard. But they had to walk for hours to get there. There were 26 acres and one acre cost $500. At the end of the evening a couple came forward and said to us, "We've just inherited some money. We would like to buy them an acre." And they gave us $500!

That was fantastic. And they sponsored a child. This couple had never travelled. Then one day they bought backpacks and they

DOROTHEA AND BARRY LEACH WITH THE DALAI LAMA

This photograph was taken at the inauguration of the new monastery at Dekyiling, Dehra Dun, in the fall of 1992. Barry Leach was a far-sighted environmentalist and college lecturer who established British Columbia's 850-acre George C. Reifel Migratory Bird Sanctuary in 1961, along with newspaper publisher Fred Auger. To do so, they approached George H. Reifel, owner of most of tiny Westham Island at the mouth of the Fraser River, and persuaded him to lease his land next to the crown tidal flats for a dollar a year. Eventually Reifel gifted a large portion of his family property to the Canadian Government for a permanent bird sanctuary, to be named in honour of his father. Dr. Barry Leach became the founding director of the Institute of Environmental Studies at Douglas College in 1970, continuing in that capacity until his retirement in 1990. He died five years later, at age sixty-five. As president and newsletter editor, he was chiefly responsible for shifting the focus of TRAS to include environmental projects in the Himalayas.

went to visit that orchard and their sponsor child. And they had a wonderful time! They just loved it. This is what I always like. The possibilities from a small seed.

TWIGG: How did you meet your husband?
LEACH: After Scotland, I went to college back in Germany for two years and became an interpreter. I was twenty-four. I was posted to a British garrison near to where we lived. Barry was an officer there and he spoke fluent German. So did his father. And his grand-father. He loved being in Germany. He understood the Germans.

TWIGG: How did you meet the Woodcocks?
LEACH: Well, I was always interested in that area of India and Tibet. My father was in the coffee business, so I grew up with names like Mysore and Sumatra. I just loved exotic places. Around 1964 or '65, Barry and I went to a lecture at UBC. John Conway was there trying to sell Tibetan Christmas cards while the man was speaking at the front. He said he belonged to an organization that was helping Tibetan refugees. I said, "Can anybody join?" He said yes. "How much to join?" Two dollars, he said. "Here you are—two dollars." I was in. I met the Woodcocks perhaps two years after that.

TWIGG: Under what circumstances?
LEACH: We used to collect things and send them to Inge for the flea markets. Barry did his Ph.D. at UBC so he would always go by their home. We were living on the other side of the Nicomekl River on a farm at the time—God knows why. At first, Barry didn't know that the Woodcocks usually stayed up 'til three or four in the morning, so he came by at ten in the morning. That was far too early for them. But just because he had the boxes, he didn't get scolded. [laughter]

I got involved with our camper, the Volkswagen van. I'd pick up Inge at eight o'clock on Sunday mornings and we'd go out to the Lougheed Drive-In, where there was a flea market at which we could sell things. And while we were driving along, of course we chatted. That is how I got to know Inge. And by the time we came back at five, George had coffee ready. Inge counted the money. If we made over $200 we were very pleased. It was a really good day.

TWIGG: How often would you do that?
LEACH: For three years, almost once a week. It depended who phoned, who had stuff to pick up. The Woodcocks knew so many people. They knew every artist from Abbotsford to Horseshoe Bay. So Ingeborg would say, "Oh, they have a very nice table." So off we would go to fetch it. Everything went into the Woodcocks' basement. Everything was very tidy. She was a good *Hausfrau*, I'm telling you. Once a week we met at one o'clock to price everything.

TWIGG: So Ingeborg was definitely the leader.
LEACH: Oh, yes! She made us feel we had to do it. We rummaged through all our stuff. And she would cajole Jack Shadbolt and other artists to give a painting. There was a famous glass blower in White Rock. Inge visited him and picked up this beautiful vase or whatever it was. And he had to give it to her. He couldn't say no to her. She wouldn't accept a no. She would just say, "We need the money. You give something." That was it.

I remember once we needed some money for something. One of these professional people gave something and Inge said, "You can have your cheque back. You can give more." That sort of thing Inge could do.

TWIGG: Do you think you had a special relationship with Ingeborg because you could understand where she came from?
LEACH: Absolutely.

TWIGG: Did you speak English or German?
LEACH: We always spoke English, except when a German expression was needed that might explain something better. Of course she was disappointed I had three children. She thought there were too many people in this world. Maybe I shouldn't say this, but Inge

twice had a miscarriage. With her first husband. And with George. It wasn't because she had to abort.

TWIGG: Having babies is a phenomenon that's pretty hard to stop.

LEACH: Yes, but she thought we should be intelligent enough not to put more people into the world. At the same time she was very kind to my children. Sometimes we felt we were a favourite niece or nephew, or something like that—because they were so kind to us. She liked my daughter and our younger son but she didn't like our older son so much because she was always worried he might disturb George. [Laughter] He was a bit of a loud child. But thousands of children benefited from their compassion, their willingness to help.

TWIGG: What was their general reputation at the time?

LEACH: Highly regarded. Everyone felt the same. George became, as you know, very well known. But there were no airs. You remember the little house? Inge never spent much money on clothing. But she was a wonderful hostess. Of course they knew the Shadbolts and the Onleys and so on, long before we met up. We felt very privileged and honoured that they took such an interest in us. Although they knew they could depend on us not ever to say no! [Laughter] Our van was really very useful, I can tell you. This would be in the late '60s or early '70s. In the early '70s they asked me to be a director. I was very shy. I didn't know all the Tibetan names. I was dumped in and felt very ignorant. Everyone else was a professional.

TWIGG: What were the early meetings like?

LEACH: There would be coffee and cookies. I think George was chairman and John Conway was vice-chairman. [George Woodcock was vice-chairman and John Conway was secretary.] I remember the first time we got money from CIDA, Inge phoned and said, "You won't believe it!" I think we got 28 or 32 thousand dollars. It was matching funds. I think, one-to-three. It was wonderful. Then George had a heart attack. Really, George was her baby. They were so close. He always called her "Darling." And she called him "Darling." She looked after him totally. The heart attack stopped the flea market. Inge said she couldn't do it anymore. She was on the phone the next morning. She phoned one of our directors in the Waldorf School on the North Shore and they came and got the whole basement full of all our collected stuff. Everything went. Barry and I were a little annoyed because we could have sold that stuff. We could have gone on with it.

TWIGG: From the Lougheed Drive-In to Ottawa, that's a pretty big step for funding. Was there any discussion about whether or not they should accept government money?
LEACH: I don't think so. No.

TWIGG: There has been very little recognition of Ingeborg. She was so radically private.
LEACH: Ingeborg was like a lot of Germans after the war when they realized what had happened. . . . She was a little bit . . . well, what was the word. . . ? I wish Barry were here. Barry taught history. He'd say, "Don't forget: not every German was a Nazi and not every Nazi was a German." The Dutch and the French, so many joined with them. Mostly fighting against Russia. Most people assumed Inge left Germany because of the Nazis. But, in fact, her parents suggested that since she was good at languages she should pursue that course. She liked the idea of being a foreign correspondent.

Her uncle had some contact to an elderly lady in England. So he arranged for her to go to England two years before the war. To improve her English. She worked for these two old ladies. Like an *au pair* girl. It wasn't very nice. They really exploited her. She was only eighteen. So she left there and met a young Englishman and married him.

TWIGG: She became British and therefore was not interned.

LEACH: Yes. I sometimes wonder if that happened because she didn't know what else to do. The marriage didn't last very long. She said it was not a good marriage. I think she was married just before the war started. She told me once it was very short. She left him and went to St. Ives. Then she met George in London. They got married and because he was a conscientious objector, they were always on the move. They lived somewhat underground.

TWIGG: In those days it was not simple to get a divorce.

LEACH: That's right.

TWIGG: Was she interested in Buddhism at that time?

LEACH: When I knew her, Inge had for a long time been interested in India and Tibet. I've got books she gave me about reincarnation. After George and [the Indian writer] Narayan were interviewed on Indian radio and they met [Lobsang] Lhalungpa, Inge told me once they were all invited to a big party with all sorts of interesting people. Writers and so on. A very beautifully dressed Indian woman sat down beside Inge and started talking about parents and grandparents and so on. Inge wasn't sure why she was being told these things, so the woman said, "Oh, I apologize, but in a previous life we were sisters. And I thought you had to know what happened to the family." By the time I met her, Inge was very, very interested in that. And open to that.

TWIGG: Could you explain more fully what you mean when you say Inge was a good *Hausfrau*?

LEACH: She was very particular. Everything had to be just so. She painted the inside of the house. She had no plants. Only cut flowers. With cooking, she had eight dishes she did well. And she made hors d'oeuvres always, which you had to finish. I remember she made crepes served with shrimp.

When George died we told her, "Inge, you need someone in the house." She tried one or two but it didn't work. Inge could have

A TRAS partner for thirty-nine years, Mrs. Rinchen Dolma Taring visited the home of Dorothea Leach in White Rock in 1999. The beloved Mrs. Taring died in 2000. "When you stop and think about it," says Leach, "the far-reaching effect of the Woodcocks has been really quite fantastic."

had a cleaning lady all the time but she didn't want anybody in the house. Then finally we got this wonderful Tibetan woman, Tsering [Samang]. My goodness me, nobody was like Tsering in caring for Inge. From the sale of the books they had, there was $6,000, and she [Inge] gave it all to Tsering because Tsering was going to take her family back to Tibet for a visit. That was just before she had to buy her tickets.

TWIGG: Ingeborg was so particular. But in the end, their base-ment was full of mice.
LEACH: Yes. That's true. Because she would never kill anything. That was how she was. They had squirrels, too. And their cat, oh, it was a spoiled thing.

TWIGG: But George and Inge were intellectuals, not nature buffs.
LEACH: That's true. She might say, "Yes, we went into the country. It was lovely." But really that means she just drove through the country. And she smoked all the time. So in the middle of the day, they didn't really go for a walk. Sometimes they would go to Bellingham to this dreadful motel, by the I-5 highway, and they would watch television all day long, because of course they had no television in Vancouver. They went for 48 hours so Inge could buy cigarettes. We had a cabin down there [across the border] so there was a standing order, to bring back cigarettes.

TWIGG: I thought George wasn't supposed to go into the United States—because of his anarchism.
LEACH: But they did slip in, just for a while. They would cross the border via Aldergrove, then go to Bellingham. There was a big grocery store, Meyers. The motel is still there, between the I-5 and Meyers. Every time I go by it I think of them. We once went there to celebrate George's birthday. We happened to be down there. That's how I know they enjoyed the television.

TWIGG: That was their idea of a risqué getaway.
LEACH: [Laughter] Yes, I suppose so.

TWIGG: How was she in the nursing home?
LEACH: When I went there, I would have to go to the reception area, then she would get two cigarettes. There was a little smoking area. But she was very gracious. We were the last people to see her; it was two days before she died. As we were leaving she said, "I'd love to go outside."

So we got a blanket and pushed her in her wheelchair. We went all the way to Granville, to a shoe store, where they had shoes with very pointed high heels. I remember we said to her, joking, this is what you need. We all had a laugh. I held her hand. She said, "It's so comforting to hold your hand." It made me sad.

DAPHNE HALES

Volunteer project manager Daphne Hales has worked tirelessly for TRAS for more than 30 years, visiting projects in the Himalayas, as well as editing and writing much of the superb Trans-Himalayan Aid Society newsletter, a major source for this book. As with TRAS co-founder Ingeborg Woodcock, and TRAS patron Dorothea Leach, Hales' connections to Tibetan refugee relief work can be traced to the repercussions of World War II.

Born in Liverpool as Daphne Miller, she was evacuated from Liverpool, at age two, during World War II, along with her brother and mother, to live for four years in Peterborough, Ontario. Her grandfather, as head of the Rotary Club in Liverpool, had accepted an invitation from a Canadian he had met at a conference, Fred Roy, head of the Rotary Club in Peterborough, to keep his and other Rotary children out of harm's way. In 1944, she was reunited with her father in Jamaica, where he worked for two years for British naval intelligence. She always vowed that she would one day return to Canada, just for a visit.

It didn't quite work out that way. After receiving a degree in Modern Languages (French and Italian), Daphne Miller fulfilled her promise to revisit Peterborough in 1960, but then she drove across North America with friends to Vancouver. Like so many before her, she was dazzled by the beauty of the place, and felt an urge to stay.

Her introduction to Tibetan refugees occurred prior to her introduction to TRAS. During a trip to India, when border conflicts prevented her from visiting the Himalayas in northern India, she and her travelling partner, Ann Feiber from Louisiana, learned it might be possible to visit Nepal instead. At the Nepalese consular office in New Delhi, they spoke to the gardener who told them everyone else was out celebrating a Nepalese holiday. They waited. Eventually the visa officer and the consular party returned, all very drunk, and they were happily granted travel visas on the spot. The flight on Royal Nepalese Airlines in a DC3 airplane from New Delhi to Kathmandu was deplorable. The pilot was dishevelled, there was vomit on the floor, and they feared for their safety. But in Nepal they had the unforgettable experience of visiting a Red Cross refugee camp for Tibetans.

The following summer, two friends in Vancouver, Sue Rigg and Judy Brown, suggested she accompany them to the home of Ingeborg Woodcock to place price tags on items that were to be sold to raise money for Tibetan refugees. Daphne Miller didn't require much convincing. At a Christmas party in 1961 she met her husband-to-be Don Hales, and discovered that, coincidentally, he was sponsoring a Tibetan refugee child through the auspices of TRAS. Daphne and Don Hales have been involved with TRAS ever since.

Daphne Hales was interviewed by Alan Twigg in West Vancouver.

TWIGG: Can you summarize the current TRAS agenda?
HALES: Well, basically it's a small Vancouver-based NGO that sup-

"Go through the local women," says Daphne Hales, a former TRAS president and sponsorship secretary. It has been an unofficial TRAS philosophy since 1962. Her daughter Jennifer Hales became TRAS president in 2009.

ports health and education for children and youth in the Himalayan regions of India, Nepal and Tibet. We mostly partner with local NGOs and schools, often in extremely remote areas. Generally we provide teacher training, vocational trainings for students, library books, computer literacy, as well as maintenance for two daycare centres and a small school in the old Tibetan part of Lhasa. Health care services are also funded in two boarding schools, one in Kathmandu and the other one in the inaccessible Spiti Valley in north India.

Each TRAS director, with the exception of the president and treasurer, is in charge of looking after some projects. This keeps our interest level high and also gives us all a personal contact with what we are supporting. Over the years many of us have taken on a variety of jobs on the board—it's a bit like musical chairs. It's a cooperative rather than a hierarchic structure. At every board meeting, we update our list of current projects. Each project is given a number. We're now up to 291. But there were more before we started counting. It's roughly seven new projects a year. A lot of these projects are three-year or five-year projects. If it's renewed, it keeps the same number.

TWIGG: If enough individuals are helped, does TRAS ever have a hand in transforming an entire community?

HALES: That sounds a bit grand. But there have been some dramatic changes. In the Spiti Valley, for instance, the people have been classified as a "scheduled caste," meaning that the government believes they are not worth educating. The elementary schools are rarely staffed, and there is only one high school for the valley. Basically the educational system is pathetic. Everyone expects the kids to return, after a brief schooling, to work on the arid, rocky little family plot to eke out a meagre living. So we have been involved with running a school with the Rinchen Zangpo Buddhist Society, whose lama was sure the kids were capable but just lacking opportunity. TRAS has supported the Munsel-Ling School in the Spiti valley for the twelve years of its existence.

The school now has 380 children, most of them boarders from remote tiny villages. The first class of undernourished, poverty-stricken children has now graduated, and TRAS members are supporting the first four admitted from that region to universities and colleges to train as doctor, nurse, administrator and artist. We have photos of them as little urchins in grade one and as handsome, competent teenagers now. All plan to return to their valley to work. TRAS trained the first six teachers—all local women. The training was done by a German woman who lived there for a year to help them. Then we trained the housemothers to look after the kids. We provided and stocked the library, the computer room, a small healthcare centre, trained two community health workers, built a greenhouse (the first of seven) and are now about to fund the water storage and distribution system.

TWIGG: So it amounts to about 300 projects overall?

HALES: Yes. Some of them are large, integrated development schemes; others are tiny. The very last one on the list involves obtaining books for a remote school of 162 children in Miao. It will fund about 400 books to create a school library. But over the next ten years, that's going to be several hundred children. Half of the books will be Tibetan and half of them will be English. The Tibetan ones are mostly printed in Dharamsala. There are Tibetan-English dictionaries, Tibetan-Chinese dictionaries, grammar books, myths and legends of Tibet and comic books galore. They have a huge sense of humour and they love teaching through humour.

They have all sorts of comic books to help the children be good citizens and to look after the environment. In this project, they plan to open the school library after hours to encourage the adults to read because in this little settlement, there's 50 percent illiteracy among the adults. They hope the adults can come and start reading the simple books with their children. It could end up that these books help the whole settlement to become literate.

TWIGG: Would you say that working with the women is the most cost-efficient way of generating social progress?
HALES: Yes. What we've found is that when you start women empowerment groups or adult literacy groups, in the beginning the people often can't come because they have so many jobs, particularly in the Indian villages, but they come a bit and they begin to read. And then we are asked to create a little library for them. I've got a photograph. There's a tiny room with two little shelves chock-a-block full of the Indian equivalent of Harlequin Romances. Because this is what the women want. They want escapism. But the man who runs it says, "The cunning thing is, as soon as I get them hooked on reading, I slip in some pamphlets on primary health care and agriculture."

TWIGG: So the women are the primary catalysts for change?
HALES: Yes. You go through the local women. Local NGOs will have a meeting of the village women and they'll ask, "What's the

most important thing to you?" It nearly always turns out that the health of their children is the most important thing for them. So you say, "Okay, if we brought in a community health worker, would you listen to her?" Through some very basic primary health care, the women start to realize the value of outside help. Then the NGO can start daycare centres so that the women can earn a bit of income, often just by sitting at home doing the traditional weaving. And then they set up a little shop to sell it. And then they set up a bank account for each woman so she has her own money for food and medicine. It doesn't go on drink and gambling and so forth.

Our local partners tell TRAS that children who attend daycare centres are more likely to go to school. And mothers who start to earn a little income, while the kids are in daycare, push to keep their daughters in school. Those girls want careers, they marry later and have babies only after their bodies have matured, thus producing healthier children, and fewer of them.

Women husking corn, camp #1,
Mundgod, 1968

TWIGG: So how does it usually work? Do local people "on the ground" hear about TRAS and apply for help? Or do you seek out these situations?

HALES: We never seek out situations. We have never imposed what we feel they need on them. We've always had the requests come from them. So we work through small Indian NGOs. And we work through the Tibetan

Here women prepare wool for weaving in the Kangra Valley.
In 1976, when Muhammad Yunus of Bangladesh provided a personal loan to 42 women making bamboo furniture, he was following the ideas of Dr. Akhtar Hameed Khan, founder of the Pakistan Academy for Rural Development (now the Bangladesh Academy for Rural Development). Thirty years later, Yunus, a Bangladesh banker and economist, received his well-deserved Nobel Peace Prize for founding Grameen Bank, a system of micro-banking whereby small loans are provided to the poor—particularly women—in order to effectively reduce poverty. This system of empowering women to generate income mirrors many of the micro-projects undertaken with TRAS support in the Himalayas. The empowerment of women was identified by TRAS as "the way to go" in the 1960s—before Muhammad Yunus' admirable initiative in Bangladesh.

Government-in-Exile. And in Nepal we've worked through this big school, the Buddha Academy Boarding School. And there's also a little society, a local NGO, Nagarik Aawaz, that has done wonders for the widows from the Maoist conflict.

TWIGG: So it's generally health and education related?
HALES: Not necessarily. For instance, Barry Leach was at an environmental conference. Nepal had woken up to the fact that if you wanted to create a beautiful park for the tourists to come, you couldn't just tell the local people to move out. It didn't work. It's a disaster if you do that. So they had this conference to figure out how to manage the local people. Barry told them the way to do it is

to get the local people to manage the park. Train them in good environmental practices. And when they have the livelihood, they can stay put. They are part of the local colour that people come to see. And it works beautifully. This is what has happened all around the Annapurna Range in Nepal. The locals have become the lodge operators and the suppliers of kerosene and the guides. They build the campsites for the tourists to stay in. They build better paths.

TWIGG: There must have been a trial and error period to evolve these funding strategies.

HALES: Yes. CHIRAG, one of the organizations we've worked with for years, once made the grave mistake of bringing in a male doctor. And of course the women wouldn't go. So they had to bring in a female doctor instead. And then it started to work. That was back in the 1980s. They made that mistake even though they were all Indians themselves. CHIRAG stands for Central Himalayan Integrated Rural Action Group. It was started by Kanai Lall, a wealthy Indian who worked for a big American company in New York, in order to "give back" something to his own people. He retired to a small town near Nainital, where he and his wife built a house. Since then CHIRAG has done some wonderful things.

TWIGG: Can you recall any details of that refugee camp you visited in 1961?

HALES: That happened because we met the head of a local Red Cross team. I remember the Tibetan Refugee Camp mostly consisted of leaky old army tents. One of their leaders was a noble Tibetan woman who had received her schooling in Darjeeling so she spoke English very well. I distinctly remember she was teaching English using a textbook from Victorian England. In those days, Kathmandu was tiny and medieval. They gave us tourist forms to fill out made of rice paper. Ours were numbered 164 and 165, so I suppose we were the 164th and 165th persons allowed to officially visit during this period of opening up the country to foreigners. While we were there, we saw the first flower-painted Volkswagen bus roll in. After that, the flood of hippies began.

TWIGG: What else do you recall of the early days?

HALES: I remember I helped with some of the flea market sales and the book sales that were overseen by Ingeborg. I also began to hold silent auctions of children's outgrown clothing twice a year. All my friends crowded into my or someone's basement and we would stock up—mostly on good quality Marks and Spencer clothing our respective mothers had sent in previous years from England! For several years, my children would mention with pride at school that THEIR clothes came from the Tibetan sale. It was the GAP of the day to them! Then raising children intervened. I sort of backed off until my youngest was in kindergarten in 1976. I guess I've been at it ever since.

One memory is very clear. In the mid-seventies, the Woodcocks managed to arrange for a planeload of Tibetan refugees to come to Canada, and they had rented the Seventh Day Adventist Camp near Hope for the winter. That way, with TRAS and others helping, the Tibetans could be taught English and eased into a new lifestyle as a group, so they wouldn't be too homesick. But at the Vancouver Airport, the B.C. government would not allow the Tibetans off the plane. Frantic phone calls were made to Ottawa. The plane took them all to Alberta, where the Tibetans were dispersed far away from each other. Some went to Japanese beet farms, where they couldn't communicate with their bosses. Gradually the Woodcocks and the Leaches brought some of the families back to B.C., with Inge rallying her friends around to scrub out houses and find jobs for the Tibetans.

TWIGG: Are you ever able to keep track of how some of the individuals have been affected by TRAS projects?

HALES: Yes. One of the girls that we sponsored, Sonam, was in the Tibetan Homes Foundation. She did vocational training. TRAS supplied the workshops and paid for the vocational training. She then was married to a Tibetan farmer down south, in one of the

Tibetan settlements. They had two children. One tragically died. For his graduation ceremony they had gone for a hike and he fell off the mountain. But now we have sponsored the daughter, Tenzin, as a nurse. She is now fully independent, with a job. She is looking after her parents as well as herself. So you can see how helping one person, thirty years ago, can help a whole family. And of course Tenzin is also doing good work in the community.

TWIGG: Are you hopeful that the work of TRAS can continue? Is there a younger generation of volunteers on the way up?

HALES: Several B.C. schools have supported TRAS work and, interestingly, the impetus has often come from the students themselves. At Argyle Secondary School in North Vancouver, one student, who decided she wanted to help children in poorer parts of the world, formed a small group to run a Himalayan Evening for students and adults, preparing a wonderful Nepali meal, and arranging entertainment and talks. This project is now in its fifth year, raising funds to support the vocational training program at Buddha Academy in Kathmandu.

"This is my all-time favourite photo," says Daphne Hales. "They're both barefoot. And you suddenly realize that this tiny kid is carrying an even smaller baby on her back. This photo, circa 1960, says to me, 'Where's our future? Where are we going?'"

The Student Council at Sutherland Secondary School in North Vancouver took up the same challenge and has shown great initiative in putting on a fabulous fashion show, book sales, and information stalls at fairs, to raise funds each year. This is their fourth year for it now. So it keeps growing. We've also had an adult-initiated art exchange between two classes of youngsters in Vancouver and North Vancouver and two schools in India and Tibet.

TRAS has never been a high-profile organization, but as long as we continue to support students' efforts with talks, slide shows, displays, newsletters, and letters from the field, I hope there will always be new people to pick up the torch.

Things continue to happen serendipitously. Three-and-a-half years ago TRAS had to leave the Lutheran Campus Centre at UBC because the building was condemned due to mould. So we moved to Columbia Street, but that building's owner sold the building after one year. Our new office manager called MPS, an office space company. The manager of their Oak Street offices was so warm and interested that MPS donated the proceeds from their year-long bottle collection to TRAS.

So we moved again. As we unpacked all our colourful handicrafts, a charming man called Mark Dwor walked past, looked, and stopped. He has been a friend to TRAS ever since. About 18 months ago he suggested we contact a woman called Shirley Giggey, who belonged to Libraries Across Borders (LAB), which creates libraries for poor communities in B.C. and abroad. She told me to fill out an application form on their website—which I did. Now we have received grants to provide school libraries for two very poor, remote Tibetan settlements in north-eastern India.

Shirley then asked me to speak at their fundraiser last November and show slides about TRAS. A quiet, bearded man walked in just as I began. He came up to me afterwards and suggested I contact him at the end of February. It turns out he is the main donor for LAB. I met him yesterday and he has had a large signed poster photo of George Woodcock down the hall from his office for many years. He knows and respects Mark Dwor, and he thinks highly of Shirley and LAB, and now he's going to give us several thousand dollars! And all because of mould in the UBC building.

Twice TRAS has taken groups of Grade 11 students from B.C. to
Nepal to study international development first-hand. These students
visited the Annapurna Conservation project.

GEORGE WOODCOCK

"I began even as a boy to realize how wide the world can be for a man of free intelligence." — G.W.

Beyond their meeting with the Dalai Lama, what motivated the Woodcocks to create TRAS? What made them tick? Little is known about Ingeborg's early years, but here is a brief biographical summary of George Woodcock's origins and his development as a man of letters, followed by edited excerpts from an interview conducted by Alan Twigg in 1994 for the CBC-TV documentary *George Woodcock: Anarchist of Cherry Street,* made by director/producer Tom Shandel.

George Woodcock's father Arthur Woodcock was a music-oriented second son and would-be writer who rebelled against his conservative Shropshire coal merchant father to pursue the arts. George Woodcock has described him as an impoverished bibliophile and an astute philatelist. Rejecting an offer of partnership in the family coal business, Arthur Woodcock left for Canada in 1907, via Liverpool and New York, and took a train from Montreal to Manitoba.

In Winnipeg he met the vaudevillian Charlie Chaplin and took various jobs, eventually becoming a bookkeeper/accountant for the Canadian Northern railway.

Obliged to send for his betrothed, Margaret Gertrude Lewis, a dour milliner's apprentice, Arthur Woodcock married her in May of 1911 but the union was never happy. When their only child was born on May 8, 1912, in Winnipeg's Grace Hospital, she disallowed her husband's inclination to call the boy George Meredith Woodcock, in honour of one of his favourite novelists, and so for the rest of his life George Woodcock would enjoy carrying an invisible middle name, one that connected him to the spirit of his adventurous father, and distanced him from his undemonstrative mother. "I suppose I am a man whose psychic arrangement is Jungian rather than Freudian," he once wrote. "I loved my father and always disliked my mother."

One Manitoba winter on Portage Avenue was one too many for Margaret Woodcock, who took their only child back to England in the spring of 1913, but it would be sufficient for George Woodcock to one day leave England—as his father had done—to claim his Canadian birthright. After Arthur Woodcock acquiesced to his father's offer of a junior partnership and dutifully reunited with his family in England, he led a mostly dreary and sickly existence. Prior to his death of Bright's disease at age forty-four in 1926, he instilled in his sympathetic son a shared dream of going further west in Canada. "An extrovert who turned inward with misfortune is how I see him," George Woodcock wrote. The son not only revered the father; George Woodcock was inspired to succeed in Canada to recompense his father's failures and dashed ambitions.

Small wonder George Woodcock could write so knowingly about Thomas Hardy's Wessex for his introduction to a Penguin edition of *Return of the Native*. Woodcock fully comprehended the hereditary weight of sorrow, of disappointment, of class consciousness, of stilted emotions, jilted love and stunted ambitions. The plight of Arthur Woodcock was Hardyesque, both noble and pathetic.

George Woodcock was raised in various Shropshire and Thames Valley towns within a literate, impoverished family. At school he was particularly averse to sports. The Depression prevented him from continuing his formal schooling as he would have liked. George Woodcock ended his formal schooling in 1928. His coal merchant grandfather offered to pay his tuition for Cambridge on the one condition that he would become an Anglican clergyman. It is sometimes suggested that Woodcock, like his father before him, rejected coercive assistance on principle to preserve his selfhood, but to his credit he once flatly eschewed this interpretation of events. "I refused," he wrote, in an essay called "The Land of the Lost Content," "not because of any free-thinking implications (those came later), but from sheer timidity; I could not see myself developing the self-confidence needed to stand in a pulpit and lecture my fellow men on the will of God."

Instead, he became mired for eleven unhappy years in a futureless job for Great Western Railway as a clerk at Paddington Station, a prisoner of timetables and protocol, like his father before him. If there was a turning point in George Woodcock's life, other than returning to Canada, it was perhaps reading William Morris' socialist writings on the train to and from work. With access to books and anarchist circles afforded to him by a German exile named Charles Lahr, proprietor of the Blue Moon Bookshop, Woodcock became a devotee of the British philosopher Herbert Read and joined a circle of friendships with young "progressives" such as V.S. Pritchett, W.H. Auden, Stephen Spender, Malcolm Muggeridge and George Orwell (Eric Blair).

Woodcock could be fastidiously judgmental when it came to writers. He most admired Orwell, but disliked Auden. "I resented him, his bogus Marxism, his perverted Oxbridge snobbery, but I was fascinated against my will by his poetic skill, and how he gave new life to traditional forms."

Woodcock later claimed Orwell was the only writer in England with the political prescience to recognize fully the totalitarian threat.

This was most fully seen in Orwell's *Coming up for Air* (1938), written prior to *Animal Farm* and *Nineteen Eighty-Four*. "We talked to him as George," Woodcock recalled fondly, "and many of us did not even know that he was also Eric."

The source of Woodcock's title for his subsequent biography of Orwell, *The Crystal Spirit*, reveals both the character of its subject and the biographer. As Orwell described at the outset of his Spanish Civil War memoir *Homage to Catalonia*, when he went to the Lenin Barracks in Barcelona to enlist he shook hands with an Italian refugee and had an unforgettable moment of fraternalism "as though his spirit and mine had momentarily succeeded in bridging the gulf of language and tradition and meeting in utter intimacy." Orwell recorded this encounter in a poem that ends:

> But the thing that I saw in your face
> No power can disinherit:
> No bomb that ever burst
> Shatters the crystal spirit.

Woodcock also established lifelong friendships with the likes of Alex Comfort and Julian Symons, and went boozing in Soho with Dylan Thomas. All the while he participated in the political ferment of the 1930s and '40s by contributing to various literary and anarchist periodicals.

When his mother died in 1940, he inherited £1,398. That same year he published his first collection of verse, *The White Island*, and filed for exemption from military service as a conscientious objector. He agreed to perform alternative civilian service with the War Agricultural Committee. Deeply influenced by the fate of idealists during the Spanish Civil War, Woodcock was initially assigned to farm labouring in Essex, but his acquiescence to alternate service soon disappeared. Instead, Woodcock used a trust fund established for him by his grandfather to try his hand at making his living as a fulltime writer in London, mainly by establishing and editing *NOW* (1940–1947), an eclectic mix of anarchist, pacifist and anti-Soviet socialist commentaries. He was also co-editor of *War Commentary*.

As he endured a precarious and frugal "underground" existence, Woodcock became increasingly infatuated by a beautiful Italian anarchist in London, Marie Louise Berneri, who was married. She was the daughter of a recently martyred Italian anarchist named Camillo Berneri. Marie Louise, her husband and two others were charged with causing disaffection among the troops by denouncing the war effort in print. The offending handbill for which they

George Woodcock is accompanied by his first great love, Marie Louise Berneri, and his second, Ingeborg Linzer Roskelly (striped sweater) during a light-hearted moment in Cambridgeshire, in 1946.

were arrested was allegedly typed on George Woodcock's typewriter. His lifelong sympathies for outlaws such as the Métis military leader Gabriel Dumont, Gandhi, the Dalai Lama and Gitksan fugitive Simon Gun-an-Noot partially arose from these war-time experiences as a dissident.

During the war George Woodcock also met his future partner Ingeborg Linzer Roskelly, who had briefly been married to an English journalist. They quickly became lovers and an inseparable team. After the war, when George Woodcock's *NOW* magazine floundered, he turned his hand to writing the first serious study of the Restoration playwright Aphra Behn, one of the first English women to live professionally by writing, and Ingeborg briefly returned to Germany as a correspondent for *Peace News*. At the Freedom Press bookshop he met Serbian refugee Ivan Avakumovic, who became an essential colleague for books about Peter Kropotkin and the Doukhobors.

The final issue of *NOW* appeared in 1947. Marie Louise would never be his. And conscientious objectors with German-born wives were none too popular in England, George and Inge Woodcock left the London literary scene and sailed for Canada, arriving in Halifax in 1949 with $750, ostensibly to emulate Doukhobor pacifists who had sought freedom in Canada some fifty years before. The Doukhobors had been encouraged and subsidized by Tolstoy near the turn of the century. "I realized that the Doukhobors were something more than nudist shovellers of snow when I began to read Tolstoy and Kropotkin," he later wrote. "They regarded them as admirable peasant radicals and Nature's anarchists."

More specifically, the Woodcocks were directly influenced to start anew on the West Coast of Canada by a young Canadian anarchist in London, Doug Worthington, who offered them free access to land. Coming to Canada entailed a revival of his father's failed idealism, and Woodcock had also been impressed by depictions of Western Canada that he'd found in a Frederick Niven novel called *The Lost Cabin Mine*. As the Woodcocks arrived in Halifax, he had a premonition that something terrible was happening to Marie Louise Berneri—to whom he would dedicate his book on Kropotkin. As they rode the CPR train to Victoria, she died at age thirty-one of heart failure.

George Woodcock gamely tried his hand at homesteading near Sooke, about 25 miles from Victoria, on Vancouver Island, clearing some land for a market garden and building a small home with Inge on Church Street (now 2271 Church Road). On a census he listed his occupation as "sign wrtr" to avoid suspicion of being an intellectual. The isolation and poverty were disturbing. The nearest Doukhobor settlement was at Hilliers, near Parksville. Not suited for subsistence farming, George Woodcock contacted the poet Earle Birney at the University of British Columbia six weeks after his arrival in Sooke. Birney visited the Woodcocks, and contacts with CBC and other writers were subsequently made.

One night in 1951 Woodcock was at a party when someone passed along the news that George Orwell (Eric Blair) had died. It was a shock. He said it was as if a bridge had been removed behind them.

In 1952, Woodcock published the first of his many books pertaining to British Columbia, a travelogue called *Ravens and Prophets: An Account of Journeys in British Columbia, Alberta and Southern Alaska*. He would publish *The Doukhobors* (with Ivan Avakumovic, 1968), *Victoria* (with Ingeborg Woodcock, 1971), *Amor De Cosmos: Journalist and Reformer* (1975), *Peoples of the Coast: The Indians of the Pacific Northwest* (1977), *A Picture History of British Columbia* (1980), *British Columbia: A Celebration* (1983), *The University of British Columbia: A Souvenir* (1986) and *British Columbia: A History of the Province* (1990). There is also a rare, limited edition of 85 copies of *Letters from Sooke: A Correspondence Between Sir Herbert Read and George Woodcock* (with an original etching by Irmgard Benedict as a frontispiece) published by the Victoria Book Arts Club in 1982, now available for approximately $500.

Worthington would later describe them as "very much churchmouse poor." Woodcock eked out a living by shovelling manure and contributing to CBC and some periodicals, selling their cabin to finance travels in the United States, and returning to a borrowed cottage at Saseenos, in Sooke. During this period he gained a Guggenheim grant of $3,000 to complete a biography of Pierre-Joseph Proudhon, enabling them to live in France for most of a year. The couple returned to Sooke to build another home at Whiffen Spit.

They were rescued from their privations in Sooke by the generosity of the painter Jack Shadbolt and his wife, Doris. Woodcock later recalled, "We wouldn't be in Vancouver if it hadn't been for the Shadbolts. When my wife and I were living in frustrated isolation in a small Vancouver Island village, Jack and Doris Shadbolt suggested we should come to live in Vancouver. At that time Capitol Hill, where Jack and Doris lived, was mainly bush, and Jack suggested that he might get us the loan of a cabin there, which he did, and our life on the mainland began in a stretch of woodland, now long vanished, where the pheasants still called and the tanagers still nested."

In August of 1954 George Woodcock succeeded in obtaining a year-long teaching position at the University of Washington in Seattle. During this year in Seattle, Ingeborg first met some Tibetans and began to study the Tibetan language and Tibetan customs. Then, in 1955, George Woodcock was barred from continuing his teaching at the University of Washington when he was denied an immigration visa as a result of his connections to a 1944 anarchist pamphlet, *Anarchy of Chaos*. As an alien who had advocated "opposition to all organized government," Woodcock was banned from United States entry by the McCarran Act in the wake of McCarthyism. His vigorous lobbying efforts to overturn the decision were to no avail.

With the crucial assistance of Earle Birney, he was rescued from his predicament with a teaching post from the Extension Department of UBC in January of 1956. That year he increased his affiliations with the CBC and befriended the essayist, conservationist and lay magistrate Roderick Haig-Brown of Campbell River. He later wrote, "Rod strikes me as one of the wisest men I have known, and sometimes, when I have committed some gross verbal irresponsibility, I see his ghost rising to admonish me with a quiet, smiling remark between puffs on the pipe that was rarely away from his mouth."

Woodcock was thus able to lecture at UBC, where he would teach both English and comparative literature. He had never attended university in England and liked to refer to himself in late years as an "autodidact," someone who is self-taught, giving rise to his affinity and correspondence with poet Al Purdy.

In 1959, Woodcock accepted the part-time position of editor of *Canadian Literature*, the first periodical to be entirely devoted to Canadian writing. He did not, as is sometimes assumed, found the publication, which he edited until 1977.

Canadian Literature was created largely under the auspices of Roy Daniells, head of the UBC English department. Woodcock's role would lead to a deep schism with the university many years later when he decided to sell his personal papers. UBC took the position that all papers pertaining to Woodcock's tenure at *Canadian Literature* were not saleable because they had been derived from his UBC employment. Woodcock had resigned his Lecturer status in 1963 to concentrate on writing, but the university had retained his services as an independent editor for the publication.

Greatly disappointed, Woodcock sold most of his literary papers to Queen's University in Ontario. Only after his death were some of his books and personal effects, including his typewriter, donated to UBC Special Collections.

George Woodcock edited 73 issues of *Canadian Literature* and was followed by W.H. New who edited 72 issues.

At age sixty, Woodcock wrote in the preface to his essays in *The Rejection of Politics*: "I began as an internationalist anarchist. I have ended, without shedding any of my libertarian principles, as a Canadian patriot, deeply concerned with securing and preserving the independence of my country (which cannot of course be divided from the in-

"George Woodcock probably made more people around the world aware of anarchism than any other twentieth-century writer except perhaps Kropotkin."—Tony Gibson, *Freedom* (February 1995)

•

"He did more than anyone else of his time to make anarchism familiar and friendly to ordinary people." —Nicholas Walter, *Independent* (February 1995)

dividual freedom of its inhabitants), and within that country the integrity—physical and aesthetic—of my mountain-shadowed and sea-bitten patria chica on the Pacific Coast."

Although something of a workhouse-hermit in his later years, Woodcock developed an extensive range of contacts among writers and other artists, particularly visual artists in Vancouver such as Jack Shadbolt, Toni Onley, Gordon Smith, Joe Plaskett, Jack Wise, Pat O'Hara and Roz Marshall. In particular, the Woodcocks maintained their close, four-way friendship with Jack and Doris Shadbolt. Neither couple had children so they often spent Christmases together.

For more than 40 years the Woodcocks had lived in an old craftsman-style cottage at 6429 McCleery Street, formerly called Cherry Street. Woodcock was particularly fond of an ancient cherry tree in their backyard, likening it to Malcolm Lowry's relationship with his beloved pier in Deep Cove. The Woodcocks once made arrangements to meet the Lowrys, their cross-town literary counterparts, in a downtown lounge, although in fact the authors mostly ignored each other, leaving their wives to manage forced conversation. But after Lowry died, Woodcock was not averse to editing a reprint of *Malcolm Lowry: The Man and his Work* (1971).

To honour George Woodcock in conjunction with his 82nd birthday and the 10th annual B.C. Book Prizes, hosted by Pierre Berton, *B.C. BookWorld* instigated and coordinated a series of events in 1994. First, the city conferred "Freedom of the City" on George Woodcock on April 12, 1994. "Thank goodness for Vancouver," wrote Mark Abley in the *Montreal Gazette*, "which has recognized —and none too soon—that it's home to a regional, national and international treasure." Greetings were sent by the likes of Julian Symons, Ursula Le Guin, Jan Morris, Timothy Findley, Mel Hurtig, Svend Robinson, the spokesperson for the Doukhobors in Canada and a representative of the Dalai Lama.

The B.C. Minister of Culture, Bill Barlee, addressed the B.C. Legislature on May 6th and invited all MLAs to join in recognizing

George Woodcock's achievements. CBC Radio's Peter Gzowski devoted one half-hour of *Morningside* to the Woodcock celebration on May 11, 1994:

GZOWSKI: You never sought publicity, so how are you feeling about all the wonderful tributes to you?

WOODCOCK: I have two points of view about what's going on. I'm deeply touched that all my life's work should be suddenly acknowledged in this expansive way. I'm also touched by the fact that I have so many friends popping up. I haven't made as many enemies as I thought! On the other hand I had a friend say to me the other day, "George, you're the luckiest man on earth. You are going to be at your wake, as it were. You get to hear what people will say about you."

GZOWSKI: You get to hear the nice stuff.

After being interviewed by Alan Twigg for the documentary film
George Woodcock, The Anarchist of Cherry Street, George Woodcock signed
several copies of the 6' x 4' INSPIRED BY GEORGE posters that were displayed
at bus shelters around Vancouver to advertise George Woodcock Day.

WOODCOCK: Quite.

GZOWSKI: You once quoted Orwell as saying, "No decent person gives a tuppence for the opinion of posterity." How do you feel about posterity?

WOODCOCK: I remember Stendhal's remark: "I have taken out a ticket in a lottery to be read in 100 years' time." I've taken out that ticket, too. So I do attach some importance to posterity.

GZOWSKI: You're the man who turned down the Order of Canada but last month you accepted Freeman status given by the City of Vancouver. What's the difference?

WOODCOCK: I think there's a considerable difference. The Order of Canada to me is just a holdover from feudalism. It's just an imitation order of knighthood, with all the ranks, the royal patron and whatnot, whereas this is an honour offered to me by my own community. Which is quite a different thing. And as an anarchist I place much more importance on local units than on nations.

GZOWSKI: What's your vision for the Woodcock Centre for Arts and Intellectual Freedom?

WOODCOCK: I think it should be a gathering place for writers and for people concerned with civil liberties. I would like to see a building large enough for organizations to take part, like the civil liberties groups. But one of the most important things is that it should be a kind of refuge for writers, in other words, writers who find their circumstances intolerable should be able to rent a room at a nominal cost. And as Alan Twigg says, we must have a bar called The Woodcock. (Laughter).

GZOWSKI: I hope that a lot of people get to toast you in a bar called The Woodcock.

WOODCOCK: So indeed do I.

A two-day symposium was held at Simon Fraser University, May 6–7, 1994, to examine George Woodcock's career. The Bau-Xi Art

WE MUST HELP ONE ANOTHER OR DIE

"'We must love one another or die,' said W.H. Auden in the early days of the last World War. What we have learnt since then is that we must help one another or die. The evidence of ecology, as much as the lessons of history, demonstrates ever more clearly how much our own well-being is dependent on the well-being of other human beings and of the very planet on which we live.

"The world has evolved over the millions of centuries, a balanced natural economy in which plant and animal species (humanity among them) exist in a delicate equilibrium with inanimate forces. The links are so intimate, the balances so perilously liable to be disturbed, that the very fabric of the mountains can be changed by an apparently humble cause like goats browsing off the vegetable cover of the soil and exposing it to erosion. The destruction of the great forests of Brazil is a matter of concern not only to the people of Brazil but to the people of the whole world whose patterns of rainfall it can drastically change.

"We can carry the matter a stage farther. If the gap between poverty and wealth in any country is extreme, that equally is the concern of the whole world. Just as weather patterns are disturbed by the poverty of the soil, so political and social stability are disturbed by the poverty of a people; the effects do not halt at frontiers."—*George Woodcock, in the CIVA Board of Directors' manual.*

Gallery hosted an exhibit of original art honouring George Woodcock. More than 1300 people attended a celebratory gathering at the Vancouver Law Courts, on May 7th, that included an unprecedented display of 152 different titles bearing George Woodcock's name, making it one of the largest exhibitions of books by a living author. The mayor of Vancouver attended and proclaimed George Woodcock Day.

Woodcock could not attend due to failing health. In a speech read on his behalf by Margaret Atwood, Woodcock recognized how the climate for literature had changed since his coastal arrival. "When I reached Vancouver at the beginning of the 1950s, one could count on one's fingers the serious writers here: Earle Birney, Dorothy Livesay, Ethel Wilson, Roderick Haig-Brown, Hubert Evans and a few younger people. There was virtually no publishing going on locally, and the one literary magazine was Alan Crawley's historic *Contemporary Verse*. Now, as tonight's gathering gives witness, there are hundreds and hundreds of writers working west of the Great Divide, there are scores of local publishing houses, large and small, and there are dozens of literary magazines, some of them of national and international importance. . . . I think the conjunction of the literary arts and the concept and practice of freedom is an essential one; in fact, I believe it is the key to my own work, which has always moved between the poles of imagination and liberty."

Margaret Atwood reading Woodcock's words at the May 1994 symposium

Lilia D'Acres and the West Coast Book Prize Society established a fund for donations to help establish a George Woodcock Centre for Arts and Intellectual Freedom in Vancouver. More than $20,000 was raised. When a heritage building could not be obtained for a Woodcock Centre, all monies raised were donated to the University of British Columbia to establish a permanent George Woodcock exhibit and the George Woodcock Canadian Literature and Intellectual Freedom Endowment Fund.

Woodcock remained indefatigable, attempting to realize his long-held ambition to complete a new translation of *Swann's Way*, the first volume of Marcel Proust's *Remembrance of Things Past*. He was also working on a novel. After George Woodcock died at home on January 28, 1995, Ingeborg Woodcock undertook retyping the manuscript of the Proust translation, completing and altering her late husband's project. Much to her disappointment it was never published. She became dismissive of the venture, but a copy of the manuscript was provided to the Queen's University archives. Don Stewart of Macleod's Books purchased Woodcock's valuable collection of anarchist publications from the estate.

George Woodcock took it as a matter of professional pride that he could write a book on almost any subject that required his services. His omnivorous intelligence had led to an invitation from Mel Hurtig in 1974 to edit Hurtig's then-proposed Canadian Encyclopedia, an invitation that Woodcock reluctantly declined. History, travel, biography, literary criticism, politics and poetry were his main subject areas. His first important book was a biography of *William Godwin* (1946), followed by the first book-length study of England's first professional female writer, *The Incomparable Aphra: A Life of Mrs. Aphra Behn* (1948).

Robin Skelton commented: "A great many of George Woodcock's books are essential reading. I would instance his work on George Orwell, William Godwin and Aphra Behn, and his many contributions to the exploration of anarchism and to the study of Canadian history and Canadian writing. His industry is as astounding as his humility; he has never turned away from a task because it lacked obvious importance but has performed the most menial of writers' tasks with the same enlightened efficiency as he has tackled the major challenges. George Woodcock is a very great Man of Letters, and he is more than that. He is a National Treasure and in a properly constituted society his 80th birthday would have been celebrated with the issuing of a postage stamp, the striking of a medal, and a burst of cannon fire on Parliament Hill."

As Skelton indicated, Woodcock was ideologically and temperamentally in favour of writing for small and obscure publications, crediting his Welsh ancestry for his outsiderism. He once wrote, "The really independent writer, by the very exercise of his function, represents a revolutionary force." He was known to use the pseudonym Anthony Appenzell. For several years he contributed an "As I Please" column to the *Georgia Straight* and later served as the poetry columnist for *BC BookWorld*. It has proved impossible to trace and compile all the freelance articles he published.

His oft-reprinted *Anarchism* (1962) remains a standard history of libertarian movements, readable and important for the way Woodcock demystifies anarchism and views it as constructive. His fair-minded *The Doukhobors* (1968), with Ivan Avakumovic, is the definitive study of the Doukhobors in Canada. The agrarian sect was so relieved to have their story finally told with some depth of understanding that Woodcock was offered a permanent place of residence in the Kootenays if he wished to live among them.

Woodcock's studies of William Godwin, Oscar Wilde, Aldous Huxley, Mahatma Gandhi, Pierre-Joseph Proudhon, Aphra Behn, Peter Kropotkin and the Trappist Thomas Merton (whom Woodcock never met) are less well-known than his biography of his dear but difficult friend, George Orwell, *The Crystal Spirit*, that earned him a Governor-General's Award in 1967.

Woodcock liked to say he rejected honours bestowed by governments but he was willing to accept juried awards and grants determined by peers. In fact, he accepted three Canada Council travel grants (1961, 1963, 1965), a Canada Council Killam Fellowship

(1970–71), a Canadian Government Overseas Fellowship (1957–58) and a Canada Council Senior Arts Award. He also won a Molson Prize in 1973 and a Canadian Authors Association Award in 1989. He twice won the UBC Medal for Popular Biography (1971, 1975). In 1992, *Maclean's* magazine recognized George Woodcock as one the country's ten most significant citizens. In 1994, he enthusiastically accepted Free Man status from the City of Vancouver, linking the roots of the word *civitas* to the development of freedom.

Preferring not to be known too well, George Woodcock published three works of less-than-revealing autobiography. The first was *Letter to the Past: An Autobiography* (1982), mainly about his life in England. It was followed by *Beyond the Mountains: An Autobiography* (1987) and *Walking Through the Valley* (1994). George Fetherling, writing under the name Douglas Fetherling, produced the only book-length biography of Woodcock to date, *The Gentle Anarchist* (Douglas & McIntyre, 1998), based largely on the accumulation of Woodcock's papers at Queen's University. Woodcock invited Fetherling to undertake the task, and gave him free rein.

TWIGG: Can you tell me about your relationship with the Dalai Lama?
WOODCOCK: I find it very hard to analyze. We're very warm and close to each other. He regards us in a very friendly way because we were one of the first people that sought him out and saw what his problems were and started to work on them. He fled in 1959 and we went to visit him in '61. We had a long talk in Dharamsala and we promised to come back and do something. And we did it. I heard that a lot of people promised to do things and never did, but we did. And I think he's treasured that.

TWIGG: So you sent money directly to the people who needed it?
WOODCOCK: Yes. Through TRAS, a non-governmental agency. We are only patrons in that now. We've withdrawn and we are

involved in another society we founded that deals with people in India [Canada India Village Aid Society]. We have managed to create a small working anarchist affiliation group. No vote is ever taken. We arrive at every decision by consensus argued through, and it's become an extraordinary kind of thing.

TWIGG: You have purposefully tried to set up an anarchist framework?
WOODCOCK: Yes, an anarchist framework it is essentially.

TWIGG: Your partner in all of these remarkable undertakings, Ingeborg, likes to shy away from the public limelight. . . .
WOODCOCK: Indeed she does.

TWIGG: So forgive me, Ingeborg, but I'd like you to speak very briefly about her importance to you.
WOODCOCK: Well, she's been a wonderful partner for me in my career. She cares for me in sickness and all that kind of thing. She gives me ideas which I sometimes badly need and, on the other hand, with the organizations, she is a superb organizer. I am the ideologue of the group and she is the organizer. Not so much lately, but in the beginning she was.

TWIGG: When I read through your autobiographies and your books of poetry, it strikes me that there is a great deal more revealed of your emotions in your poetry. Would you agree?
WOODCOCK: Yes, I would. But then you see people only read what they want to read. Because I am not primarily recognized as a poet, they don't read my poems. They'd learn a lot more if they read my poems.

TWIGG: Well, along those lines I conclude that one of the most influential people in your life as an artist was the anarchist Marie Louise Berneri. You were also a friend of her husband, who was a publisher. Could you tell me a little bit about who she was?
WOODCOCK: Marie Louise Berneri was the daughter of a very

famous Italian anarchist, a professor who had to flee from Italy for his beliefs and who was slaughtered by the communists in Spain. She was an admirable person, very beautiful and intellectually extraordinarily bright. In a sense she was the chief personal influence bringing me towards anarchism.

TWIGG: During the war, her husband was charged with sedition.
WOODCOCK: She was, too.

TWIGG: But there was some English law that says a husband and wife cannot be tried for the same crime. . . . Is that correct?
WOODCOCK: Yes, and so she was let off, which annoyed her thoroughly. Nevertheless she and I carried on the whole operation of the anarchist press until the others came out.

TWIGG: For a time you had to go underground in England. That influenced your life-long anarchism, being essentially an outlaw.
WOODCOCK: Yes, actually it did. Of course I do have the outsider mentality. That's why I welcome the development these days of the underground economy and that sort of thing. This is the kind of world I like.

TWIGG: What does it mean when you refer to yourself as an anarchist in the 1990s?
WOODCOCK: It means, I suppose, a person for whom freedom is the most important thing—intellectual freedom and, as far as possible, physical freedom. You can be bound by physical things, as I am by certain sicknesses, but nevertheless you can, within yourself, still be free to recognize that all initiatives really come from yourself if you don't depend upon structures of government or structures of any kind. Structures are fine as long as they are controlled by the people who actually work within the structures, but they're dicey even there. You live as you wish to do and, if a job is oppressing, you leave it. I've done it on several occasions. I broke with the university. It's a derogatory thing to say it's a form of evasion, but you evade those unpleasant choices, you evade situations

in which you are insubordinate, you evade situations that will offend your dignity.

TWIGG: Can you give me some specific examples?
WOODCOCK: My split with the university was over the fact that I had become involved with helping Tibetans in India. I went on a year's leave to India. I let a year pass and then I asked for a year's unpaid leave. For some reason the new president had decided that unpaid leave could only be granted through the decision of a council that consisted almost entirely of scientists and, of course, they couldn't understand my reasons for wanting to go. So they said no, no unpaid leave. So I immediately resigned. When you act dramatically in that way it often has a consequence that is very negative. I was editing *Canadian Literature*. I didn't want to let *Canadian Literature* go, so they reached a nice compromise by which I received half a professor's salary. I was allowed to wander where I wanted. Here is a case in which you search for your independence and allow something creative to come out of that.

TWIGG: You rejected the Order of Canada but you are willing to become the first writer to be accorded Freedom of the City. Why?
WOODCOCK: Well, I think there are all kinds of traditions involved here; first of all the Order of Canada is really a replica of something. We don't allow people to be knights, to be knighted by the Queen of England, but we do allow them to become members of the Order of Canada. It even has the same phraseology as the English orders of knighthood, companions and this sort of thing. What I'm going to be given, I gather, is not the key to the city, which in many cities is the case. It's the freedom medal, and for me freedom has always been associated traditionally with the city: think of the Greek city-states where they developed all the ideas of democracy; think of the medieval cities where the serf could flee from his lord's estate, and once he got through the gates he was a free man. This is an important tradition, the link between the idea of the city and the idea of freedom. That's why I've accepted it.

TWIGG: What accounts for your endurance and your stubbornness to be "a man of free intelligence?"

WOODCOCK: Partly I suppose my Welsh ancestry, partly the fact that I am a Taurean. I think one of the basic things in my life is the death of my father who died young. He was a man of enormous talent, particularly musical talent, but he never had the chance to develop. I think that after he died I was impelled by the idea of completing that life in my life.

TWIGG: You've written that creativity often comes out of early wounds. What were your early wounds? Beyond the death of your father?

WOODCOCK: My early wounds were the English school system among other things. It wasn't merely the discipline; it was the ways in which the boys got what was called the school spirit. In most English schools it is a brutal kind of pro-sporty spirit that militates against the intellectual who is looked on as a weakling. I was unpopular at school just because I was an intellectual. I always answered all the questions off the top of my head; I didn't swat up the material. But they nevertheless resented me because of that.

TWIGG: Your relations with your father were obviously respectful but your relationship with your mother was more fractious. What type of woman was she?

WOODCOCK: She was a woman, when I look back, of great high principles and that was her trouble. She carried those into all kinds of literal interpretations, so that you are forced to be a liar by her and her demands.

TWIGG: Would you agree you've inherited her principled nature?
WOODCOCK: Yes, I'd agree.

TWIGG: What do you mean when you refer to George Orwell as your dear but difficult friend?

WOODCOCK: I thought I called him my dear, dour George in

one of my poems. Orwell was the sort of man who was full of grievances. He was very loyal. Once he got to know you, he was extremely loyal. He hated passionately and irrationally. I remember people who were really quite decent people who tagged along a bit with his bandwagon, and Orwell was full of contempt and fury against them. I used to tolerate them because I thought they were benighted souls, and might someday see the light, but Orwell didn't. He just hated them with a bitter fury.

TWIGG: So is Orwell still with you as an influence?

WOODCOCK: I think he is. I remember Herbert Read saying to me, "Whenever I reach a decision these days I feel Orwell's ghost admonishing me over my shoulder." This was the effect he had on people. You thought about him and even after he was dead you began to judge your actions by his standards. Orwell was very eccentric. He never peered over my shoulder as he did over Read's but nevertheless I've thought about him.

TWIGG: And now you're translating some Proust.

WOODCOCK: Yes. A lot of writers like Nabokov complain about the translations. It was translated during the 1920s and it followed the English idiom of translations. It was very sentimental, Elizabethan sentimental. The very title, of course, *Remembrance of Things Past*, has nothing to do with the real title, which is *In Search of Lost Time*. So I decided it was time to do a new one.

TWIGG: And you also have a new autobiography that is forthcoming.

WOODCOCK: Yes. The title is *Walking through the Valley*, meaning walking near to death, the valley of the shadow. It's a summing up in a sense. It's an account of the things I've done in the last fifteen years, but it's also a reflection on life as a whole. I say a lot about the process of autobiography and what I think writing a biography does to you, and how it does change your perspective. You realize your life in fact, as you conceive it, is a great fiction.

PART THREE

THE HOME FRONT

Ingeborg and George

KNOWING THE
WOODCOCKS

She was a Buddhist. He was an anarchist. Together Ingeborg and George Woodcock were a tag team of activists—you and me against the world—who called each other "Darling," drank a lot of martinis, worked exceedingly hard and were mutually dedicated to helping others. "They're so close," observed Joan Symons, George Woodcock's secretary for *Canadian Literature* magazine, "that when one of them breathes out, the other one breathes in." Even though they founded three still-functioning charitable initiatives and have affected the lives of millions of people, the world knows precious little about them as a couple.

UP CLOSE
Sylvia Rickard likes to tell the story about how George and Ingeborg met at a garden party in London. According to Inge's version of events, they were attracted to one another quickly. After several hours of "winking and drinking," trying to find a way to speak to one another, George finally summoned up the liquid courage to

introduce himself. Ingeborg's first words to the great love of her life were, "Excuse me. I think I'm going to be sick."

Inge vomited. And that was the beginning of their romance.

Born in Toronto in 1937, Sylvia Rickard first met George Woodcock in 1957 and Ingeborg Woodcock in 1965. Like Sarah McAlpine (neé Proctor), she was something of a surrogate daughter to them, probably more so to Inge than George.

While studying languages at UBC, she was told by a friend in 1957 that she must take a class from George Woodcock. She audited his 20th Century European Literature in Translation course. It included—she recalls—Tolstoy, Proust, Ibsen, Camus, Chekhov, Turgenev, Dostoevsky, Strindberg and Malraux. "As a professor," she says, "he was always very modest to a fault."

Rickard's career as a composer lay ahead of her. She took one course from Jean Coulthard, visited England, returned to Canada when her adopted mother was dying of cancer, took another course from Coulthard, lived in France, attended Stanford from 1961 to 1963, and then went to India. Her daughter Janine was born there in 1964. For fourteen months Rickard lived mainly in Rohtak, 44 miles west of Delhi, before returning to Canada with her infant daughter. Rickard took private instruction in composition from Coulthard in 1975, tied for first in a music competition and de-

Sylvia Rickard

cided to pursue music composition seriously at age 35.

At this juncture, TRAS member Judy Brown, having known Rickard in a UBC sorority, suggested she might like to attend a TRAS meeting. "I said, 'Oh, I really like George Woodcock.'" Rickard recalls, "So I went to their house where Inge started assigning everyone jobs. They were selling 25-cent raffle tickets. She asked me where I lived. At the time I was living in

Hycroft Towers. There were nine floors. She was delighted. Of course I was conscripted on the spot. Inge told me I had to go door-to-door in my building. I was painfully shy but I approached everyone with the raffle tickets because I was so scared of Inge. I didn't want to let her down!"

Rickard joined Inge's crews who helped prepare housing for Tibetan refugees. In particular, the Woodcocks were keen to assist their friends from Delhi, the Lhalungpas, who had first lived at UBC's Acadia camp upon their arrival in British Columbia. Having arranged for Lobsang Lhalungpa to teach at UBC, George Woodcock then found him a placement to teach Tibetan studies in Madison, Wisconsin, but Lhalungpa failed to make the most of this opportunity. The Woodcocks subsequently received financial aid from Rickard and others to help purchase a house for Lobsang Lhalungpa and his wife Dekyi on West 18th Avenue in Vancouver.

"I remember one time," says Rickard. "A bunch of us were cleaning up a house for Tibetans in Surrey. We were on our hands and knees, performing chores, scrubbing the refrigerator, things like that, and there was Inge, standing in the middle of it all, supervising. One job wasn't done well, so she snapped, "Who did dat!" Everyone froze. We were all petrified. Finally one of us confessed. Years later, when I was at the Woodcocks' house for dinner, I reminded Inge of this incident. She was absolutely horrified. She turned white. She leaned over to me and said, with great sincerity, 'Thank you, Sylvia, for holding up the mirror.' We ended up laughing. But she recognized the German boss in herself, and she didn't like it."

The Woodcocks were always kind to Rickard's daughter, Janine, buying her Christmas and birthday presents. "I think it was probably because they both had such unhappy childhoods themselves," she says. Inge told Rickard how upset she had been, growing up, to see the heads of wild animals mounted as trophies on the inner walls of the house in which she lived.

The Woodcocks listened only to classical music on the radio.

George Woodcock was particularly fond of Mozart, and he once expressed a fanciful wish to be reborn as Mozart. There was a musical affinity between the couple and Rickard. She composed background cello music for a CBC radio presentation of a story by Franz Kafka called "A Breast for Beating in my Hour of Need," adapted by George Woodcock and Otto Lowy. Rickard, a vegetarian and animal rights sympathizer, also presented the world premiere of a recent composition for solo harp when Ingeborg organized an event to protest the killing of baby harp seals in Newfoundland.

Rickard frequently received unsolicited advice from Ingeborg about men. Ingeborg consistently disapproved of the men in Rickard's life and advised her to stop having relationships with men entirely. Rickard had been raised as Linda Hambley. "When I cracked my adoption," she recalls, "I was thirty-five." She clearly remembers the evening she arrived at the Woodcocks' house, overjoyed to have learned the identity of her birth mother—who had just contacted her by telephone for the first time—only to have Inge immediately pour cold water on her enthusiasm, warning her that the caller could be an imposter. Rickard resented Inge's negativity. George Woodcock ameliorated the situation, explaining that Inge was just trying to protect Sylvia from disappointment. In retrospect, possibly Ingeborg resented competition from another older, female advisor.

Family friend Tony Phillips has suggested Rickard and Ingeborg had a mother-daughter relationship. Rickard recalls Ingeborg telling her about two abortions she had "with George." Dorothea Leach has recalled a different story, involving two miscarriages. Rickard does not know when these abortions occurred, or if there were any miscarriages. "They probably would have made really good parents," she says. "But they just didn't want to."

As a fellow Taurus, Rickard was also privy to George's character. "He was dead-centre Taurus," she says. "His birthday was May 8, right in the middle. He told me, 'We are prone to self-indulgence in food and drink—and stubbornness.' Of course the other side of stubbornness is perseverance. In his quiet, sweet, bedroom slipper way, he could be like an enraged tiger. And very defiant. He hated the Fraser Institute, for example. Just hated them. Of course he could behave in a very gentlemanly way, but there were always, as he once put it, 'subterranean rumblings.'"

Rickard verifies that Woodcock greatly admired Gandhi and his non-violent pacificism. Woodcock would sometimes quote Gandhi and say, "One step is enough for me." He also liked the Gandhian notion of power arising from the bottom of society, rather than power trying to generate progress from the top.

"He had highly developed radar for pomposity," she says. "I remember him telling a funny story about some aristocratic nitwit in India. George imitated his upper class Indian accent perfectly. 'Oh, Doctor Woodcock, would you please enlighten us with your pearls of wisdom!' He could really be quite hilarious sometimes. And the humour could be biting. A far cry from gentle. I think he was not a gentle anarchist as much as he was a defiant anarchist."

Sylvia Rickard now lives in Cordova Bay, south of Victoria.

THE BROADCASTER

It is a little-known fact that George Woodcock once interviewed the Dalai Lama in the CBC Radio studios but the interview never aired.

"The Dalai Lama was not as eloquent as he is now," recalls radio producer Don Mowatt. "He was actually very shy. This was back when the Dalai Lama was still uncomfortable with his English. George was an experienced broadcaster, but only as someone to be listened to. In radio, you have to know how to listen, as well as talk. The interview proved unusable because George's questions were too complex. And the Dalai Lama's answers were far too short. He mostly replied Yes and No. Basically, the Dalai Lama was nervous and intimidated."

Born in Montreal in 1943, Don Mowatt was the son of a chaplain and medical doctor. His father instilled in him an appreciation of the arts. He entered university in Victoria at age fourteen and was among the first graduates of the newly formed University of Victoria in 1962, at age eighteen. Upon discovering he was not keen to study law at UBC, Mowatt switched to American literature and theology. He was hired by the CBC Director of Radio in Vancouver, Peter Garvie, in 1964. "In those days," he says, "the arts were still king at CBC."

As a fledgling radio producer in 1964, Mowatt first worked with George Woodcock to record his radio play about a Scottish missionary on the B.C. coast. Their professional relationship endured for three decades. "At first I found him austere and aloof. In those days, the CBC was still dominated by Britophiles, whereas I was British Columbian. To me, he always had that English sensibility about him. My opinion of him changed but it was always coloured by that."

Mowatt's intimacy with both Woodcocks increased considerably when he joined their Committee of 100, a loosely gathered consortium of highly placed citizens, such as architect Arthur Erickson and Jack Shadbolt, who agreed to protest CBC cutbacks in arts and local programming. As the executive producer of "The Hornby Collection," and president of the radio producers, Mowatt joined the fray.

Don Mowatt: "Even though George and Inge believed in being consensual, in fact, the reality of their lives was quite different."

"George was not a gentle anarchist," Mowatt recalls. "He gave the impression of that. But I discovered he was a genteel anarchist who could be quite prickly and aggressive. His whole approach to the Committee of 100 was adversarial. The CBC had just built this enormous factory in a crucial part of town, right near the post office and the Queen Elizabeth Theatre, and they were eroding regional input. So

George got on his high horse and took it out on the president of the CBC, Al Johnson. He wrote an article in *Saturday Night* that portrayed Johnson as being unsympathetic to the arts. He also wrote about Johnson's wavy hair in a highly personal way."

In fact, Johnson was supportive of the arts. The problem was really his advisor, Peter Meggs. Mowatt told George Woodcock his target should have been Peter Meggs who co-authored a report that changed the emphasis of the CBC to favour current affairs and news. Mowatt regretted Woodcock's disparaging comments about Johnson and later made peace with Johnson, who proved supportive of "The Hornby Collection" until he left the helm. The Committee of 100 had raised a considerable fuss but never succeeded in altering the erosion of the CBC's arts coverage.

When the CBC's foremost program for intellectuals, "Ideas," made a three-part program on Ontario's Northrop Frye, it was decided that a reciprocal program should be made about Western Canada's George Woodcock. Mowatt happily accepted the challenge. Having made programs that seriously showcased Woodcock's poetry, and produced programs such as Woodcock's radio play about Gabriel Dumont, Mowatt was sufficiently trusted by Woodcock for him to consider the proposal.

Woodcock and Mowatt spent a year and a half discussing how a radio autobiography could be made, mapping out areas of discussion. In these planning sessions, George was fastidious as to what matters should be addressed, and what matters should be ignored. Don Mowatt received strict orders from Ingeborg that audio recording sessions could last no longer than forty minutes—and he soon learned that Ingeborg's estimation of her husband's endurance was correct.

George Woodcock told his life story in three 52–minute programs, based on promptings from Mowatt. The sessions were recorded with one microphone in the Woodcocks' home, where Ingeborg could control the time. The result was an in-depth self-portrait that proved deeply satisfying to anyone who knew George, but for six months he refused to heed his friends' enticements to listen to it. The host of the program was Lister Sinclair, whom George loathed, and so George refused to listen, even though the program had been prepared by his friend, Don Mowatt.

Eventually Ingeborg convinced her husband to overcome his aversion to Lister Sinclair and listen to a story which, quite obviously, he already knew. When *Ideas* re-broadcast the three hour-long segments, George Woodcock agreed to listen. After the second episode, he called to apologize and agreed the program was terrific. He hadn't realized that Lister Sinclair's voice would only intrude at the beginning and end of each episode.

Having grown fond of Ingeborg over the years, Don Mowatt sent her a letter of condolence after her husband died. In it, he confided that he had initially found George's austere manner off-putting, daunting. In a long and friendly reply, she said she couldn't understand how that could be so.

"Of course she wouldn't see it," Mowatt says, "because it was *she* who could intimidate *him*."

Don Mowatt of North Vancouver retired from the CBC in 1997 and taught at UBC's Creative Writing Department for nine years.

THE HANDSHAKE

"Sometimes a simple gesture can have great meaning," says Don Stewart. "I was putting together a display of all the books authored or edited by George Woodcock for the big celebration of his life. I visited George and Inge several times in the search for elusive titles. George was ailing and resting a lot and not very available, so I searched the house as needed. During one of our brief encounters, George suddenly asked to shake my hand. As we shook hands George said, "This handshake is two handshakes from Kropotkin." Then, the story began.

"Prince Peter Kropotkin was one of the most famous anarchists. As an activist and author who rejected his aristocratic roots, he was imprisoned in Russia, escaped and fled through Siberia to America and on to Europe. He wrote many important anarchist books, founded *Freedom* (the London anarchist journal) in 1886, assisted in the emigration of the Doukobors to Canada, and died in Russia in 1921.

"In 1946 George Woodcock was researching his future biography of Kropotkin, *The Anarchist Prince*. In June of that year Woodcock visited Switzerland (the Jura having been an early anarchist centre), and he attended the gathering of old anarchists at Berne to commemorate the seventieth anniversary of Bakunin's death. Michael Bakunin was an early Russian revolutionary and anarchist who escaped from Russia and took refuge in Switzerland. At this gathering George met and shook hands with Luigi Bertoni who, as a young man, had known Bakunin and worked closely with Kropotkin following his escape from Russia.

"To encourage the young anarchist working on a biography of Kropotkin, Bertoni warmly shook hands and reminded George of his connection with Kropotkin. At this gathering George was one of only two speakers under the age of seventy. Anarchism appeared to be dying out. George was part of the revival with his many books, including the best selling *Anarchism* which has been reprinted many times.

"The handshake from George," Don Stewart continued, "suddenly had great personal significance for me because of my own activism and interest in anarchism. I have since "passed on" the handshake to younger activists."

THE ONLEYS

According to painter Toni Onley, "George was the sort of Englishman who never really expressed much emotion." But Woodcock was not averse to demonstrating standoffishness. When Onley first attempted to meet Woodcock, he approached and said, "I'm Toni Onley, the painter." With a plummy British accent, Woodcock replied, "Indeed you are."

And that was as far as it went.

At age seventy, George Woodcock met Toni Onley for a second time at a fundraising dinner at the Hyatt Regency in downtown Vancouver. Onley remarked, "It seems to me you're piddling away your energies to raise a few dollars. Why don't you and I go to India together? I'll paint and you can write. We'll make a book together, and sell the paintings in the bargain." As a result, *The Walls of India* was published in 1985, based on their mutual tour of India in 1982–83, accompanied by their wives.

Yukiko Onley, now a photographer in Vancouver, remembers the Woodcocks often. She commented, "Inge is a saint, but she was no angel."

URSULA'S FAULT

Journalist and editor Russell Wodell first met the Woodcocks when he interviewed George Woodcock on behalf of *Monday* magazine in Victoria in 1978. Wodell subsequently edited the CIVA newsletter with Keath Fraser, and pioneered the society's website. Wodell recalls how the Woodcocks' friendliness doubled as an instinctual act of procurement.

"It is all Ursula K. Le Guin's fault," he writes. "George and Inge Woodcock were in Victoria attempting to promote George's latest book, *Faces from History*, and came to my office where they were, I felt, pleasantly surprised to encounter someone who at least knew who George was.

"The conversation turned to the history of anarchy, and we discovered a mutual admiration for Le Guin's remarkable 1974 novel *The Dispossessed: An Ambiguous Utopia.* Suddenly Inge commanded me to accompany them to a nearby café. Little did I know of the famous Woodcock ruthlessness at spotting people who could be exploited for good ends—or suspect that as a direct result two decades later I would find myself in the unambiguous dystopia of India."

When Wodell and his partner David Gordon Duke relocated to Vancouver one year later, they were invited to housesit with *de rigueur* instructions on how exactly to feed chicken livers, blended

A barefoot George walks behind stylish Yukiko Onley in 1983. Toni and Yukiko Onley twice travelled with the Woodcocks: first to India and southeast Asia for six weeks, and later to Europe for four weeks. The latter trip was more problematic. Yukiko Onley recalls, "Inge wanted everything to be done her way. We had to stick to her schedule. We couldn't delay anywhere. There were four of us in a small rented car and she insisted on smoking constantly."

with cornflakes, to Alfie the cat. The raccoons were to be fed stale Dare's chocolate chip cookies.

David Gordon Duke subsequently provided a succinct description of the Woodcock home in an obituary notice about Ingeborg. "The tiny house on McCleery Street was one of the most remarkable dwellings in Western Canada: utterly spartan, yet filled with Asian art, artifacts and crafts collected on world travels, and paintings (mostly gifts) by a who's who of the Canadian art world. There were no luxuries: Inge kept a cheap transistor radio in the kitchen tuned to the CBC, and George typed his books on a tiny plastic portable typewriter sitting atop a home-made desk. Only two "modern" gadgets stood out in this resolutely self-sufficient environment: a huge kiln in the basement (Inge had studied pottery with Bernard Leach), and in George's study an ancient photocopier on which they duplicated newsletters for the two charities they created and directed: the Tibetan Refugee Aid Society and Canada India Village Aid. Spending a couple of weeks there was an indoctrination into the Woodcock code of moral anarchism: being good meant working hard, with no complaints and no expectation of thanks."

In the early 1980s, after the Woodcocks left on their trip, the housesitters discovered Ingeborg had left them a large envelope of cash for expenses and meals. "We didn't touch it," says Wodell, "and the day after they returned, Inge telephoned in a fury. David argued back, refusing any reimbursements, and Inge finally admitted defeat, saying 'You could almost be my son, you are just as stubborn as I!'" Predictably, such intimacy led the male couple to be inveigled into helping with the first CIVA book sale, lugging books from the basement of Sarah and John McAlpine's home to St. Mary's Church in Kerrisdale. Later Russell Wodell replaced George as CIVA secretary.

Wodell has since been known to joke, with great fondness, that the heritage of the Woodcocks is the philosophy of the ruthless exploitation of your friends.

"In 1984," Russell Wodell recalls, "George approached me to

"The tiny house on McCleery Street was one of the most remarkable dwellings in Western Canada," wrote housesitter David Gordon Duke.

sponsor a screening of Shyam Benegal's film *Kali Yuga* (*The Evil Age*) as part of CIVA's ambitious India Festival, and shortly thereafter asked me to join the board as assistant secretary. Taking minutes at the meetings that followed was the best imaginable education in doing good in Orwellian times."

Wodell is one of the few Woodcock devotees willing to look below the surface of the Woodcocks' formidable and admirable activism to consider the price they paid for staying together.

"To my mind George and Inge achieved a real symbiosis," he says. "Although every word of the books is George's, it was Inge who enabled him to write them. But we must remember that while symbiosis enables two organisms to produce what neither could alone, at the same time the process distorts both organisms permanently.

"After a while the 'George and Inge' act solidified and they were to a degree trapped in their respective roles, a process I suspect they had observed in their friends Charles Laughton and Elsa Lancaster. George could never be seen to lose his temper in public, and Inge could be a sweet old lady only when she was alone with her cat.

"I suspect that part of Inge's intense need for privacy stemmed from the fact that she didn't altogether like or approve of the 'Inge' persona she was trapped in, and perhaps somewhat resented the saintly persona she allowed George to present to the world."

RELUCTANTLY GERMAN

Ingeborg Woodcock steadfastly avoided personal history. She could be like a porcupine to anyone who struck her as invasive. Her resolve to maintain privacy was such that she dissuaded George from including details about her, or their marriage, in his three volumes of autobiography. In the first volume, Woodcock was obliged succinctly to write, "In 1943 at a party in Great Russell Street, I met the very private person who became my wife, and so began the relationship that has sustained my life since then. Her exemplary desire for anonymity I have to respect, even though I do not share it."

Not even her name gets mentioned.

Later, Ingeborg Woodcock refused to cooperate with her husband's biographer George Fetherling beyond granting permission to use some photos. Theirs was an icy relationship from the beginning. She always called him Mr. Fetherling and he matched her by calling her Mrs. Woodcock. Fetherling now maintains he is glad she did not participate. Eventually George Woodcock privately bemoaned his wife's overt chilliness in a letter (that Fetherling found in the Queen's University archives), saying his wife no longer permitted Fetherling inside their home, thereby making it difficult for George to dream up new excuses to meet Fetherling secretly at the UBC Faculty Club.

It is not clear as to what extent Ingeborg's antipathy to Fetherling was personal, or principled, or fearful. Given that she was always protective of her husband, and others have described George Woodcock as Ingeborg's "baby," it is obvious she resented anyone gaining any possible access to him that was superior to her own degree of intimacy. At the same time, she was philosophically opposed to her husband taking himself too seriously, and Fetherling was clearly intent on providing the world with a very serious and insightful book about her husband.

Her disdain for overt egotism was such that she could be intimidating and over-reactive to the trespasses of others. David Gordon Duke recalls how she once stormed away from the head table at a charity banquet "when the celebrity host began praising his own charitable endeavours." Such bold judgementalism cast a shadow over her husband's memoirs—and it didn't help that George Woodcock could be discreet in print to the point of being evasive and uncooperative, particularly when discussing sexual matters. If Fetherling's tattle-free portrait is a tad dry, he is completely blameless and must be commended for doing as well as he did with a man whose autobiographies are, frankly, dull, when one considers his extraordinary life.

Meanwhile, a brief summary of her life is required, along with some reflections on her character.

Ingeborg Hedwig Elisabeth Linzer was born in 1917 in Weimar, Germany—not Austria as was often claimed—approximately 50 miles southwest of Leipzig. Weimar is one of the great centers of Europe, having been home to Goethe, Schiller and Nietzsche, with the Buchenwald concentration camp just down the road.

Reputedly the daughter of a Polish mother and a minor German aristocrat, she was adept at English and other languages. Like George, she was fond of her father but disliked her mother. According to Peggy New, "She once told us that her first awareness and interest in Tibet came from talks with her father while they walked in the Alps during her childhood. These memories of her father seemed especially dear to Inge, and it seemed that it was he who introduced her to the notion of Tibet or perhaps to a book that depicted an extraordinary people living high among the Himalayan Mountains. She said she immediately felt a spiritual affinity to Tibet even as a young girl."

Ingeborg left Germany in 1938, hoping to gain experiences that might enable her to work as a foreign correspondent, but her experiences as an au pair girl for two elderly women in Ipswich, England, as arranged by a relative, proved unsatisfactory. Against her parents' wishes, she married a British journalist, Frederick Roskelly, just prior to the outbreak of World War II. They moved to Cornwall to live among artists at St. Ives. Among her acquaintances during this period were Charles Laughton and Elsa Lancaster. She also took pottery lessons from Bernard Leach.

The marriage to Roskelly, who was a part-time journalist, was short-lived—possibly by design. This union enabled Ingeborg to remain freely in England as a British subject, without being interned, despite her origins. She was a fervent anti-fascist.

In 1943, as Ingeborg Linzer Roskelly, she met George Woodcock at a house party. The story goes they passed the night on the floor together. Because George was active as a pacifist, and he was complicit in producing anti-war literature, the couple lived "underground," frequently moving from one address to another in order to avoid police scrutiny after their mutual friend, Marie Louise Berneri, was brought before the court for the dissemination of literature that was allegedly produced on George Woodcock's typewriter.

George Woodcock had been born in Winnipeg so Canada was suitable for immigration purposes. After World War II, when opportunities proved scarce, they left the London literary scene in 1949 to homestead on Vancouver Island. An argument can be made that Ingeborg and her anarchist husband came to British Columbia in the aftermath of World War II mostly to escape from notoriety. As George Fetherling has noted, Ingeborg had "a heavy, German, music hall accent" that would have been far from welcome among Britons after Hitler's defeat. Having narrowly avoided arrest for treason as an anti-war pacifist, George undoubtedly encountered some difficulties explaining to returning veterans in the pub what he had been doing during the war effort. So, in 1949, in

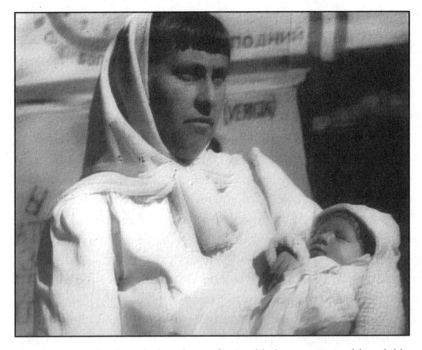

Ingeborg Woodcock took this photo of a Doukhobor woman and her child during one of several trips the Woodcocks made to the Kootenays. It appears in the first of George Woodcock's travel books, *Ravens and Prophets*. She always accompanied him on his research expeditions.

tiny Sooke, they could continue to operate beneath the radar of conventional opinions, in a town that boasted 399 mostly working class residents.

And Ingeborg Woodcock avoided the limelight, and the camera, the rest of the way.

In 1952, when George Woodcock published the first of his many books pertaining to British Columbia, *Ravens and Prophets*, it was based on his explorations with Ingeborg. George never drove, so thereafter they were partners for the research of all his travel books. She was his chauffeur as well as his cook—and his photographer. But she generally preferred not to be credited.

Even though she had been a photographer, and provided photographs for her husband's 1971 book on Victoria and several travel memoirs, Ingeborg avoided having her own photograph taken. Her aversion to the camera went deeper than the conventional vanity sometimes associated with fading female beauty. Ingeborg's distaste for photography was outwardly cranky, inwardly Buddhist.

In his foreword to *Tibetan Voices* (Pomegranate Artbooks, 1996), photographer Brian Harris has described meeting a family of pilgrims, west of Lhasa, in 1994. When this party of eight travellers, led by twin brothers, declined Harris' request to take photographs of them, Harris' translator, Nambu, told him that some Tibetans "prefer to have few remains in this world after they have died to keep them tied to their former existence." Nambu also noted that some older Tibetans are taken aback whenever they see photographs of people in newspapers and magazines that have been discarded, or trampled, because that's tantamount to disrespecting someone's likeness (i.e. making it akin to garbage).

"Perhaps one principle underlying this uneasiness about photographic portraiture," Harris writes, referring to an essay by Ananda K. Coomaraswamy entitled *The Traditional Conception of Ideal Portraiture*, "is the Buddhist understanding that our human existence is a precious and extremely rare opportunity for spiritual liberation. This principle can lead to natural concern about abusing our human state—even in the form of an exact image of oneself. To a sophisticated modern mind the reactions of traditional peoples to photography may appear to be just a quaint example of simple superstition. However, if we juxtapose this response with that encountered in 'developed' societies when our own photograph is taken or we photograph others, the degree of anxiety or self-inflation that many of our contemporaries experience is both astounding and revealing.

"Whether it is the familiar identity crisis that so many people experience in front of the camera, or the dissatisfaction with what the camera and film produces, the modern and 'enlightened' reaction may be more indicative of a fragile and superstitious sense of self than it is a calm rejection of photographic portraiture grounded in a deep metaphysical principle. The modern world has forgotten or lost the means of orientation toward its sacred and transcendent center, and this absence has led to a conception of self and other that is limited and thus fragile."

Ingeborg Woodcock would concur with Harris' view. Hers was not the coyness of an elderly Western woman concerned with wrinkles. She had the puritanical prejudices of a stern moralist who resisted luxuries and who, according to David Gordon Duke's obituary, "was notoriously sharp at the slightest manifestation of swollen ego." Her abhorrence of self-glorification and self-advertisement frequently proved problematic for her husband. Although George Woodcock, in later years, was never so gauche as to outwardly seek attention and publicity, he was sufficiently shrewd not to reject it when it came his way. In doing so, he had to be careful to avoid Ingeborg's wrath.

When George Woodcock agreed to be the subject of a documentary film, *The Anarchist of Cherry Street*, Ingeborg simply would not countenance a film crew in her house, even a modest two-person operation consisting of a sound engineer and cameraman. He was interviewed instead at the office of *B.C. BookWorld*. Once he was taken to a park on Dunbar Avenue, near his home, in order to have his photograph taken. This session was semi-clandestine because Ingeborg would not approve. But after George died, the park photograph became the focus of the shrine Ingeborg maintained in their study, looking at it every day.

HELPING THE BOAT PEOPLE

Although George and Inge were formidable, admirable and generous—and mostly good, it must be said that George was frequently capable of literary vanity. And Ingeborg was capable of arrogance. Both were prone to harsh opinions of others in unguarded private moments. He took his own dreams and premonitions seriously; she loved to listen to a late night radio program dedicated to reports of the paranormal, and she had an abiding interest in the possibility of flying saucers. Their ideas spilled into one another's heads. It might be said that George Woodcock was a philosophical anarchist, as opposed to a revolutionary anarchist; and Ingeborg Woodcock was a philosophical Buddhist as opposed to a religious Buddhist.

In 1979, Ingeborg convinced George to re-integrate with TRAS in order to respond to the needs of the Vietnamese "Boat People." As thousands of Vietnamese tried to flee their country in unseaworthy vessels after the fall of Saigon to the Communists and the end of the Vietnam War, simultaneously, many Cambodians were trying to escape from the murderous Khmer Rouge regime.

In a Special Bulletin of TRAS dated July 1979—credited to both Ingeborg and George—a "horrified" George Woodcock announced: "As you know, Inge and I first took up the cause of the Tibetan refugees when we got to know of their plight in the snow-covered Himalayas. Now another group of Asian refugees needs

"We all knew that behind this crusty façade was a kind heart and great compassion for all living things." — Dorothea Leach on Ingeborg Woodcock. This photo of Ingeborg Woodcock, c. 1979–81, courtesy of Sylvia Rickard.

our assistance: perhaps even more tragically because neighbouring countries refuse to help them. 200,000, it is claimed, have already perished at sea.

"The only chance for these refugees is to get them asylum in friendly countries. We ask for your help to bring some of them to Canada. The problem is huge, terrifyingly so. But after our experience with the Tibetans, and the generous way you have responded over the years, we know we can count once more on your help to do what we can in this new emergency.

"We are doing our utmost to raise concerns—and funds—and we have asked the present Directors of the Tibetan Refugee Aid Society to launch this appeal. We shall be working night and day to bring in initially 10 families under the Society's sponsorship, and more if funds permit.

"Will you please help us NOW?"

TRAS supporters were ultimately urged, in the final sentence, to help the Woodcocks help the refugees. TRAS responded to the pleas of its co-founders by resolving to raise $80,000 to sponsor ten families, as soon as possible. Ingeborg revitalized her fundraising gambits from the 1960s and set to work organizing a major art sale in conjunction with Paul Wong at the Bau-Xi Gallery in Vancouver. She also instigated more collections for furniture, household items, clothing and toys.

Canada had agreed to accept up to 3,000 refugees per month, and some 5,000 could come to Vancouver. Unfortunately the federal government allocated three-to-four months for processing prospective immigrants from makeshift camps in south-east Asia. By September TRAS had contributed $10,000 to an immigration sponsorship fund of $37,500. One generous donor contributed $16,000.

Names of specific would-be refugees were obtained from Reverend Stephen Lee of the Refugee Resettlement Centre in Vancouver's Chinatown, and some 25 of these were selected from one of the worst refugee camps, Nong Kai, in northern Thailand. TRAS affiliates were supplied with an extensive list of suggestions as to

INGEBORG AND THE BOAT PEOPLE

This is a rare piece of published writing by Ingeborg Woodcock. Unlike her husband, she was fond of exclamation marks.

It seems symbolic that our first two sponsored refugees to come here are Cambodians! All of us thought that the misery of the Vietnamese Boat People could not be surpassed, and each one of us in imagination saw them reach the shore, then the threatening guns, and after that the command to get back out to sea. Each one of us felt the scorching sun, the thirst, the hunger, the filth and stench on those boats. And none of us wanted to take this mental image on to its final end—the capsizing of the leaky boat and death in the sea. 250,000 human lives thus lost!

But now we learn of even greater horrors, if this is possible, where a whole people—the Cambodians—seem destined for extinction, simply for the sake of power manipulations between two megalomaniac regimes. Three million—3,000,000 men, women and children—have already died, and day by day thousands and thousands more are wiped out by starvation and disease. It is another holocaust of an even worse dimension than that of the Boat People. Where do we go from here?

Two are safe now—two young men—who escaped on foot through the jungle into Thailand. They lived on the edge of starvation for 15 months in a refugee camp on the border of Laos. A friend of theirs in the camp had what seemed the unbelievable luck to be chosen as suitable by Canadian Immigration, and when he arrived he asked us to be sponsors to his friends, Eng and Meng. Here they are now, the first two lives you and you (the donors of money and labour and kindness) have saved.

Now we await the next of our sponsored families, and then the next, and the next. I do wish we could save them all. Obviously we can't. But we can save as many as you—our donors and supporters—allow us to do. Our Boat People Fund now stands at well over $60,000, but we need to make it up to a minimum of $80,000. Please, be generous. We beg.

how to help the Boat People when they arrived. The Bau-Xi art sale occurred as envisioned, at the end of September.

By April of 1980, Vice-Chairman Conway was able report the target of $80,000 for ten families had been reached, thanks to an injection of $15,000 from TRAS reserves. Specifically, TRAS hoped to assist Vietnamese Boat People, as well as families from among the thousands of Cambodian and Laotian refugees who had fled to Thailand, and others who had sought asylum in Hong Kong. TRAS opted to sponsor an additional 50 individuals from the overcrowded camps in Thailand and Malaysia.

The Woodcocks had sounded the clarion call and the network of TRAS supporters had responded. Remarkably, TRAS assistance to refugees in India and Nepal during its 1979–80 fiscal year had concurrently reached an all-time high of $356,000, mainly for community development projects such as irrigation, electrification, dairy farming, handicraft production and vocational training. (During this period TRAS also supported a program of building schools in Nepal's remoter villages, as organized by Michael Rojik of Toronto.)

Once again, administration constituted less than one percent of expenditures. The exemplary parsimony of TRAS when it came to its management was a tradition started by Ingeborg as much as George.

"We all agree," says Dorothea Leach, "that Inge's incredible energy, her brilliant ideas for moneymaking schemes and her iron hand with which she ruled us contributed just as much to the success of the organization.

"Even if one did not feel like wrapping bulk Christmas cards or going to the fleamarket, only a broken limb would be accepted as an excuse! No matter how impatient or prickly she could be, we all knew that behind this crusty façade was a kind heart and great compassion for all living things."

But good intentions were not enough. TRAS reluctantly concluded in 1980 that its funds were more effectively deployed in the area in which they had developed expertise and local connections, the Himalayas. Even though it achieved its fundraising goal and proved highly effective in raising public awareness of a dreadful crisis, the Woodcocks' urgent appeal to help save South-Asian refugees (not just Vietnamese refugees) from a catastrophic situation in 1979–80 was ultimately deemed an administrative failure.

THE HAUSFRAU

So who was Ingeborg Hedwig Elisabeth Linzer (Roskelly) Woodcock? Her only brother has died, so her childhood cannot be recalled beyond surmise. Ivan Avakumovic knew them in England, but he has been reluctant to comment.

From England onwards, there are various clues and informants as to her personality, but unfortunately the most valuable source of sustained insight, Doris Shadbolt, died of a heart attack in Mexico in 2003.

When the Woodcocks accepted an offer from Doris and Jack Shadbolt to take up semi-permanent residence in a cabin adjoining their property in Burnaby, the two childless women, who were consistently supportive of their husbands' artistic endeavours, became best friends. Doris Shadbolt remained a stalwart supporter of the Woodcocks' charities as long as she lived. "Doris was at the top of the list of potential founding members," says CIVA's founding chairman, Tony Phillips. "Not only was she perhaps their closest friend, she also had a wealth of knowledge about India based on extensive travels throughout the country with Jack." Doris Shadbolt resigned from the board of CIVA in 1996, a year after George Woodcock's death. Jack Shadbolt died in 1999. Ingeborg was therefore the last surviving member of a potent quartet.

Ingeborg's secondary preoccupation, after caring for her husband, was their modest house once described by her husband as "a piece of carpenter's gothic." The unpretentious two-storey house, dating from the early 1920s, had once stood alone near an orchard, the vestige of which was one lone cherry tree in the backyard, giving rise to the title poem of George Woodcock's deeply-felt,

Rarely known to speak publicly—although she always had lots to say—
Ingeborg Woodcock made an exception at the UBC Special Collections Library
when George Woodcock's typewriter was placed on permanent display, along
with an exhibit of his books, as coordinated by librarian Brenda Peterson.

final poetry collection, *The Cherry Tree on Cherry Street.* The name of the street was altered to McCleery Street to honour the Irish-born pioneer homesteader and failed Cariboo prospector Fitzgerald McCleery who had built a trail from New Westminster to Point Grey with his brother Samuel for $30 per month. After the Wood-cocks bought the house in 1959 for $15,000, they paid off the mortgage one year later.

"I remember she was very meticulous," recalls Peggy New, a frequent guest. "The house was beautifully set-up. She had a network of handymen to maintain the place and she was sharing a cleaning lady with Leila Vennewitz (Heinrich Böll's translator). Inge explained all the needs of the house. She always kept the windows open so it was very fresh. She explained that the floors were covered in sisal. She liked that because it did not require a vacuum cleaner.

"George and Inge didn't believe much in the way of electronic devices. It might have been suspicion about modern technology but they also came from very frugal beginnings. They never had a vacuum cleaner while we were there. Nor was there a washer. They took their laundry out to the drycleaners in Kerrisdale. And they had no television. They had a refrigerator that was old with no real freezing compartment."

There was only one bathroom—upstairs—and the Woodcocks retained their black, rotary dial telephone, refusing to switch to a newfangled push-button model. Low tech was *de rigueur*. New recalls: "Later on, we were at their house and Inge was complaining that the stove wasn't working and she was going to have to go and replace the stove because the burner was going. I said, 'Inge, I think that burner is replaceable. Let's go and look.' She was astonished when I removed the burner. For twenty dollars it could be replaced. She had no idea. That's the way they were about technology."

The house on McCleery became famous for its parties, or salons, over which Ingeborg presided. Frequently her guests went home startled by some of her comments. "We were once invited to drinks with several other people," recalls Russell Wodell, "and among them a lady who was bursting with pride over the birth of her third or fourth grandchild. Inge became furious and said, 'I don't know how you can be so callous as to bring children into this world. Look at David and Russell, you don't see them having children!'"

THE ÜBERMOTHER

The word for angel in German is *Engel*. So, linguistically, Inge was almost an angel. Family friend Angela McWhirter fondly recalls that once there were three Georges and two Angelas—and an Inge— in the same room. Inge and George Woodcock. Angela and George McWhirter. Angela and George Bowering. All three Georges had prodigious literary outputs, encouraged by their wives.

"Women like her are made to spoil writers and artists," says Angela McWhirter. "George was *so* lucky. She devoted her life to her darling George. Although she had no children, she was ironically a very motherly woman, an *Übermother*. It is ironic because she decried us all here in the First World breeding when there were neglected, needy babies in India, Tibet and elsewhere.

"It was impossible not to her admire her energy! All that time they lived on McCleery, the house paintwork sparkled with never a chip to be seen! She was an artist in her own right—but she put her art into fabulous open sandwiches, full of cholesterol and satisfying taste. And she did things. She found jobs for Tibetan refugees, she looked after stray cats. I remember once we were there with Al Purdy, another 'auld poet,' but, Philistine that I am, I remember my ear just wanted to be titillated by Inge's fiery, firm beliefs."

But Ingeborg's strong opinions were not always welcome. McWhirter also recalls: "She once threw a bucket of cold water on my delight at being a first-time grandmother. That soured my feeling for her somewhat. And trying not to argue about her and George's ridiculous regard for the rats that they trapped and let loose in the 'wild.' I have a phobia about rats and I want them dead."

The McWhirters nonetheless happily allowed Ingeborg to smoke in their living room, keeping a special ashtray set aside for her visits. She smoked Benson and Hedges cigarettes, buying them by the carton. Lung cancer be damned. In a *Vancouver Sun* obituary, David Gordon Duke would describe her as a lifelong defiant smoker.

THE NEWS

Two people who knew the Woodcocks well for many years were Bill and Peggy New. Bill New first became acquainted with George Woodcock when he became Assistant Editor of *Canadian Literature* in 1965, spending many hours at the Woodcocks' dining table helping George and Associate Editor Donald Stephens assemble the paste-up before an edition went off to Victoria to Morriss Printers. During those sessions Inge would keep "the chaps" well supplied with coffee and hors d'oeuvres and dessert treats.

In 1966, when George Woodcock had a heart attack, Bill was asked to help prepare the next issue of *Canadian Literature*. "George being George, he wanted to see what I was doing before it went over to Charlie Morriss, the printer," he recalls. "Despite being fiercely protective always of George's welfare, Inge allowed me half an hour in the hospital, mainly because I had already been going over to the house to help before that." Bill New would later serve as the editor of *Canadian Literature*, for a seventeen-year period, from 1977 to 1995.

As George Woodcock was making a good recovery during the spring and summer of 1967, the Woodcocks were considering a trip to Lake Lugano in Switzerland to allow him to continue his recovery and to test whether he could tolerate travel again. Bill and Peggy New, as newlyweds, returned from San Francisco and were flattered to be offered the chance to live in and care for the Woodcocks' house from September to April in 1967–68, enabling them to escape from a tiny apartment. But Inge needed to meet Peggy before entrusting the house to them.

"It began with a nervous tea party that resembled a formal interview but rapidly dissolved into laughter and shared intimacies," says Peggy. "Far from the remote figure of literary, professorial, and broadcasting fame, George was warm and welcoming and displayed his quietly ironic sense of humour. When I was introduced to Inge, I took my cue to pronounce her name, as George did, 'Ing-a,' although many others have pronounced it 'Ingh-a.' Never did I hear her referred to as Ingeborg by any of her friends."

At first Peggy found Inge to be formidable. "Her demanding standards for keeping her spotless and shining household were based on utter practicality," says Peggy. She used only the most basic and sensible of cleaning materials long before our current wave of ecological awareness. For her, these methods were a matter of efficiency and economy.

"Inge ran the house in a very labour-intensive fashion, meaning that she worked very hard at it scrubbing, sweeping, polishing—or she hired the occasional cleaning lady to do so. During our winter there, Inge asked us to keep on the cleaning lady she shared on alternate weeks with Leila Vennewitz. In those days she would make hand-shaped, hand-painted pottery beads for sale as part of her fundraising. I remember the closet in their bedroom had no door, just a lovely screen of those beads in a curtain."

Like most visitors to the house, the News were struck by the Woodcocks' love of animals. Peggy New writes: "George and Inge doted on each of their successive pet cats for whom they always chose generic names like Kitty or Tiger. Our duty over that winter of 1967–68 was less to mind the house than to pamper their cat, Pussy. She was allowed the special privilege of climbing onto a portion of the kitchen counter to witness the ritual cutting up of her prescribed diet of premium calf's liver that we were to purchase at a particular butcher.

"They would go to any extreme to treat a pet animal with the utmost kindness. And even any insect. I remember one evening while preparing dinner, Inge emerged from the kitchen to tell her guests that she had been stung by a wasp. When we all expressed our alarm, she batted away our concern and wouldn't allow the sting to bother her, would not blame the wasp, nor would she find and destroy it. 'Wasps are my friends,' she declared.

"It was only a few years later that Inge began cultivating an entire family of nomadic raccoons over its many generations by feeding them each evening off the back porch. She delighted in observing their personalities and their family relationships and, as she saw it, their gratitude at receiving their regular meal which they unfailingly appeared for.

"One other characteristic made clear to us from our first meeting with the Woodcocks was their selfless generosity. When renting the house to us, George and Inge insisted that the rent be just enough to cover their taxes, considerably less than a standard rental in Kerrisdale would be. This generous assistance to a couple just starting out made it possible for us to save enough for the down payment on our own house that next spring.

"That cosy, quirky house on McCleery Street ended up meaning a great deal to us. The cottage had a creek running under it. You could hear it sometimes. And when you came into the house, you got this whiff of apples, something never explained. Despite the fact that Inge was a heavy smoker, the house always had that refreshing apple scent. There was the cherry tree in the back which burst out in festoons of white blossom every spring just outside George's office window. In the backyard there was also an apple tree. Because Bill's family grew orchards in the Kootenays, he knew that it was an unusual apple—a Leathland [Lievland] Raspberry. Inge loved these apples, and she was most impressed that Bill knew their name. She always made sure that we were given a supply of Leathlands when they ripened every summer."

That first meeting between the News and the Woodcocks set the tone for a very fond friendship that lasted through the next thirty or more of George and Inge's remaining years.

Inge turned out to be every bit as impressive as George in her quest for knowledge and her wide interests. Conversations with the Woodcocks could leap from their preference for the Swiss voting system as a solution to Canada's separation dilemma of the '90s—Canada should adopt a canton type of representation—to Margaret Atwood's consistent generosity to other writers, to admiration for the paintings by local artists which graced their walls—like the luminous John Korner abstract above the mantel.

Inge's strong opinions included her attitude toward children. Peggy New writes: "They were so disturbed by the often terrible conditions wrought by the excessive growth of the world's population that they could see no benefit in contributing more people to it. That meant that we, like many other of their young friends of the time, underwent a pretty rigorous questioning from Inge when we were expecting our second child. She certainly hoped that we were not entertaining the idea of adding any more to the family! And yet, they were unfailingly kind to children. They loved engaging them in conversation. They always remembered them with unexpected gifts. On a higher level, they had decided that their legacy should lie in benefiting not themselves nor a family of their own, but other people."

Ingeborg Woodcock was fascinated with the all-night American radio talk show Coast to Coast AM with Art Bell that catered to insomniacs, UFO enthusiasts and conspiracy theorists. This home-produced show focused on bizarre and unexplained phenomena, typically postulating that spacecraft rode the tailwind of the Hale-Bopp comet and that the U.S. government was concealing evidence of life forms from beyond the planet. These broadcasts emanated from more than 300 radio stations via Bell's own KNYE 95.1 FM station at Pahrump, Nevada.

"The radio revelations provoked many a controversial discussion," says Peggy New, "as we, the Woodcocks' guests, were encouraged to jump in with an opinion, to query or puzzle or verify or even ridicule an Art Bell idea—but the fun of such a provocative evening was that George and Inge welcomed all opinions and responded with great interest and respect. Inge would not accept the paranormal or any other phenomenon without a characteristically thorough investigation."

The Woodcocks hated unnecessary social rituals but this lack of pretension often conflicted with their innate generosity and civility. "At Christmas there could be no more generous friends," Peggy New recalls. "They remembered all their wide circle with carefully chosen and beautifully wrapped gifts which they hand-delivered all around town in the days leading to Christmas, much to our dismay as their health difficulties increased. They imposed this ritual upon themselves, yet they hated the commercial and ritualistic aspects of Christmas. They tried their best to escape the whole ceremonial side of it by taking off for the day, often driving along deserted rural roads like Zero Avenue, one of their favourite escape routes."

The Woodcocks' compassion extended to any worthy cause, or any friend in need. In early 1979, for example, George and Inge were puzzled and upset to hear of the disappearance of their good friend Betty Belshaw in Switzerland. As this mystery continued over many months, and her husband Cyril presented himself to Swiss authorities for questioning, George and Inge mounted a campaign of support by urging his friends and colleagues to write letters affirming his good character. Cyril Belshaw was not convicted of any crime and he returned to live in Vancouver. (Ellen Godfrey documented the trial in *By Reason of Doubt* (Clarke, Irwin, 1981), which won her an Edgar Allan Poe Mystery Writers of America special award for true crime.)

"Whenever they heard any tale of discomfort they took it as their personal mission to alleviate the problem," Peggy New writes. "We were once unexpectedly recipients of such largesse. During their visit with us in Cambridge in 1971, we jokingly confided that it was very difficult in Britain to find products common in Canada like peanut butter or apple juice for our toddler. Not long after that, we received a 'Care' parcel shipped to us from Canada, carefully made up by Inge, containing all of the longed-for items."

The News don't recall the Woodcocks ever showing off travel

snapshots from their trips. It was contrary to their nature to take travel photos as souvenirs. Bill New says he cannot recall ever seeing a colour photo taken by Ingeborg nor does Peggy New ever recall seeing a photo album in the house. Some private photos did exist—and these mostly ended up in the archives of Queen's University—but Ingeborg's penchant for photography evidently petered out shortly after she showed great enthusiasm for a small Minolta camera purchased for a trip to Australia in the late 1980s.

"They were so intrepid," recalls Peggy New. "Aging never deterred them from taking the next adventure. They even went to the South Pacific and explored many of the emerging island nations for a CBC television documentary. Despite Inge becoming very sick on that trip and having to take time out to recover in Australia they continued to love travelling.

"The Woodcocks had no tv set, so we invited them over to see the first show on our colour set—an old tube version. Having just spent the afternoon in the editing room poring over tiny screens, they were looking forward to seeing the real thing. We started to watch the show and Inge said sternly, 'There's something wrong with your television! I've seen those pictures and they don't look THAT colour!' [laughter] And she was right, of course. The colour on our set was distorted. And so the least technical person in the room instructed us, or rather chided us, about the need for a new tv set!

"Even after visiting New Guinea, Australia and India in those years, they were thrilled by the thought of being able to celebrate George's 75th birthday "on the road" on yet another trip, to China. It was like watching young kids on their first adventure to see them relish the idea that perhaps George's health would allow them this one last big trip.

"Inge was always extremely humble about her contributions to George's career, but at the same time you knew that she didn't want to be ignored. Despite her being so self-effacing, I think Inge wanted people to recognize what they had accomplished together. We, Inge's friends and admirers, were to know her legacy; we were just not supposed to talk about it. And she never felt comfortable revealing much about herself, except perhaps in the occasional offhand remark. At various times, we were led to believe that she might have Danish or Austrian heritage. She hated, not just the Nazis but the idea of state control over private behaviour, which she equated with a sort of Nazism.

"When she was gently questioned about her heavy smoking habit and the possibility of her having self-inflicted damage and about all the mounting evidence of the dangers of second-hand smoke, she countered that if cars could spew pollution, then so could she. 'Smoking in public is my civil right. I don't want some bus driver telling the public what it can do. That's creeping Fascism.' And she continued to smoke. That, too, was Ingeborg Woodcock."

"One of our fondest memories of Inge will always be her love of flowers. The best thing you could take to Inge was a bouquet of fresh flowers," says Bill New, "especially sweet peas. Only cut flowers, no potted plants. And she liked bouquets that were multi-coloured. She said, 'My mother never allowed mixed colours. She insisted on bouquets of one-colour only.'"

GRANVILLE LODGE

Ingeborg Woodcock rarely consented to see a physician until friends arranged for one to make house calls after George died. Although she preferred to be stoical about the maladies that afflicted her—such as arthritis and ulcers and cataracts—she did, however, once accept an offer from the Dalai Lama to have his personal physician treat her arthritis. After taking a distasteful concoction and being adversely affected by the treatment, she was heard to loudly proclaim, "These eastern doctors, they don't know what they're doing!"

She felt her arthritis benefited from a Nuu-chah-nulth drumming ceremony on Vancouver Island, and she favoured the healing properties of Manuka honey from New Zealand (which helped ease the stomach ulcer she suffered as a result of allopathic treatments for arthritis). But her diet, her smoking and her loneliness took their toll after George died.

At first she busied herself with writing some poetry and completing George's unfinished translation of Proust. When she discovered publishers were not interested in the completed manuscript, she abruptly turned her back on the enterprise and did not want any fuss made about it. (Without her knowledge, a copy of the manuscript found its way to the Queen's University archives.) Her main caregivers, Sarah McAlpine and Tony Phillips, have retrospectively wished they had encouraged Ingeborg to continue translating more volumes of Proust's masterpiece.

"She went through a very rough patch," says Phillips, diplomatically. "It was very, very sad. Inge was drinking too much. She was not in very good shape and the house fell apart. She wouldn't do the roof. It had a tarp on it. It was infested with squirrels and rats. The whole bloody thing was imploding."

Phillips, McAlpine, Dale Rolfsen and his wife Gloria were all called upon to make emergency visits to rescue Ingeborg from bad falls and other troubles. "She kept saying she had no reason to live," McAlpine recalls. "She'd been a caregiver for years and it was over. It was like losing her child and the only thing she had in her life at that point was the cat. I think she was also eating less. You can't really have an interest in eating when you ate what she did. Liver paté. I'll remember the grocery list forever. Lemon cake, spaghettios—awful ravioli in a can."

Ingeborg became reclusive. Sometimes even her best friends were not able to enter the house with ease. "There came a point where Inge was clearly unable to maintain herself," says Phillips. "We tried to talk her into keeping the house, getting it refurbished, keeping it as a heritage house. But she and George were adamant about the money having to go into a trust for writers. She also knew it would cost a helluva lot of money to refurbish the house."

Phillips, McAlpine and others became concerned about Ingeborg's hermit-like existence. Half the time she wouldn't allow them into the house. Groceries would be left at the doorstep. After many alarming incidents, Ingeborg burned herself on the stove and her clothes ended up on fire. Dale and Gloria Rolfsen rushed her to the hospital. It was the beginning of a harrowing decline.

"She finally fell and broke her upper arm," McAlpine recalls. "And she went kicking and screaming the whole way. She curled up in her bed. She wouldn't talk to anybody in the hospital. She was rude to the doctors, rude to the nurses. She'd say to them, 'I can't hear you."

The situation went from bad to worse to frightening. After Ingeborg's friends cautioned the doctors about her inability to be left to her own devices, a psychiatrist at the UBC hospital decided that Ingeborg was experiencing dementia. He declared her to be incompetent and made her a ward of the state. For an anarchist couple like the Woodcocks, such a fate would be beyond Kafkaesque. The state would have the power to control their estate, controlling decisions and taking 5 percent when Ingeborg died.

Fortunately Tony Phillips had the wherewithal to launch a hasty appeal. With his connections with the head of the UBC Psychiatry Department, Phillips was able to arrange for one of British Columbia's foremost geriatric psychiatrists to interview Ingeborg and obtain a second opinion. Phillips and McAlpine both visited Ingeborg in advance, sternly spelling out the crisis.

Ingeborg passed her interview with flying colours. She was entirely sane—and simply uncooperative. Remarkably, the incompetency verdict was reversed in about a month. After that, Ingeborg was relatively docile. She accepted a new life within the restrictions of Granville Park Lodge where she avoided other residents and kept re-reading one book, Heinrich Harrer's *Seven Years in Tibet*.

"Inge had always been a very private person," recalls Dorothea Leach, "and she never made any friends there. But she appreciated the excellent care given by the staff and continued to indulge in her lifelong passions of reading and smoking! As she tired easily and had impaired hearing, she liked only some close friends to come for short visits. Inge always had been a perfect hostess and even here was gracious, never complained and showed a lively interest in the latest news of TRAS and CIVA."

"She was always open to new possibilities," says Peggy New. "On a spiritual level she was looking for something that would explain the universe. When George died, she had her picture of him there and she would put her hand on it and say things like 'I know he's waiting for me.' Buddhism, thoughts of reincarnation, that was a part of her, even though she was entirely sceptical about other things. She had great faith that there was something beyond, and she knew that she and George were in unison on that."

Ingeborg Woodcock died peacefully in her sleep, of cancer, on December 11, 2003.

She had specified that no memorial service be held for her but Tony Phillips—one of the few people who ever stood up to her—hosted a gathering at his home. The Dalai Lama sent this message: "I am deeply saddened to learn of the passing away of Mrs. Woodcock, in Vancouver on 11 December 2003. I would like to express my deep condolence to family members and friends. Mrs. Woodcock and her husband, the late Prof. George Woodcock, because of their deep concern for the plight of the Tibetan refugees formed the Tibetan Refugee Aid Society in order to provide the basic daily necessities to the Tibetan refugees in the early years of our exile. It is because of the selfless efforts of people like the Woodcocks that we have been able to establish a viable community in exile. We Tibetans owe a great deal of gratitude to these two kind souls in Canada for their interest, sympathy and dedication in helping the Tibetans for many years. The memory of the Woodcocks will always be cherished by the Tibetan refugees."

Friends spread the ashes of George and Ingeborg Woodcock at Anarchist Mountain in British Columbia.

CANADA INDIA
VILLAGE AID

Tony Phillips, the first president of Canada India Village Aid, remembers how and why the Woodcocks left TRAS to start CIVA, the second independent non-profit charitable society they co-founded.

"I first got involved with TRAS at George's behest," he says. "George was persuading various people to go on the board of TRAS to counter-balance the influence of John Conway. This was in '78 or '79. I recall Shirley Rushton joined the TRAS board when I did. The Woodcocks had been off the TRAS board. What caused the creation of Canada Village Aid was their friend in India, Patwant Singh, who had created a small hospital called Kabliji. They had need of a generator. George made a request to TRAS to fund this $20,000 generator. We could see the pros and cons of it, frankly. The upshot was that TRAS decided they were not going to fund the generator. So then it was all-out war. The Woodcocks decided there was a need to create a society for the rural India situation and that's what triggered it. The generator."

John Conway recalls the Woodcocks wanted money from TRAS immediately. He tried to explain to George that the TRAS funds had already been allocated in the budget for projects aligned with CIDA, and therefore he could not eradicate those commitments in favour of a spontaneous request. Having promised they could help their friend Patwant Singh—who had smoothed the way for them in their travels and meetings in India—George and Ingeborg decided they had to find another way to raise the funds.

Started in 1981, and very much like TRAS—but with its emphasis on rural India—CIVA adopted a mandate to foster self-help and self-reliance through sustainable development and women's empowerment, usually partnering with local organizations in areas of economic development, education, health care and environmental concern.

CIVA has often operated in conjunction with Seva Mandir, an Indian non-profit organization that was introduced to the Woodcocks by John Friesen. Seva Mandir mainly assists the rural, predominantly tribal population in the Udaipur and Rajsamand district of southern Rajasthan.

"Operating from Udaipur and working among tribal peoples, notably the Bhils," George Woodcock wrote, "Seva Mandir strengthened our belief in an approach based on helping the people pick their own goals and helping them achieve them; there was nudging, shall we say, but not shoving."

Here is George Woodcock's first-person account of how and why CIVA was created—with no mention of the generator.

VOTELESS MEETINGS: THE FOUNDING OF CIVA

It was friendship that aroused and has supported Inge and me in what has been the main cause, outside of literature, of our recent years, the small organization, unpolitical and unliterary, known as Canada India Village Aid.

It all began in the early summer of 1981 when Patwant Singh emerged from our past. Patwant is an Indian writer and editor of

Design, his country's best magazine of architecture and planning. His father was one of the Sikh contractors who, under the direction of Sir Edwin Lutyens, built the dramatic complex of rose-coloured buildings in the centre of New Delhi that was designed to enshrine the authority of the British Raj as successor to all the alien rulers of India, and is now the node of power in independent India. Through a mutual friend's letter of introduction, we met Patwant Singh an hour after landing in Bombay on our first Indian journey; like many Sikhs, he was a tall man; his mobile, intelligent face was framed between a black turban and a black, carefully tended beard which I later learnt he kept in a net when he slept.

Within a week he and my old London friend Mulk Raj Anand, now in Bombay, had introduced us to all the local writers, artists and filmmakers. A couple of weeks later, in Delhi, Patwant performed the same service all over again with almost Mogul lavishness, introducing me to most of the people we wanted to meet (though Nehru would not bite) and giving enormous parties to which everyone came because nobody wanted to be left out. There we encountered not only great Indian writers like the superb novelist and tale-teller R.K. Narayan, but also great foreign writers like Octavio Paz, who was then Mexico's ambassador to India.

Patwant's social adeptness, his extravagant self-projection, and his love of pleasure made one think of him in those days that extended over almost the first two decades of our friendship as the intelligent playboy, capable of writing a good book on Indian politics, which he did, of editing an elegant magazine for sophisticates, and of wearing his highly starched black turban in elegant combination with his Gucci shoes as he skittered over the tragic aspects of Asian existence.

He mocked gently our efforts to help Tibetan refugees; he refused to admit, out of nationalist pride, that poverty was a word to be applied to India; and it was I, not he, who noticed that his night watchman had no shoes and was wearing the most wretched of worn-down open sandals in the bitter cold nights of a Delhi December.

About 1980, all this seemed to change dramatically, as life does so often among Indian men who approach the darker verges of middle age, and all at once become aware of the power of karma and the relation between present and future lives. Patwant suffered a heart attack. Recovering from it, he found himself considering what would have happened if he had been a peasant farmer from one of the poverty-stricken villages near his country house of Ghamroj in Haryana, sixty miles or so from Delhi. Almost certainly he would have died, for there was no hospital near enough to save him. The thought nagged, as thoughts do on sleepless hospital nights, and when he recovered Patwant went out to look at the areas near his leisure farm with a new uneasy eye. He found the villages poorer than he had assumed, the land arid, or salinated from bad irrigation; eye diseases caused largely by diet deficiency were so prevalent that any child who survived infancy had a ten-to-one chance of eventually contracting cataract or glaucoma; survival beyond infancy was itself reduced as a possibility by the high rate of gastroenteritis; tuberculosis was on the upswing among cattle and hence among human beings. The women were still in semi-purdah, living withdrawn and repressed lives inaccessible to family planning instruction, for though these people were Jats of Hindu faith, the area had been for centuries under Moslem domination.

The decisive incident came one night when Patwant was driving back to Delhi, and came upon a group of peasants at the roadside and among them a woman in agonized labour; she needed help urgently. Patwant got the peasants to load her into his car and drove to the military hospital in Delhi where he had connections; the woman's life and her child's were saved. He decided immediately to found a small hospital so that such a situation might never again occur among what he rather patriarchally regarded as his peasants.

He got to work immediately, calling in the debts of years of lavish hospitality. He badgered the state government of Haryana into giving a piece of land he specified must be barren. He persuaded architect friends to design an open campus of small pavilions to be built

GEORGE WOODCOCK AND THE OLD EMPIRE

Travelling in India, according to George Woodcock, "was like coming home." As Don Mowatt explained on CBC's *Ideas*, "India had long fascinated George. He had grown up in the same Shropshire town as Robert Clive, the great hero of the British Raj. And later he had pored over the career and writings of Gandhi, eventually writing a small book on the Indian leader."

Woodcock had remained in correspondence with Indian writers he met in London, and he felt comfortable in a country that enabled him to converse in English much of the time. "It may be an old fashioned English [in India]," he said, "and when you ask questions they may say to you, 'Yes, that would be two furlongs to the right, and seven furlongs to the left,' so it may be archaic, but still it's English. You're at home in the sense that if you've lived in the dubious, gaudy glories of the Raj in any sort of way, you see them surviving in extraordinary manners. In other words, the old empire is not dead. It's still kicking around."

Despite witnessing severe poverty in India, George Woodcock experienced none of the intense aversion to brutality and sense of cultural alienation he had experienced in Mexico in the early 1950s. He fully understood India's recent history and saw that India had its own imperial headquarters in Delhi.

"It's colonialized in the sense that Delhi tries to maintain a power over the rest of the country," he said. "Native rulers have just replaced the English rulers. And they're using the same laws! When Mrs. Gandhi declared an emergency, she declared that emergency not under any law passed by the Indian parliament, but under a decree passed by the Viceroy of India in the 1930s. You'd think that in Gandhi's country they'd be a little more compassionate, but the penalty of hanging, which is abolished in Britain and all the other former British possessions, still operates in India.

"When we went back in the 1980s, centralized power had grown. You had the big roads. It lost a great deal of its variety, and therefore its charm and interest."

Sarah McAlpine primarily oversaw the affairs of Ingeborg Woodcock after George Woodcock's death. A former student of George Woodcock and a CIVA president, she was acknowledged by him as "a person of great vitality and variety, loyalty and generosity."

Psychologist Tony Phillips remains a key figure in CIVA despite his concurrent responsibilities as Scientific Director, CIHR Institute of Neurosciences, Mental Health and Addiction, Department of Psychiatry, Faculty of Medicine, University of British Columbia.

cheaply of local materials. He talked manufacturers into giving him beds and sheets and cement. He recruited retired army doctors to staff his hospital and charmed Delhi specialists into offering services at nominal fees. He persuaded a couple of English nurses travelling in India to stay on and help start up the hospital.

Above all, he turned to the vast international circle of friendships he had built up in the years of pleasure and embarked on great annual pilgrimages to collect funds in Britain, the United States and especially Canada, where he tapped the consciences of lumber-rich Vancouver Indians and persuaded the Canadian International Development Agency that his Kabliji Hospital and Rural Health Centre was a voluntary venture worth supporting.

At this point Inge and I became involved. As old friends we were astonished at his apparent transformation, but rejoiced in it. We got together some other Old India Hands, like John and Marta Friesen; some doctors including Shirley Rushton and Douglas Forbes; a few other friends like Doris Shadbolt and Tony Phillips, a psychologist who became our first chairman; like the accountant Hari Varshney who became our treasurer; like Sarah McAlpine and Judy Brown who had attended my lectures long ago at UBC and had worked with us for the Tibetans. We called the little organization we founded Canada India Village Aid.

Here we had our first small difference with Patwant, who wanted us to call it Friends of Kabliji, which we pointed out would be meaningless to Canadians. In any case we had been attracted to Patwant's suggestion that his experiment was replicable and we joined to that a basic philosophy drawn from Gandhi's argument that village regeneration was the real foundation of India's regeneration, an idea long and fatally neglected by Indian politicians. We hoped the opportunities would come—and they quickly did—for us to extend our help beyond Patwant Singh's experiment. In fact Canada India Village Aid became a (major) factor in our lives. . . .

CIVA's first major fundraising gambit was the book on India that Woodcock co-authored with Toni Onley. Woodcock's narrative was combined with twenty-four watercolours by Onley as they travelled from Rajasthan, south towards the green lagoons of Kerala, eastward to the temple centres of Orissa and ending in the Himalayas. "True to his word, Toni donated all the paintings he did in India to CIVA," recalls Sarah McAlpine. Sales exceeded $125,000, launching CIVA as a viable organization.

Through its contacts with Seva Mandir, CIVA began to turn away from authoritarian doctor-oriented approaches towards more libertarian ideas based on recruiting villagers to accept training as health workers, and then sending them them back among their own people. Its fundraising activities became more varied. Here is how George Woodcock explained the situation:

Toni Onley became George's closest painter-friend towards the end of his life. The Woodcocks liked the outspoken Onley partly because he was not tight-fisted.

Our first major effort was actually a training scheme of this kind, which produced a significant improvement in local treatment of sicknesses, in public health, and even in nutrition through the encouragement of composting and kitchen gardens. When a drought began in the areas of Rajasthan where Seva Mandir operated, we expanded into the environmental area, forming a partnership between Seva Mandir, which provided the technical services, the villagers who offered their labour, the Indian government which opened its granaries to compensate them, and we who provided the cash for buying the stone and cement (an expensive commodity in India) and transporting it. We built ten dams, each of which served a thousand people and their animals as it filled with ground water and the occasional rain.

Through the summer of 1984 we worked on an Indian festival for the autumn. We had the cooperation of the India Music Society, with which we collaborated in importing an Orissa dancer and a noted India sitarist; Pacific Cinémathèque, which put on Indian films during the week; the Vancouver Art Gallery, which hosted an exhibition of Toni Onley's Indian paintings, and Xisa Huang of the Bau-Xi Gallery who did the same for a show of paintings donated by artists from all over Canada, including Alex Colville, Tony Urquhart and Ivan Eyre as well as the current Vancouver masters; finally, we held a great book sale, and with all this and a generous grant from the Canadian International Development Agency (CIDA), we were able to start our training scheme.

The artists, including the writers, continued to support us over the years, and two years afterwards we organized a nationwide poetry competition. Two poets who lived in Vancouver (George Bowering and George McWhirter) joined us in organizing the event and giving a first reading of the thousands of poems, good and bad, that were pouring in. Margaret Atwood, Al Purdy and I were the final judges, and the whole affair culminated in a poetry reading in 1988 that was organized by Greg Gatenby at Harbourfront, where Margaret and Al and I read in company with John Pass, the first-prize winner, and the other five winners.

The poetry contest, with a considerable supplement from CIDA, enabled us to build our ten dams in Rajasthan, around which Seva Mandir contoured the land and planted trees chosen for shade and fruit and forage. When he saw the first photographs of the dams, George Bowering said, "Now, that is concrete poetry." The winning poems were eventually published in *Dry Wells of India: An Anthology against Thirst*, which Howard White brought out and Margaret Atwood introduced.

Two years later the same group, Bowering and McWhirter, Inge and I, would launch a similar competition for anecdotes, led to the idea by an evening drinking Bushmills when the tales flowed free. What we found was that poetry, despite the recent craze for oral readings, remains a written art with thousands of people treasuring manuscripts, while the anecdote is essentially an oral art and—surprisingly—a shy one, for people are rarely inclined to put on paper the tales they tell. So we had a far more limited response than we had from the poets two years before, and in order to make a good anthology I had to invite my friends in the literary world, such as Margaret Atwood and Timothy Findley, Ronald Wright and Dorothy Livesay, Julian Symons and Eric Wright, to send us their tales as guest writers. They responded generously, and so a book finally appeared in 1991 with George McWhirter's introduction [the curiously titled *The Great Canadian Anecdote Contest*].

For me one of the splendid features of our work with Canada India Village Aid was the way it created or extended friendships, which I believe was due to the open style of our organization, or persistence in discussion until consensus was reached, and there was never any anger of the defeated at the end of our voteless meetings.

Since its beginnings in 1981, CIVA has since worked tirelessly to maintain the ideals established by the Woodcocks, helping rural communities all over India. Typically, in 2008, CIVA assisted two

Indian NGOs, Rashtra Seva Dal (RSD) and ASHA, to cope with emergency situations caused by the Kosi River floods of August and September 2008, in the Bihar area of northern India, one of India's poorest states, as well as flooding in the state of Orissa, bordering on the Bay of Bengal. In 2008, it was estimated that two million people were left homeless and many were killed by the worst flooding in India in half a century. Indian Prime Minister Manmohan Singh called it a "national calamity."

The Bihar tragedy occurred after the Kosi River, swollen by monsoon rains, burst an upstream dam in Nepal. Experts said that a river embankment in Nepal, for which the Indian government was responsible under a treaty between the two countries, failed on August 18 when the river was flowing at only about a sixth of the design capacity of the defense. Locals who had noted the river was about to breach the embankment three days before it happened were ignored.

The death toll rose significantly as water-borne diseases took hold and adults and children, already weak from malnourishment, were unable to access food and shelter. In addition, food riots broke out in several areas. Unlike the situation in Indonesia, where televised reports of a horrific tsunami had mobilized world aid for Indonesians, when the interior areas of Kisangunj, Katiyar, Arrariya, Madhepura and some parts of Purnea were flooded, the world took little notice.

CIVA became involved as a result of a simple letter from RSD's trustee Sudha Varde:

"We would like to request CIVA for a sum of Rs.10,00000 (ten lakhs). Ideally, we would like to use Rs. 4,00000 for rebuilding the schools (= 20 X Rs. 20000) and the rest for helping the community members to replace their huts and the most essential things that they are missing and this includes books and school supplies. . . . Our request to CIVA is confined to an absolute minimum that we require to put our project back on its feet. Education is the hope for these children and we do not want the lamp of hope that we lit so many years ago to be extinguished simply because a river changed its course."

CIVA had already been involved with Sudha Varde's RSD. In 1993, RSD had started a camp for Moslem and Dalit women with the dual purpose of impressing upon them the importance of education and being organized for their legal rights. CIVA, as a result, later funded a similar camp in another part of Bihar. RSD had also started twenty schools in Bihar for child labourers by persuading the community to donate small pieces of land for construction purposes. Similar structures were built to hold meetings of women's groups. All these structures were washed away by the flooding, as well as most of the huts of poor farmers. Knowing that RSD was a worthwhile partner, CIVA responded quickly and fully to the funding request. CIVA also fulfilled a funding request from the ASHA society.

"We take the view that our role is not to provide top-down direction," says CIVA's website, "but rather to stand back and allow the people who are directly affected come to us and tell us what they need. . . . As CIVA has no paid staff every dollar donated goes directly to India to help foster self-help and self-reliance among some of the world's poorest people."

This is the Woodcockian model. All work is done by volunteers, chiefly the board of directors. These individuals also bear the administrative costs of the society. In 2008, the board of directors consisted of Judy Brown, Suzy Buckley, John Harriss, Ashok Kotwal, Sophie Low-Beer, Sarah McAlpine, Essop Mia, Amir Mitha, Anne Murphy, Tony Phillips, Drew Stewart, Cathy Strickland, Russell Wodell and Hari Varshney. Organizational mainstays have included Tony Phillips and Sarah McAlpine.

Past directors have included Bill Bruneau, Barbara Chilcott, Marnie DiGiandomenico, Johanna Duprey, Bahman Farmanara, Hannah Fisher, Katherine Fletcher, Dr. W.D. Forbes, Keath Fraser, John Friesen, Marta Friesen, Genise Gill, Patricia LaNauze, Charlotte Mitha, Toni Onley, Robert Philips, Dale Rolfsen, Shirley Rushton, Doris Shadbolt, Giles Shearing Somers and Max Wyman.

Sponsors for CIVA have ranged from the industrialist J.V. Clyne to environmentalist David Suzuki.

As noted in George Woodcock's memoir, CIVA has also benefited from the contributions of many artists such as choreographer Anna Wyman, novelists Margaret Laurence and Timothy Findley, composer Harry Somers, architect Arthur Erickson, and painters Gordon Smith and Jack Shadbolt. CIVA also received royalties from books, most notably editor Keath Fraser's hugely successful collection of travel misadventures, *Bad Trips* (Vintage Books, 1991). Published in England as *Worst Journeys: The Picador Book of Travel* (1992), this bestselling anthology has generated more than $150,000 for CIVA.

Drs. Kathleen W. and Robert G. Langston of Naramata gave generously towards CIVA's health training project in Rajasthan and left a generous bequest in their wills, as did supporter Elizabeth Rose of California. While the economy of India is booming, almost one quarter of the world's poor live in India where more than 78 percent of the population lives on under $2 a day (at the purchasing power parity). In response, CIVA favours modest undertakings with Indian organizations at the grassroots level.

The constitution of CIVA was written with the advice and aid of Stephen Owen, who later became Ombudsman of British Columbia, a federal MP for Quadra and Commissioner on Resources and

Royalties since 1991 from Keath Fraser's *Bad Trips* now constitute the largest single donation to CIVA.

Environment to the provincial government. Among the witnesses for the application were poet Earle Birney and Ingeborg Woodcock. Signatories for registration were William Forbes, Shirley Rushton, A.G. "Tony" Phillips, John Friesen and George Woodcock. Doris Shadbolt and Ingeborg Woodcock were also originating members, joined soon thereafter by Sarah McAlpine.

The first chairman was Tony Phillips;

Shirley Rushton was vice-chairman; George Woodcock was secretary; Hari Varshney was treasurer. The secretary's job was apportioned to Russell Wodell.

"The CIVA Board has long shared a deep-seated mistrust of international bureaucracy and a zestful glee at manipulating it into concrete benefits to some of the world's most neglected citizens," recalls Wodell.

"I was hooked at once by accounts of a recent scheme to sell simple dhurries through the Bau-Xi Gallery: local artists contributed designs which were woven by village widows, and their work sold in Canada at roughly 1000 percent mark-up, which paid for the materials for further rugs. Nothing was said to the funding agencies about the fact that this scheme quietly subverted the caste system, by making the harijan women weavers the richest people in their villages. . . .

"Most of us have probably been burned more than once by the astonishing egotism of self-proclaimed do-gooders. On the CIVA board I found a refreshing and above all good-natured pragmatism. One of our projects identified a need for sanitation facilities, and accordingly a series of deep concrete latrines was constructed. 'Hurrah!' said the villagers, and promptly filled the latrines with potatoes, now finally safe from marauding rats. The board laughed in unison and agreed that this demonstrated a far greater need for secure food storage."

The treasurer's job was later handled by Amir Mitha, an Ismaili accountant from Uganda who was associated with the India Music Society. He says, "Most of the people who joined CIVA were brought in personally by George and Inge. I've been on the board close to thirty years. And if you ask me what keeps me going still, it is, in some sense—and I'm very careful in using the word—an obligation to George which we owe. It requires us to continue.

"That's partly why these two organizations have survived and thrived. It is because of the inspiration that George and Inge left with us."

EXAMPLES OF TYPICAL CIVA PROJECTS

■ The Women's Income Generation project in Trivandru, Kerala, was designed to provide a seven-month training period for 50 women to empower them to carry on weaving in their own homes. It also provided funds from a working capital pool to buy raw materials so that products could be sold to the Mitraniketan Women's Cooperative Society. The training procedures took fourteen months, split into two periods, from May 1996 to November 1996, and from December 1996 to June 1997. It was the first CIVA project in Kerala, at the southern tip of India.

■ A sustainable energy program with CHIRAG was commenced jointly by CIVA and TRAS in 1993. CIVA was the first organization to provide funds to CHIRAG after it was registered as a non-profit society in 1986, funding a community health project. The Ford Foundation, Oxfam and other funding agencies subsequently partnered with CHIRAG, most notably the Swiss Development Commission (SDC), as of 1990. Numerous CHIRAG programs in health, education and forestry have been funded by CIVA and TRAS in the Nainital District. Following an inspection of the CIVA-sponsored rural health centre in Sitla by Tony Phillips, CIVA supported the creation of a second clinic in the village of Khasialekh. Of the total cost for the scheme of $98,388, CIVA and the Canadian International Development Agency jointly bore $86,672. The total CIVA contribution was $31,084.

■ In villages surrounding Coimbatore in Tamil Nadu state, CIVA partnered with Shanti Ashram on literacy and income generation projects for Harijan (Untouchable) women from lower caste families. A "spiritually motivated" Gandhian organization headed by Dr. M. Aram and his wife, Shanti Ashram provided vocational training to more than 3,000 women in 29 villages. CIVA representatives made several inspection visits in the early 1990s to ensure funds were well allocated.

■ In association with Father Burns, a long-time associate of the Woodcocks, CIVA partnered with the Darjeeling Jesuits of North

Bengal to improve health services for 150,000 families in the Darjeeling district by providing courses for paramedic/midwives who deliver primary health care in the region. Again, a CIVA representative visited the project, based in Hayden Hall, in 1995.

■ CIVA and TRAS have both partnered with Sister Victorine, the Indian Carmelite nun in the south Indian state of Karnataka, whose Carmelite Sisters of the Incarnation Convent built a health centre and dispensary in the Geddalahalli Village region near Mysore. After a visit by Jennifer Hales of TRAS, who stayed for six weeks working with Sister Victorine, CIVA sponsored a second facility for 150 families in Jettihundi, 11 kilometres from Mysore. She saw how the Carmelite nuns work with Hindu, Muslim, Buddhist, Jain and Tibetan people. "Sister Victorine is easily one of the most caring and resourceful women I have ever met," Hales reported. "As others have said, she can make a dollar go further than anyone we know, doing an incredible amount with a tiny bit of money to benefit the poor. Her compassion and commitment are endless."

For more information about Canada India Village Aid society, visit www.civaid.ca.

George Woodcock accepted the UBC Medal for Popular Biography in 1973 (above) and in 1976, as well as the Molson Prize in 1973, Freedom of the City of Vancouver in 1994 and Fellowship of the Royal Society of Canada in 1968. He is also known for refusing awards given by the Canadian state, including the Order of Canada.

THE WOODCOCK FUND
& WOODCOCK AWARD

The proceeds from the sale of the Woodcocks' home on McCleery Street in Vancouver have been donated to generate a $2.3 million endowment (as of June 2009) that provides financial aid to writers during times of unforeseen financial hardship.

The Woodcock Endowment Fund for Writers in Financial Distress was established by the Woodcocks in 1989. "Part of the reason they set up this fund," suggests Tony Phillips, "was the Shadbolts were setting up the Shadbolt Centre and their own trust fund. In essence, I think George and Inge probably said, 'Well, Jack and Doris are doing this, so we should really be thinking about what we're going to do. They're supporting artists. So we'll support writers.' They were idealists. Their idea was simple: If somebody has fallen on hard times you just give them a helping hand and everything will straighten out."

The Writers' Trust of Canada, formerly known as the Writers' Development Trust, subsequently received $1 million from the Woodcock estate in 2005, followed by $876,000 in 2006, and a final installment of $683 in 2009. "Writers are one of Canada's greatest exports," said Don Oravec, Executive Director of the Writers' Trust of Canada, in 2006, "yet many endure near poverty. This increased support of the Woodcock Fund will encourage and preserve our literary heritage by rescuing those works that might otherwise be abandoned." These bequests, overseen by estate executor Sarah McAlpine, constitute one of the largest private donations to the literary arts in Canada, if not the largest.

Between 1989 (when it was activated) and 2009, the Woodcock Fund dispersed a total of $647,404 to 1489 writers who applied. "An endowment was built up from '89 to '05," says James Davies, senior program manager, "while at the same time the Fund dispersed between twenty and forty thousand dollars each year." To be eligible for assistance, the writer must be working on a book that, without the grant, would be imperiled or abandoned, and the writer must have already published a minimum of two works, as well as face a financial crisis that exceeds the ongoing, chronic problem of making a living. The fund chiefly serves writers of fiction, poetry, plays and creative non-fiction.

"The Woodcock Fund is one of the many enduring legacies funded by the Woodcocks' generous, passionate and unflagging engagement with the world," says Ronald Wright, who knew the Woodcocks for twenty years prior to serving as Chair of the Writers' Trust Woodcock Committee. "Many authors received the Woodcocks' encouragement and friendship, which are rare gifts, and especially so from our heroes."

In his remarks to celebrate the inauguration of the Woodcock Endowment Fund for Writers in Financial Distress on May 24, 2006, family friend and author Keath Fraser noted that George Woodcock "grew up in poverty and endured the costs of this, in one way or another, for more than half a lifetime. It's no wonder in remembering the value of a shilling he refused to forget that the worth of a dollar increased when it was shared."

Fraser quoted from a letter written by George Woodcock to Sir

Herbert Read that describes his impoverishment in Sooke and the importance of charity: "A few weeks later we were again out of paper money and down to nickels and pennies. This time we went over to the Englands to try and borrow a couple of dollars. They too were broke again. . . . Having told us this, Jean went without another word to her cupboard, took out her meager stores, and divided them, tin by tin and packet by packet. Then she took the children's money box, silently opened it, counted out the contents, wrote an IOU, and then divided the cash so that she and Inge had about $4 each. It was the most shining act of mutual aid I have ever experienced."

George and Ingeborg Woodcock learned the importance of charity the hard way, and they would always remember, as Keath Fraser made clear at the closing of his remarks:

"George never forgot 'the culture shock that often comes from the first encounter with deep poverty.' He was referring to his first trip to the less developed world, Mexico, in the summer of 1954. But his allusion might just as well apply to the culture shock of returning to Canada in 1949, where he encountered the deep poverty of having to buy his time as a writer by digging septic tanks and shovelling turkey shit.

"The Woodcock Fund is characteristic of George and Inge because it reflects their capacity and moral desire to remember others . . . never to forget, as George put it, 'the less fortunate.' Having done their best for impoverished Tibetan refugees and tribal Indian villagers, their own tribe of writers is what they chose to remember in their will.

"In setting up this legacy, they were really remembering their anarchist roots. No red tape or state intervention, thank you, just mutual aid among writers. No hierarchy among applicants, but rather an evaluation by peers. And no publicity about the grants given; instead, anonymity guaranteed."

George and Ingeborg Woodcock undoubtedly looked favourably on the Toronto-based Writers' Trust, registered as a non-profit organization in 1976, because it was conceived by writers Margaret

The Woodcocks' extreme poverty in Sooke has been cited as one
of the reasons they donated most of their estate to the Writers' Trust to help
other writers in financial distress. The Woodcocks built this second cabin in
Sooke at Whiffen Spit, not far from the present site of the Sooke Harbour
House five-star restaurant. Sooke, coincidentally, was the site of the
first homestead built by a European landowner on Vancouver Island,
independent of the Hudson's Bay Company.

Atwood, Graeme Gibson, Pierre Berton, David Young and Margaret
Laurence. He was especially fond of Margaret Laurence, with whom
he had corresponded, and Atwood, who taught at UBC in 1964–65
while writing the first draft of her novel, *The Edible Woman*. Atwood
felt indebted to Woodcock for writing a highly favourable review
of her work in the *Toronto Star* near the outset of her career.

Visit www.writerstrust.com for further information.

WOODCOCK LIFETIME ACHIEVEMENT AWARD

In 1994, in the aftermath of civic events held to recognize the
literary career of George Woodcock, *B.C. BookWorld* began working in partnership with the City of Vancouver (Mayor of Vancouver's office), the Vancouver Public Library and a non-profit society
(Pacific BookWorld News Society, founded in 1988) to jointly spon-

Jane Rule (seated) was the second recipient of the Lifetime Achievement Award
now named after George Woodcock. Rule's partner Helen Sonthoff (standing)
and Jane Rule befriended the Woodcocks not long after the lesbian couple
arrived in Vancouver in 1956. Both taught in the UBC English department.

sor and present an annual prize to a senior British Columbia author whose enduring contribution to the literary arts spans several
decades. Initially the corporate sponsor for this undertaking was
BC Gas, later renamed Terasen. This sponsor would not agree to
have the award named in honour of George Woodcock, as was first
envisioned. But, in 2007, the Terasen Lifetime Achievement Award
was renamed the George Woodcock Lifetime Achievement Award,
as originally intended. Each year another commemorative marble
plaque is installed in the Writers' Walk—or Woodcock Walk—at

the Vancouver Public Library on Georgia Street in Vancouver. The Mayor of Vancouver, or his representative, attends a presentation ceremony and issues a proclamation in honour of the recipient, who receives a cash award. Winners are announced with press releases and full-page notices in *B.C. BookWorld*. The recipients of the annual award have been: Eric Nicol (1995), Jane Rule (1996), Barry Broadfoot (1997), Christie Harris (1998), Phyllis Webb (1999), Paul St. Pierre (2000), Robert Harlow (2001), Peter Trower (2002), Audrey Thomas (2003), P.K. Page (2004), Alice Munro (2005), Jack Hodgins (2006), bill bissett (2007), Joy Kogawa (2008) and W.P. Kinsella (2009).

Visit www.georgewoodcock.com for further information.

TIBETANS
& THE DALAI LAMA
IN BRITISH COLUMBIA

Tibetans in British Columbia have been part of an extended family, including TRAS, since George and Ingeborg Woodcock facilitated the immigration of their friends Lobsang and Dekyi Lhalungpa in the 1960s.

Born in 1924 into a prominent Tibetan family, Lobsang Lhalungpa had worked for the Dalai Lama's secretariat in the Potala palace, once he came of age. Following the incursions of the Chinese in 1950, Lhalungpa decided not to return to Tibet while undertaking a diplomatic mission to India.

He taught at St. Joseph's College in Darjeeling, translated a biography of Gandhi into Tibetan, co-authored a Tibetan-English Grammar and set himself the task of preserving Tibetan wisdom, lore and history by meeting with exiled lamas. He and his wife Dekyi had children in India. After the Lhalungpas met the Woodcocks in 1961, they moved to England for a short time before the Woodcocks were able to sponsor their immigration to Canada. It is believed they became the first Tibetans to live in Canada.

During a multicultural parade in Vancouver in the mid-1970s, these Tibetans were alarmed to be walking in front a Chinese delegation because they did not wish to be associated with China in any way. From left: Dolma Tsering, Kesang Tsering, unknown, Tsega Garie, unknown and Dekyi Lhalungpa. The Tibetan Cultural Society of B.C. was later founded with 35 members in January of 1981 to preserve culture, religion and language.

Having helped Lobsang Lhalungpa secure a teaching position with the Asian Department at UBC, through his connections with the university president (who was also the honorary chairman of TRAS), George Woodcock relied on Lhalungpa to add his considerable charm and unrivalled knowledge to enhance presentations about Tibet made to support the work of TRAS.

Lhalungpa became associated with the Smithsonian Institute as a scholar and he remarried. His first wife, Dekyi, who worked for many years at the Naam restaurant in Vancouver, died in 1995. Lobsang Lhalungpa moved to New Mexico where he was killed in a car accident on April 28, 2008, at age eighty-four. Hundreds attended his funeral in Sante Fe. His son, Tenzin Lhalungpa, remains active in Tibetan affairs as president of CTC in Vancouver.

Each Tibetan immigrant has his or her own story to tell.

Phuntsok Kakho recalls being met at the Vancouver International Airport by the Woodcocks and the Lhalungpas in September of 1971, when several Tibetan families from India were admitted to Alberta. They flew onward to Calgary, then were taken by bus to Tabor, where they were given jobs as farmers, and were taught English.

Between 1972 and 1974, Tibetan families from Alberta came to British Columbia and were helped to find jobs by TRAS and the Lhalungpas. Phuntsok Kakho arrived with his family in 1975 and settled in Surrey. There were 56 members of the Tibetan Cultural Society of BC (TCS), including children, by 2002, when Phuntsok Kakho was its president—at which time he estimated there were 115 Tibetans living in British Columbia.

The TCS has donated funds to a settlement project in Ladakh, hosted nuns and monks from India and Nepal, and co-hosted the 1993 visit of the Dalai Lama with the Canada Tibet Committee.

Tibetan families in B.C. come from Tibetan communities such as Lhasa, Lethang, Amdo, Kham and Sekha Che. Some lived as nomads, others worked for the Tibetan government. Others were traders or farmers. They celebrate the Dalai Lama's birthday, Tibetan New Year and other Tibetan religious holidays. Prayer meetings have been held on a rotating basis in different homes. One of the goals of TCS is to establish a Tibetan Cultural Centre.

"Most of us miss having tea at the shops and chatting with our family and friends," says Kakho, "going to the monastery to do offerings, and circumambulation, practising our religion, the spicy and homemade food, and the close knit community of family and friends. The list can go on and on. But on the whole we are very happy that we have come to Canada in order to give the children and ourselves a good life and education."

When extras were needed for the filming of an outdoor skating scene for the Brad Pitt movie *Seven Years in Tibet*, outlining the life

All sponsored by TRAS, these orphans with the Tarings (back row) in Mussoorie include Dawa Dolma (small girl at front) who now lives in Surrey, B.C.

of Heinrich Harrer and his friendship with the teenaged Dalai Lama, members of the Tibetan community in B.C. were hired to portray Tibetans for scenes filmed on a frozen lake near Williams Lake in central B.C. Phuntsok Kakho briefly imagined he was back in Tibet until he noticed all the buildings were made of cardboard.

During World War II, Harrer reached Tibet after escaping from a British detention camp in the Himalayas with several of his German-born and Austrian-born mountain climbing companions, notably Peter Aufschnaiter. After his eight years in Tibet, Aufschnaiter became a Nepalese citizen. Fluent in Tibetan, he gathered medical supplies for Tibetans living near the border of Tibet and Nepal. The Woodcocks met Peter Aufschnaiter in Kathmandu.

Better-liked by the Tibetans than Harrer, Aufschnaiter was equally famous in Germany where his book about his Tibet experiences has been considered superior to Harrer's account. The Brad Pitt movie, in which Pitt depicts Harrer, shows that Aufschnaiter resented

Harrer's stubborn egotism, but it invents a romantic entanglement for Aufschnaiter with a Tibetan woman.

One of Harrer's and Aufschnaiter's comrades, Hans Kopp, also escaped to Tibet but left Harrer and Aufschnaiter to go to the remote kingdom of Mustang, where he was recaptured by the British. Hans Kopp later immigrated to Canada and lived in Richmond, B.C. Kopp subsequently attended a talk by Barry and Dorothea Leach about TRAS and thereafter remained in contact with them until his death in the early 1970s. His memoir *Himalaya Shuttlecock* is now available in an English translation.

TSERING'S STORY

Born in Darjeeling, India, as the son of Tibetan parents, Rinzin Samang still vividly recalls George Woodcock's return visit to Mrs. Taring's school in Mussoorie where he and all the other children waited at attention for a very long time, as well-behaved as possible, in order to greet properly the revered "Dr. Woodcock." Today he smiles to remember how this distinguished visitor from Canada was accorded almost as much respect as the Dalai Lama.

Some forty years later, Rinzin Samang now owns a large, new home in White Rock, British Columbia, with two cars inside his heated garage. Clearly he has worked very hard and prospered. Now he and his wife Tsering have been blessed with fine, well-behaved young teenagers, Yeshey and Tara, whose respectful manners seems almost non-Canadian. Above a large sofa in the living room is a panoramic colour photo of the Potala that was purchased in Dharamsala. The entire family visited Dharamsala for several months in 2008.

Rinzin met Tsering, his wife-to-be, in Vancouver. Born in the tiny village of Light, she and one of her brothers escaped from Tibet, via Nepal, in 1984–85, with fifteen others, at age seventeen. The group of Tibetan refugees drove to the border in a truck, then trekked through the mountains. She was sponsored to immigrate to Canada in 1987 by an older brother—who was friends with

Rinzin in Vancouver. Her older brother in Vancouver was allowed to sponsor her as a guardian because both Tsering's parents died when she was twelve, and she had not yet to turn eighteen.

In 1994, only a few years after her twins were born, Tsering Samang was asked by long-time TRAS supporter Dorothea Leach if she would like to earn a little extra money by doing some housework for her. Having only recently arrived in Canada, Tsering was understandably reluctant. She could not speak English well and she was not familiar with Canadian standards of cleaning. It seemed bizarre to her that Canadians wanted to keep everything so relentlessly clean.

Dorothea Leach generously coaxed her along. One day Tsering was asked by Dorothea Leach if she might consider going all the way into Vancouver to meet someone named Ingeborg Woodcock. Even if Rinzin Samang had not witnessed the Woodcocks' visit to Mussoorie when he was a boy, most of the people in the small community of Tibetan refugees in British Columbia knew about TRAS and the Woodcocks.

Tsering was told that Ingeborg Woodcock's husband had recently died. She needed someone to help her with some basic housework, as well as shopping. Despite the fact that Ingeborg had the reputation of being difficult to work for, Tsering knew in her heart as soon as they met that Ingeborg was a good person. Thus began a friendship that became integral to Ingeborg for the rest of her life.

Tsering always came on Wednesdays, when the gardener came. She was supposed to work for three hours each time, attending mostly to minor tasks. Much of the time there wasn't a great deal required, so Ingeborg would ask Tsering to wash her little car in the garage. But Ingeborg would never allow Tsering to work for more than an hour and a half before she insisted Tsering stop working so they could have coffee together. It was their little ritual. The cat would immediately jump onto Ingeborg's lap and the two women would talk. At first they had cookies and other baking; then one day there was cheesecake. "I told her, 'I love cheesecake!'" Tsering recalls. After that, Ingeborg always bought cheesecake for Tsering's visits.

Ingeborg frequently told Tsering about her first husband, Roskelly. Chiefly she was dissatisfied with him because he was irresponsible, even lazy. As a journalist he would be expected to jump into action at all hours of the day. Ingeborg was irritated at his unwillingness or inability to do so. She had to rouse him, goad him, to do his job properly. "When she met George Woodcock," Tsering says, "it made her happy." Here, by contrast, was a writer who knew how to work.

Then calamity struck. Ingeborg had a stroke. It was Tsering who discovered Ingeborg's naked body in the study. "I didn't want to have a key to the house," she recalls, "so I would always phone on Tuesdays to tell her I was coming. But this one time, when I called, the phone just rang and rang. No answer. It was very strange. She was nearly always at home. The next day when I arrived, I knocked on the door. I knock. Knock. Knock. Maybe ten minutes. I am very worried.

"I got down and looked through the mail slot. I call inside. I listen. I can hear something. Her voice. I go around to the back. I look inside. I go next door to the neighbour. I know her. She calls 911. They come and break a window. We find her there, where she has fallen. She has been there for maybe 36 hours. Or maybe she fell when she tried to get to the phone when I called her. We don't know.

"The flowers have fallen onto the floor. And George's ashes have been knocked onto the floor, too. She is lying beside the ashes of her husband. I am a Buddhist. I think maybe he has come back to visit her, to take her with him."

The medics revived her but Ingeborg strenuously objected to being taken to the hospital. She pleaded for Tsering to stay, to look after her. But Tsering was frightened. She could not stay. She had two small children at home. And she did not have any experience as a nurse.

Clearly, Ingeborg was very ill. Tsering asked one of the emergency response workers to come into the kitchen. She asked him to take Ingeborg to the hospital. They were fully in accord. It would

THE SHRINE

Housekeeper Tsering Samang was fascinated by the modest shrine that Ingeborg constructed around this black and white photograph taken by Alan Twigg in 1994. As he peers directly towards the viewer, supported by a cane but still strong in his mind, one can see that the expression on George Woodcock's face is both kind and inquisitive. Alongside his ashes and the photo, Ingeborg also kept freshly cut flowers and a copy of *The Cherry Tree on Cherry Street*. This thin collection of poetry from Quarry Press is seldom recognized as a "major" work, but it contains much of George Woodcock's most intimate writing, including love poems to their friend, Marie Louise Berneri. Ingeborg frequently talked to Tsering about George, referring to him as her baby. The more they talked, the more Tsering began to understand the nature of their love.

be necessary for Ingeborg to have medical attention for a prolonged period, otherwise she could die.

Ingeborg spent several weeks in the hospital. After that, once she returned home, the old, black, manual style rotary telephone on the wall was replaced with a new telephone near her bed, and the awkward bathroom facilities were finally improved. Tsering resumed her visits. She increasingly took charge of the shopping.

Tsering would drive them in her own car for groceries. Mostly Ingeborg liked to buy whiskey, Johnny Walker. She also liked white fish. But her needs remained both frugal and uncomplicated. She would buy chocolates for Tsering to take home to Yeshey and Tara, whom she never met.

"She live for other people," says Tsering. "Not much people do this. Most people enjoy themselves first."

In Ingeborg's closet were two grey wool sweaters and a long beige jacket. "She had only two lipsticks," says Tsering. "One in the washroom and one in her purse. I had never seen her wear pants."

Knowing Ingeborg's habit of frugality, and to balance her habit of philanthropy, Tsering volunteered to bring her fresh cut flowers from Surrey, where she could buy them more cheaply. Each Wednesday she would arrive with new flowers and a bill; Ingeborg would reimburse her.

Ingeborg gave advice about raising children. Don't spoil them. And sometimes she reminisced. She recalled once having difficulty with immigration officials at an airport in Tokyo, but when the airport officials learned that George Woodcock was an internationally known intellectual, the Woodcocks were suddenly accorded special treatment. Ingeborg was disdainful, objecting to the fact that anyone, including themselves, should be worthy of elitist privileges.

Tsering had lost her mother at age twelve, and Ingeborg never had children, so their familiarity went beyond employer/employee. Occasionally they would trade Tibetan words, and Tsering once made her Tibetan tea, with butter and salt. But Ingeborg was limited to one cup.

After the Dalai Lama's doctor examined Ingeborg for arthritis, he prescribed medicine to be sent from India. When the medicine arrived, Ingeborg took it, but the results were dire. "She was throwing up. She was sick. I think the people in India sent the wrong medicine. I was scared. I told her to go to Mexico, better climate. But she said, no, I'm okay. She just wanted to stay home.

"I know her personality. I know she feels very bad. I know her feelings. She doesn't want me to help her. I told her, 'Nothing to shame.' She still doesn't want me to help. You have to show some anger. I tell her we have to become children again. That is the way. In Tibet, we do not have hospital or nursing home. The children look after the parents.

"I tell her that my brothers look after my parents this way. It is natural. I get her clothes off. I wash her. When the nurse come, I tell her to cut the toenails, to put them in warm water. It is not enough to comb the hair."

Tsering visited Ingeborg for about five years, on an ongoing

Tsering Samang (front) and her husband Rinzin (right) live in White Rock with their son and daughter, who have visited Tibet with their parents.

basis, before Ingeborg went into a care facility where Tsering also visited her.

Tsering was one of the few people who could tease Ingeborg. In her room once, before they went downstairs to the smoking area, Tsering told Ingeborg she should put on some lipstick, some make-up, because there were many women in the building and very few men, so the woman had to try very hard to get the men to notice. Ingeborg expressed mock horror at this suggestion, but she had a hearty laugh. Downstairs, Ingeborg told a fellow female smoker about Tsering's advice to her, chortling again at the absurdity.

About a year after Ingeborg died, Tsering was contacted again by Dorothea Leach. She and her husband were invited to the Leachs' home.

"I had heard the Dalai Lama's brother was in Vancouver," Tsering recalls, "so I thought we were being invited to meet him. My husband and I dressed up." But when they arrived at the Leachs' home, the Dalai Lama's brother was not there.

Instead, Dorothea Leach gave Tsering an envelope with a note from Sarah McAlpine, an executrix of Ingeborg's will. Although the Woodcocks had decided they ought to donate the bulk of their money, and the proceeds of the sale of their home, to the Writers Development Trust to help Canadian writers, Ingeborg ensured that her housekeeper was to receive the proceeds of the sale of many books purchased en masse by the antiquarian bookseller Don Stewart of Macleod's Books, an expert on anarchist literature. Dorothea Leach passed along a cheque from Ingeborg's estate to Tsering for more than six thousand dollars, enabling the family to plan a trip to India together.

"They work hard for people," Tsering says. "They never work hard for themselves. It is very hard to find this kind of people. Sometimes the wife, sometimes the husband, they want to work hard for themselves. The Woodcocks different. Both have the same kind of feelings. Same feelings, same heart."

The Dalai Lama has always attracted sold-out audiences in Vancouver: "We cannot achieve world peace without first achieving peace within ourselves."

THE DALAI LAMA IN VANCOUVER
"My religion is simple, my religion is kindness."—Dalai Lama

Karmic links brought Victor Chan to Dharamsala—according to the Dalai Lama. And those karmic links, in turn, have repeatedly brought the Dalai Lama to Vancouver.

The year was 1971. Needing a break from his studies in Canada and the U.S., Victor Chan bought a VW bus in Utrecht and planned to make his way overland to India. A few months into the trip he found himself spending nearly half a year in Afghanistan, then a haven for dropouts and would-be adventurers.

"I was abducted," he recalls, "together with two fellow travellers, Cheryl from New York and Rita from Munich, by three rifle-wielding Afghan men. Somehow we managed to escape and Cheryl and I decided to continue to India together. It turned out that she had a letter of introduction to the Dalai Lama."

In March of 1972, Chan sat face-to-face with the exiled Tibetan leader for the first of many encounters. "Somehow, unexpectedly," said His Holiness, "something brought you here. Your being kidnapped in Afghanistan. There may be karmic links in many past lives."

Since then Victor Chan has written an extraordinarily detailed, 1,100-page guide to pilgrimages in Tibet. He has also co-authored the *Dalai Lama's Wisdom of Forgiveness*, and he has thrice helped to arrange the Dalai Lama's itinerary for visits to Vancouver—in 2004, 2006 and 2009.

The first time Chan saw the Dalai Lama speak in Vancouver, he stood nearby as His Holiness spoke without notes in his idiosyncratic English: "Some of you come with certain expectations of the Dalai Lama. The Nobel laureate give some kind of exciting information or something special. Nothing! I have nothing to offer. Just some blah, blah, blah."

Then he went on to reiterate a favourite theme: "We have to make every effort to promote human affection. Promote a warm heart; look at humanity as a whole. Today's reality: whole world almost like one body. One thing happens some distant place, the repercussions reach your own place. Destruction of your neighbour as enemy is essentially destruction of yourself."

Born in Hong Kong in 1945, Victor Chan was a particle physicist before he decided to escape from graduate work at the University of Chicago and travel to Asia. In 1984, Chan made his first visit to Tibet, covering 42,000 kilometres on foot, by horse, by yak, by coracle, by truck and by bus. He returned in 1990 to walk the pilgrim trails, becoming the first person to reach Lhasa from Kathmandu by mountain bike. In 1994 he was touted as the only non-Tibetan to have made all three of the sacred Tibetan pilgrimages to Kailash, Tsari and Lapchi.

With Pitman Potter, director of the Institute of Asian Research at UBC, Chan was instrumental in helping to establish a Tibetan studies program at UBC and he co-founded the Dalai Lama Center for Peace and Education with His Holiness in 2005. Their Center is also instigating the Vancouver Peace Summit: Nobel Laureates in

Dialogue, September 26–29, 2009, featuring Archbishop Desmond Tutu and former Irish President Mary Robinson.

Chan previously coordinated the Balancing Educating the Mind with Educating the Heart dialogues at UBC in 2004 that included Nobel Peace Prize winner Shirin Ebadi, a voice of conscience in Iran, and Archbishop Desmond Tutu, who was pleased to introduce the Dalai Lama.

Tutu told Victor Chan: "Isn't it extraordinary, in a culture that worships success, that it isn't the aggressively successful, the abrasive, the macho, who are the ones that we admire? We might envy their bank balances, but we do not admire them. But we revere the Dalai Lama. He has this incredible sense of fun. He laughs easily; he is almost like a schoolboy. The Dalai Lama makes us feel good about being human. About being alive at a time when someone like him is around. He is about the only one, one of the very, very, very, very few, who can fill Central Park with adoring devotees." The Dalai Lama's mini-Woodstock event in New York's Central Park was arranged by actor Richard Gere.

Vancouver's Victor Chan and His Holiness, in Dharamsala.
The two have co-founded The Dalai Lama Center for Peace and Education.
Chan has coordinated three of the Dalai Lama's visits to Vancouver.

In 2004, the Dalai Lama's two public talks in Vancouver were sold out in advance within 30 minutes of the tickets going on sale. These talks were to be presented in a 4,000-seat building at UBC but the location was changed to the 12,000-seat Pacific Coliseum. Again, all 12,000 seats were sold quickly for each event. TRAS president Marion Tipple presented her Tibet photographs at the Vancouver Public Library, and TRAS was invited to mount a display at the Bank of Hong Kong's Pendulum Gallery.

Chan was once curious if the Dalai Lama ever wondered why he is such a people-magnet. In one of their get-togethers, Chan said, "I'd like to ask you a silly question." His Holiness was sitting cross-legged in lotus, as usual, in his corner armchair inside his residence in Dharamsala. "Why are you so popular? What makes you irresistible to so many people?"

He didn't brush Chan's question aside with a joke, as Chan thought he might. He was thoughtful as he replied, "I don't think myself having especially good qualities. Oh, maybe some small things. I have positive mind. Sometimes, of course, I get a little irritated. But in my heart, I never blame. I never think bad things against anyone. I also try to consider others more. I believe others more important than me. Maybe people like me for my good heart."

He rubbed his cheeks with his fingers and continued, "Under this skin, same nature, same kinds of desires and emotions. I usually try to give happy feeling to the other person. Eventually many people talking something positive about me. Then more people came, just follow reputation—that also possible. But there may be other factors. Maybe some karmic link, something more mysterious."

The Dalai Lama first formally met TRAS as an organization on September 4, 1979, during his first visit to the United States. Billed as a private tour, this little-publicized tour enabled His Holiness to meet people in forty different centres. In Seattle, he received an Honorary Doctorate and he gave audiences to the local Tibetan refugee communities, including twenty-five TRAS representatives.

The meeting with TRAS members, arranged by T.C. Tethong of Victoria, was held in a large hall where a dais had been erected draped with a yellow canopy. A lovely old *thanka* (religious Tibetan wall-hanging) decorated the back wall, in front of which stood a throne covered in brocade.

His Holiness sat in front of the throne on a chair which was almost hidden by beautiful Tibetan rugs. Flags of the United States, Canada and Tibet and potted palms flanked the dais.

John Conway has recalled how members of the Tibetan communities in B.C., Alberta, Washington and Oregon, most of them in national dress, sat together on the floor in front of the dais, and on both sides chairs had been placed for the many western guests.

Sharp at nine o'clock a hush fell over the large assembly and the Dalai Lama entered the hall followed by several red-robed monks, Tibetan officials and American bodyguards.

"We all sat down and watched in silence while H.H. was served a ceremonial cup of butter tea and tsampa (roasted barley flour) on a beautifully carved Tibetan table. After a sip of tea H.H. threw a few grains of tsampa into the air as an offering and then ate some.

"Through an interpreter the Dalai Lama welcomed all and expressed special recognition of the interest the western guests had shown in the Tibetans and the help given in the past for the rehabilitation of his people in exile. H.H. then turned to the Tibetan community and talked to them for over an hour.

"Although not able to understand what H.H. was saying, we enjoyed listening to the sound of his voice and watching his lively gestures. At times he seemed like a father giving good advice, serious or smiling, at other times he shook his finger at his listeners just like a teacher admonishing his students, and then he seemed to turn into a marvellous story-teller, slapping his knee, or both hands emphasizing a point, laughing and looking around at his attentive audience.

"With a charming grin he suddenly turned to us and said in

THE DALAI LAMA

MESSAGE

I would like to express my deep appreciation to the Trans-Himalayan Aid Society for the help you have given Tibetans since your foundation as the Tibetan Refugee Aid Society forty years ago. We Tibetans are passing through a very difficult period and shouldering very difficult tasks with many obstacles. But these factors do not discourage us, because our goal is just and true.

Beginning from 1959, when we first came into exile, we calculated that our struggle may take a long time and we have prepared carefully to meet that challenge. We decided that providing our children with a good education, a modern as well as our own traditional education, was a priority so that even if the struggle is prolonged, a new generation could replace the older one and take responsibility for our cause.

I am grateful to all of you for the help you have given our refugee community, particularly your direct interest in the specific needs of the various settlements, and hope we can count on your continued friendship until our goal is won.

June 7, 2002

Letter from his Holiness the Dalai Lama

English, 'You are not boring?' Seeing smiles on our faces convinced him that all was well and with a hearty 'O.K,' he addressed the Tibetans again.

"Later H.H. spoke to the TRAS members for 25 minutes. At first he thanked us through an interpreter for the help given to Tibetan refugees in the past by TRAS. He stated that of the 100,000 Tibetans living in exile, mainly in India, about 7,000 were still in need of rehabilitation.

"The greatest concerns, however, were for educational and medical facilities. H.H. then explained, speaking now in good English, that Tibetans are very prone to T.B. as they have no resistance to that disease.

"Barry Leach informed H.H. that TRAS recognises these concerns and, thanks to a generous benefactor, has established a scholarship fund for vocational training. When we expressed our concern for Tibetans in Bhutan, H.H. described the situation as 'very difficult through misunderstanding.' The Bhutanese government was demanding that all 4,000 Tibetans living in that country should become citizens. Very few complied with this, because most wished to remain Tibetan.

"H.H. did not criticize this demand; he recognized that the two cultures were very closely related. However, he felt the Tibetans should be given more time instead of being forced to decide immediately."

Local Tibetans organized the Dalai Lama's first visit to Vancouver in October of 1980.

After initial plans were made by the Office of Tibet in New York, the Dalai Lama's itinerary was arranged and organized by twelve Tibetan families in British Columbia. They were responsible for "accommodation, travel and bodyguards." TRAS helped with some of the planning. A lecture to the Vancouver Institute on the UBC campus drew 2,000 enthusiastic listeners. It was followed by a reception at the Hotel Vancouver for 250 guests, including TRAS members, Mayor Mike Harcourt and his Council.

The highlight of that inaugural visit for TRAS directors was the possibility that His Holiness might attend a board meeting. Daphne Hales remembers how everyone waited on tenterhooks, not sure if he would really appear. Suddenly the door of a small meeting room opened and several Tibetans arrived, followed by the Dalai Lama, who promptly sat down at the table and talked with everyone about important issues facing Tibetans. The unprecedented TRAS meeting included George and Ingeborg Woodcock. In 1980, the Dalai Lama also attended an inter-faith service.

Having received the Nobel Prize for Peace in 1989, His Holiness made his second visit to Vancouver, again organized by local Tibetans, in July of 1993, lecturing at the Pan Pacific Hotel and meeting with the Woodcocks in private. Dorothea Leach recalls, "When the Dalai Lama was here, and George and Inge had a private audience, the Dalai Lama pointed to George's leg. At first George thought there was a stain. He was going to clean it off.

"And the Dalai Lama said, 'No, no, no.' It was a ladybug. So one of the monks with the Dalai Lama had to take it down and release it on Granville Street, or wherever they were."

The Dalai Lama was making arrangements to see Ingeborg Woodcock in 2004 when he learned of her death in December of 2003.

"Everything the Woodcocks did was built on friendship," says Tony Phillips. "They were past masters at creating friends. They nurtured the social net. When you became their friends, it was a lifelong commitment on their part to be your friend. And if you ever needed anything, or got into trouble, they would be right there. It was just a case of, 'Well, my philosophy says I should do this.' This is how they lived their lives. And so everybody who became a friend, stayed a friend."

Including the Dalai Lama.

A 1993 portrait of the Dalai Lama in Vancouver, by Doane Gregory ▶

THE FINAL MEETING

"I will always remember when the Woodcocks had their last audience with the Dalai Lama," says Margo Palmer. "It was at the Hotel Vancouver.

"We were waiting for them in a long, echoing, hotel hallway, very wide. They came out after seeing him. They started walking down that corridor. They were quite happy. Tony and I were a little distance away and they were walking towards us. I looked up and I saw the Dalai Lama was there behind them, with just one aide. George and Inge had their backs to him.

"They didn't see him. He had come out of the room to watch them leave. They had done their farewells. And the Dalai Lama just stood in the middle of the corridor. He just watched them walk away.

"He waited until we had all walked off before he turned away. And you knew from his stance and his face that he was concentrating so powerfully on them. And who they were, and what they had done.

"Because he knew he was unlikely to see them again."

For more information about TRAS, visit www.tras.ca.

The TRAS-supported Buddha Academy Boarding School [BABS] in Kathmandu has been run by Principal Dorje Namgyal Lama since 1991 for destitute children. Under his direction, the Nepalese school has been expanded from 60 students to more than 500 students. Founded in 1989, BABS is a charitable English-medium boarding school, started by the All Nepal Himalayan Buddhist Association. Dorje Namgyal Lama escaped from Tibet as a youngster and was educated in Mussoorie, sponsored by a TRAS member.

Old People's Home in Mussoorie, built and maintained by TRAS.

AN INVENTORY OF
TRAS PROJECTS

In the 1970s, TRAS partnered with the Incarnation Convent in Mysore where Sister Victorine (above) raised and educated Tibetan orphans. With no interest in converting them, she referred to them as "our little Buddhists." TRAS President Jennifer Hales worked with Sister Victorine for several months and met graduates and children sponsored by TRAS members. Sister Victorine has since become the Superior General of the Carmelite Sisters of St. Teresa.

After the Indian government gave 400 acres to Tibetans at Kollegal, supported by TRAS, elephants ravaged the crops. Captain Bill Davinson of MYRADA
instructed farmers to dig a ditch seven kilometres long and six feet deep,
planted with sisal that hurt the elephants' feet. Night watchmen in the few
remaining trees fired warning shots whenever herds of elephants approached.
TRAS supported the Tibetans at Kollegal as well as displaced Indians, providing
housing. Consultants were brought from Thailand to teach the displaced
Indians how to learn silk weaving after mulberry bushes were planted.

TRAS PROJECTS PRIOR TO 1967

Children's School, Mussoorie: food and clothing
Children's Home, Dharamsala: food and clothing
Children's School, Mussoorie: new roof
Maple Leaf Hospital, Kangra

102 TRAS-FUNDED PROJECTS 1967–88

North India Projects: 1967–88
Anand Nagar, Indore: 1978–79
Bankura, W.B.: 1977
Bhutan: 1971–78
Buddhist Dialectics College, Dharamsala: 1978–79
Centre for Indigenous Rural Development and Awakening: 1980
Choephelling Settlement, Miao, Arunachal Pradesh: 1976–80
Choglamar, Leh, Ladakh: 1975–79
Clement Town, Dehra Dun: 1976

Darjeeling: 1976–78

Dhar Leprosy Treatment Centre: 1977

Dukpa Dungsey Association, Darjeeling: 1973–74

Dukpa Dungsey Association, Kalimpong: 1975–76

Herbertpur: 1977–79

Himalayan Marketing Association, New Delhi: 1974–1980

Ichi Workshop: 1972–73

Indo-Tibet Buddhist Cultural Institute, Kalimpong: 1964–79

Jubar Sanatorium, Simla: 1971

Kabliji Hospital: 1977–78

Kabliji Hospital and Sardarni Harnam Kaur Trust: 1982–83

Ludhiana School for the Blind: 1978

Mainpat Tibetan Settlement: 1973–76

Marine Production Complex, Pataupakali, Photograph Book: 1981

Nehru Memorial Foundation, Clement Town, Dehra Dun: 1972–73

Nepal: 1970–79

Nepal School Building Programme, Kabhre Vocational Training: 1978, 1985

Ngor Evan Institute, Bir: 1969

Nim Tea Estate, Darjeeling: 1971

Nyingmapa Lamas' College, Clement Town, Dehra Dun: 1969–72

Rajpur: 1977–78

Rajpur Old People's Home (Mrs. Taring)

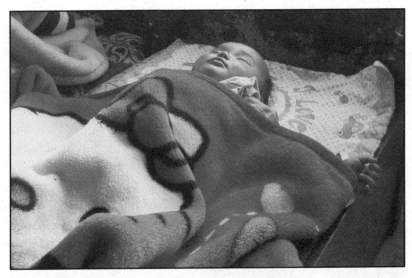

As evidenced by this 2009 photo, TRAS has long supported the Little Flower Crèche, in McLeod Ganj, near Dharamsala, as part of the Tibetan Government-in-Exile complex, for the young children of government workers.

TWO HANDS CLAPPING

Tsetan Chonjore has been communicating with his TRAS sponsor Peggy Larson of Victoria for more than 40 years. An accomplished musician, Tsetan has devoted much of his time to teaching Tibetan children traditional Tibetan music, dance and songs. While he was teaching Tibetan at UBC, he attended His Holiness the Dalai Lama's talk in Vancouver in September 2006, during which his students performed. Tsetan Chonjore currently teaches Tibetan language at the University of Virginia-Charlottesville where he also conducts research and publishes books and papers.

"His Holiness the Dalai Lama has always had great foresight and vision in emphasizing the importance of education," he writes. "But just as one hand cannot clap, vision alone cannot bring about results. Financial and other support is needed. TRAS and its sponsors comprise the other hand. His Holiness's vision and TRAS sponsors together are like two hands clapping. I am the sound they make. I am the result. I am very, very grateful."

Here, in brief, is his story.

"I was born in Xigatse, Tibet, and left with my aunt and uncle in the early 1960s when I was 12 years old. We travelled on foot and by vehicle into Nepal to a Tibetan refugee camp in Kathmandu where I learned my first 'ABCs' in the refugee school. From Nepal, I moved to Dharamsala and from there to the Tibetan settlement in Mussoorie in northern India where I studied at the Central Tibetan Administration School and boarded at the Tibetan Homes Foundation (THF) run by Mrs. Taring. One day, we children had our individual photos taken. We weren't sure why. We were simply told the photos were 'for sponsorship.' A while later I received a letter from a Mrs. Peggy Larson in Canada. I wrote back to her,

TRAS sponsor Peggy Larson with Tsetan Chonjore in Victoria in 2007

and that is how the communication and relationship between me and my sponsor began. "Mum" and I have now been communicating for over 40 years. We first met in 1980 when she made a trip to India. Then in 1986, on my first trip to North America to teach Tibetan, I visited Mum and her family in Victoria. When I was at UBC teaching, I went to Victoria to see them as often as I could. I am a part of their family.

"In Mussoorie, at times we children were casual about our letter-writing, and one time I asked a friend of mine to write my letter to Mrs. Larson. Soon after, the school received a letter from her. She had immediately recognized that the handwriting was not mine, and was concerned about what had happened to me. Her response surprised me. I had not expected her to pay such attention to me. I realized at that moment just how much my sponsor cared for me, my livelihood, my education and my future.

"While at THF, I took every opportunity to learn new things. I played on all the sports teams and I studied music, learning to play all the Tibetan instruments. I later taught music to younger children at the school.

After I finished high school, my official sponsorship through TRAS ended. But Mrs. Larson wanted to continue to pay for my education. Because of her support I was able to study Tibetan language at St. Joseph's College in Darjeeling and obtain my undergraduate degree.

"The education I received in Mussoorie and Darjeeling while sponsored by Mrs. Larson is the reason that I have been able to pursue my passion for teaching Tibetan language, culture, music, song and dance. I am where I am today because of TRAS and because of Mrs. Larson's kind and continuous support."

A Tibetan language analyst and author of a widely-used Tibetan language textbook, Tsetan Chonjore has been teaching the Tibetan language to westerners for almost three decades.

This daycare centre is just one component of the Annapurna Conservation Area Integrated Rural Development Project in Nepal, started by Barry Leach. Lynn and Frank Beck of TRAS have directed this $900,000 effort.

Rajpur Tibetan Welfare Handicrafts Centre: 1973–75

Sakya Centre, Dehra Dun: 1967–85

Sakya Centre, Rajpur: 1978

Sakya School, Bir: 1975–79

Sanjauli Settlement, Simla: 1973–75

Samdup Tarjeyling Monastery, Sonada: 1972

Samiti Medical Scheme, New Delhi: 1979–83

Scholarships for Tibetans: 1969–79

Sikkim: 1976

Simla Handicrafts Centre: 1975–79

Tezu Tibetan Settlement: 1978–82

Thascholing Lama's Centre, Manali: 1975

Tibetan Children's Village, Dharamsala: 1969–79

Tibetan Cholgum Society, Paonta: 1976

Tibetan Craft Community, Tashi Jong: 1967–79

Tibetan Handicrafts Centre, Dalhousie: 1972–79

Tibetan Homes Foundation, Mussoorie: 1971–83

Tibetan Kham Lingtsang Society, Dehra Dun: 1971

Tibetan Khampa Industrial Society, Bir: 1971–73

Tibetan Library, Dharamsala: 1973, 1975

Tibetan Monasteries, Dalhousie: 1973–76

Tibetan Muslim Association, Srinagar: 1979

Tibetan Welfare, Delek Hospital: 1975, 1976, 1979–86
Tibetan Welfare (or Medical) Hospital, Dharamsala: 1970–72, 1977
Tibetan Women's Carpet Centre, Dehra Dun: 1973–77
Tibetan Women's Centre, Rajpur: 1978–82
Tibetan Industrial Rehabilitation Society (TIRS): 1969–70
TIRS General: 1971–80
TIRS Kumrao, Paonta: 1971–79
TIRS Puruwala: 1972–85
TIRS Tibetan Settlements, Bir: 1975–79
Visit of His Holiness the Dalai Lama to North America: 1980
Vocational Rehabilitation Training Centre, Ludhiana: 1974–77

South India Projects: 1969–86
Andra Pradesh Well-Digging Schemes: 1979–80
Asian Institute for Rural Development (AIRD)
Bangalore: 1978–88
Bhandara Settlement: 1973–80
Bylakuppe, Cauvery Valley: 1976–79
Canada-India Village, Trivandrum: 1974, 1976
Cauvery Valley: 1969–73, 1979
Chandragiri, Orissa: 1975–80
Chandrakal Farmers' Welfare Society: 1974–77
CONTAK, Bangalore: 1977–80
Cyclone Disaster Relief: 1976, 1978
Cyclone Relief Projects, Sangameshwaram, Alapadu: 1979
Huthur Cooperative: 1978–80
Kerala Balagram: 1979–82
Kollegal Farmers' Settlement (or Welfare or Cooperative): 1975, 1977–78
Kollegal Tibetan Settlements: 1976, 1978
Kushta Chikitsa Sangha Chitradurga: 1972–73, 1976
Kushta Chikitsa Sangha Divengere: 1974–78
Mundgod: 1967–74, 1978
Mysore Rehabilitation and Development Agency (MYRADA)
Kollegal: 1971–74, 1979
MYRADA, General: 1975–83
Navavikas Development Scheme: 1979
Pestalozzi Children's Village, Bangalore: 1973–79
Reddypalem Well-Digging Project: 1975
Reddypalem Drinking Water: 1979–86
Reddypalem Community Development Project: 1976–79
Tibetan Cooperative, Mundgod: 1975–79
Tibetan Rehabilitation Hospital, Mundgod: 1976–79
Virajpet Community Development, Taluk: 1975–81

Other Projects 1979–85:

Arthik Samata Mandal, Sheep-Shearing Program for Subsidiary Occupation: 1979–85

Correspondence Mr. F. Williamson (Calgary Importer of Tibetan Carpets): 1980

Dairy Farming Project, Kollegal: 1978–81

Nepal Schools: 1979–83

Records of Projects: 1980–88

Refugees in Canada sponsored by TRAS: 1980–86

Tibetan Refugee Self-help Centre, Darjeeling: 1981

Vocational Training Programme, Kampuchean Refugees: 1980–82

TRAS PROJECTS 1987–2009

1987

Navavikas Village Development, S. India

Balamandir Foundling Hospital: rehabilitation training, Madras

School building, rural development, sidars, cook and guide training, Nepal

Tibetan rural housing and provision of cows at Lama Hatta and Rabongla, N. India

Rumtek Institute Building

Bokar Destitute Home

St. Alphonsus School: husbandry training

Himalayan Foothills: feasibility study and development survey

Drukpa Tibetan Handicrafts Centre, near Darjeeling

Tibetan Homes Foundation: extension of wood and metal crafts building

April 1988

Continuing and new projects:

Tibetan Agricultural Mechanics, Community Development, Orissa

Tibetan Medical Training: nurse's aides, doctors and village health workers

Amdo Secretarial Training

CTA Dept. of Education: 20 trainees in thangka painting, calligraphy, wood carving

Sakya Centre, Rajpur, N. India

Vocational Training in South India: medical, pharmacy, nurses, teachers

Onkarnath (Indian NGO Vanguard for Peace) Health Extension Project: bringing health and income generation to 50 villages, N. India

Tashi Jong Clinic Health Care Training, N. India

Kathmandu Valley: Tibetan health worker training, Nepal

Choephelling Tibetan Settlement: housing, Miao, N.E. India

Tibetan Women's Centre: housing and weaving equipment, Rajpur, N. India.

Tibetan Homes Foundation: replacement of Home 8/18, Mussoorie, N. India

Community Health Worker Training: training CHWS for Tibetan settlements in India and Nepal, Delek Tibetan Hospital, Dharamsala

Amdo Tibetan Colony: water and electricity to 35 homes, Clement Town, N. India

Ling Gesar School Addition

Tibetan Homes Foundation: addition to old people's home

February 1991

Tibetan Cultural Training: dance, thangka painting, etc., Dharamsala

Amdo Colony Vocational Training Classroom Construction

Dekyiling Rehabilitation Training Facilities

Annapurna Lodge Operators' Training

Maternal/Child Health Project for Tibetan Settlements in Kathmandu Valley

Drikung Institute Electricity and Water Supply

Amdo Secretarial Training

Shillong Students' Hostel

Village Tree Nurseries, Ramgarth

Herbertpur Drinking Water

Doeguling Tibetan Settlement, Old People Support, Mundgod

Incarnation Convent: training for teachers and nurses, S. India

CTE (Council for Tibetan Education): nurse training, Dharamsala

Central Tibetan Secretariat: training and refresher courses

Shigatse Crèche and Health Post: with funding going through Swiss Red Cross (the first TRAS
    Project inside Tibet, at Gang Gyen Carpet Factory in Shigatse, Tibet)

Central Tibetan Secretariat: support for health clinics, Dharamsala

Puruwala Tibetan Settlement: sanitary schemes

Tinetam Homes Foundation: repairs to Home 8/18, Mussoorie

Integrated Development Program, Chusul, Ladakh

Chakpori Medical Training (traditional Tibetan medical training), Darjeeling

CHIRAG (Central Himalayan Integrated Rural Action Group), Sitla, North India: Mother and
    ChildCare Project

Choephelling Tibetan Settlement, Agricultural Transport, N.E. India

Tezu Tibetan Settlement, Agricultural Income Schemes, N.E. India

Annapurna Conservation Area Integrated Rural Development Project (ACAP) in seven villages,
    Nepal

Kunphenling Tibetan Settlement, Ravangla

Bir Tibetan Settlement Drinking Water Project

Dekyiling Tibetan Settlement: weaver training

Choeling Nuns, Dharamsala: prayer hall built with support from TRAS member

Tibetan Children's Village (TCV): tailoring course, Dharamsala

Refugee Weavers Rehabilitation Training

Ladakh Solar Box Cookers

Pelshong Tibetan Medical School: traditional Tibetan medical training for 36 students, Pelshong, Tibet

Chakpori Medical Training: continuation of 110, moved to Kathmandu

Community Health Worker Training, Delek Hospital, Dharamsala

CHIRAG Social Forestry Program, Sitla, N. India

Tibetan Nuns Project: conduit for private funds from WWFT (Women Working for Tibet)

Disaster at Chauntra Settlement: rebuilding of burned-down weaving hall

Tibetan Refugee Clothing Project: conduit for private member's funds for project

Delek Hospital Lab Improvements, Dharamsala

Sister Victorine's Home for Retired Nuns: Incarnation convent project, S. India

Sister Victorine's Novices' Education, S. India

Tibetan Homes Foundation: maintenance of old people's home, Mussoorie

ITECI School, Kalimpong

Snow Lion Foundation: irrigation project for Jampa Ling Tibetan Settlement, Pokhara, Nepal

Snow Lion Foundation: Norbu Lingka Sports Club, Kathmandu

Snow Lion Foundation: donation of motorcycle, Kathmandu

Science Books Project for Tibetan Schools, India

Sister Victorine: teacher training, S. India

Tibetan Women's Centre: renovation to Nabha House for accommodation, Rajpur

Annuity from TRAS member for sponsored youth

Private English School: rent and teaching materials for young people, Lhasa, Tibet

CTA Dept. of Education Tibetan Cultural Training: thangka painting, wood carving, Tibetan language, music and dancing, Dharamsala

Little Flower Crèche for children of government workers; annual maintenance, Dharamsala

Tibetan Environmental Education: in villages, monasteries and settlements

CHIRAG Sustainable Energy Program: bio gas plants, gas cooking stoves, rainwater collection, smokeless chulas (traditional cooking stoves), Sitla, N. India

October 1993

Sangsang Primary School Reconstruction, Tibet

ACAP King Mahendra Trust Integrated Development Project, Sikles, Nepal

Drikung Kagyu Institute Bakery

Dhogu Yugyal Ling Tibetan Settlement, Dehra Dun.

Reconstruction and Horticulture, Herbertpur, N. India

Bir Sakya Lama Society Carpet Factory Tailor Training, Kangra, N. India

Dekyiling Tibetan Handicraft Settlement, Tailoring and Weaving Training, N. India

Society for Holistic Action in Rehabilitation (SHARE), Kullu Valley: toilet construction project in villages above Manali (constructing 250 toilets away from fresh water supply), N. India

NERDA: tailoring training, Meghalaya, N.E. India

Dolma Ling Nunnery Building: medical centre and two classrooms, Dharamsala

Institute of Buddhist Dialectics: purchase of computer for production of teacher training manual to teach children in Tibetan language in Tibetan schools in India, Dharamsala

February 1995

Sonam Ling Settlement: weaver training, Choglamsar, Leh, Ladakh

Kunphelling Tibetan Settlement (CTA): typhoon damage

Tibetan New Settlement, Bylakuppe: water system for village, S. India

Buddha Memorial Children's Home: vocational training for street children, carpentry, tailoring and electrician training, Kathmandu

Incarnation Convent: elementary school start-up grant, S. India

Incarnation Convent: teacher training (12 teachers), S. India

Incarnation Convent: nurse training (12 nurses), S. India

NERDA: school renovation (four classrooms for Middle School) for Tibetan settlement, N.E. India

Tibetan Refugee Service: health worker training, Choglamsar, Leh, Ladakh

Tibetan Refugee Service: rations storeroom, Choglamsar, Leh, Ladakh

CTA Dept. of Education: Tibetan language teacher training, Dharamsala

CTA Dept. of Education: Tibetan cultural and English language training, Dharamsala

Delek Hospital: community health worker training, Dharamsala

Tibetan Environmental Network: headwork upgrade, Ladakh

Snow Lion Foundation: headwater upgrade, Pokkhara, Nepal

CHIRAG: Mother and Child Care Program II, Sitla, N. India

CTA Dept. of Information and International Relations: five-day workshop for 30 Tibetan teachers on
environmental follow-up, Dharamsala

CTA Dept. of Education: nurses training, Dharamsala

Rinchen Zangpo Society for Spiti Development: teacher training for five girls for new school for
children from remote villages, Spiti, N. India

Appropriate Agricultural Alternatives (AAA): farmer training project, Kathmandu, Nepal

February 1997

Snow Lion Foundation: renovation to Tibetan old people's home, Kathmandu

Buddha Academy: one-year continuation for current carpentry/tailoring class, Kathmandu, Nepal

NERDA: school renovations, subsidy for cost overruns, Maghalaya, India

ACAP Phase II: rural development, Sikles, Nepal

International Development Education for Young Canadians, Nepal

CTA Dept. of Education: nurse training, Dharamsala

CTA Dept. of Education: thangka painting training, Dharamsala

This English class in Lhasa, sponsored by TRAS, was the creation of
Tsarong Phungyal who had endured a long imprisonment.

Marion Tipple has directed many TRAS projects for the Munsel-Ling School.

Tibetan Homes Foundation: training of two *ayas* for one hostel, Mussoorie
Tibetan Women's Centre: carpet weaving training for 20 women, Dehra Dun, N. India
Incarnation Convent: vocational training for youth (automotive, etc.), Mysore, S. India
Incarnation Convent: teacher training, Mysore, S. India
CTA Dept. of Education: vocational training for teachers and unemployed youth, Dharamsala
SHARE: Kullu Valley Toilets Phase II (750 toilets built), Manali, N. India
Incarnation Convent: nurse training, Mysore, S. India
NERDA: Shillong School renovation, Shillong, N. India
Lhasa Yuthok Kindergarten: full annual support for school, Lhasa, Tibet

May 1999
CHIRAG: Institutional Support/Health/Mother and Child (continued), Sitla, N. India (in cooperation
 with CIVA)
Institute of Buddhist Dialectics: purchase of computer and scanner, Dharamsala
CTA Dept. of Education: training of seven thangka painters, Dharamsala
CTA Dept. of Education: training of five nurses, Dharamsala
Youth Trip to Nepal Administration
Incarnation Convent: teacher training, S. India
Buddha Academy: vocational training—carpentry, tailoring, electrical (Phase II), Nepal
Bir Tibetan Community Centre Renovation, Bir, N. India

January 2000

Rinchen Zangpo Society for Spiti Development: house mothers training, Spiti

Bir Sakya Lama Society: replacement of looms, Bir, N. India

Doeguling Tibetan Settlement: new stove for old people's home kitchen, Mundgod, S. India

Mang-Yul Tibetan Society: teaching aids, library furnishing, Leh, Ladakh

Incarnation Convent: vocational training for youth (Phase II)

Inst. of Buddhist Dialectics: computer training program upgrade, Dharamsala, N. India

ACAP, Sikles Integrated Rural Development (Phase III) Sikles, Nepal

CTA Dept. of Education: pre-primary teacher training (Phase II), Dharamsala, N. India

Lhasa Yuthok Kindergarten (Phase II), Lhasa, Tibet

CHIRAG, Integrated Health and Community Welfare, Sitla, N. India (in cooperation with CIVA)

Incarnation Convent: nurse training, Mysore, S. India

Incarnation Convent: teacher training, Mysore, S. India

Didi-la's Old People: funds for old people's home furnishing, Tibet

Buddha Academy: bridge financing for vocational training, Kathmandu, Nepal

April 2002

Rinchen Zangpo Society for Spiti Dev: computer training for Munsel-Ling School, Spiti, N. India

Nepal Model Academy: support for school, Kathmandu, Nepal

One of more than 1,000 toilets that were built by SHARE with TRAS funding in the Kullu Valley of northern India

Buddha Academy: vocational training (Phase III), Kathmandu, Nepal

November 2002

SHARE: Kullu Valley immunization for all children in 30 villages, registering 700 families in a health plan (Phase III), Manali

Lhasa Yuthok Kindergarten: sustained support, Lhasa, Tibet

CTA Dept. of Education: nurse training, Dharamsala

SHARE: Manali environmental education for schools, Manali, N. India

Tibetan Women's Centre: computer purchase, Rajpur, N. India

April 2003

Mount Carmel Convent: teacher training for girls, Kottyam, S. Kerala, India

February 2004

Incarnation Convent: vocational training for youth (Phase III), S. India

Buddha Academy Vocational Training (1), Kathmandu, Nepal

Dekyiling Tibetan Handicraft Centre: crèche maintenance, Dehra Dun

This Choglamsar project clearly recognizes its partnership with TRAS.

CTA Dept. of Education: nurse training for ten women, Dharamsala
Incarnation Convent: nurse training, Mysore, S. India
Rinchen Zangpo Society for Spiti Dev: building six greenhouses, Spiti, N. India
Rinchen Zangpo Society for Spiti Dev: stocking of library, Spiti, N. India
Mustang Girls Scholarship Fund (funds remaining in Nepal after girls were educated—to be used for
    new project. Since the unrest, it has been impossible to trace, so project is in limbo)

February 2006
Nagarik Aawaz Displaced Youth Training, Kathmandu, Nepal
Buddha Academy: rebuilding of collapsed wall, Kathmandu, Nepal
Buddha Academy Vocational Training (2), Kathmandu, Nepal
Tibetan Nuns: sewing training and supplies, Lhasa, Tibet
Nepal Medical Relief Fund (after uprising in Kathmandu), Nepal
Buddha Academy: special fund for orphans from the unrest, Nepal
Munsel-Ling School: healthcare centre building, Spiti, N. India

January 2007
Buddha Academy: HIV/AIDS training and books, Kathmandu, Nepal
CIDA/TRAS Vocational Training multi-partner project (in process of applying), Dharamsala and Manali
Jamyang classroom building and vocational training, Spiti, N. India
Munsel-Ling School toilet block construction, Spiti, N. India

January 2008
Choephelling Tibetan Settlement: library books, Miao, NE. India
Little Flower Crèche: crèche for children of government workers, Dharamsala, N. India
Lhasa Yuthok Kindergarten, Lhasa, Tibet

Dekyiling Crèche: maintenance, Dehra Dun, N. India
Buddha Academy Vocational Training (3), Kathmandu, Nepal
Munsel-Ling School: healthcare workers' salaries, Spiti, N. India

January 2009
Munsel-Ling School: first large greenhouse, Spiti, N. India
Munsel-Ling School: healthcare centre dispensary supplies, Spiti
Munsel-Ling School: new beds and bedding for 380 children, Spiti
Munsel-Ling School: water distribution system and maintenance training, Spiti
Tezu Tibetan Settlement: library books, Tezu, N.E. India
CTA Dept. of Education: nurse training, Dharamsala, N India

Photographed in 2009, these students are living at the Suja School in Bir, one of many Tibetan Children's Village (TCV) schools supported by TRAS.

"The really independent writer, by the very exercise of his function, represents a revolutionary force."
— GEORGE WOODCOCK

"For the urgent task of mankind today is surely not the spreading of the Buddhist Dharma in the West or the spreading of the Christian message in the East, but the recognition and the application of those essential truths regarding suffering and compassion, and the moral precepts deriving from them, that exist in all religions, buried—as they often are—under the dispensible debris of legend and liturgy. What Sakyamuni taught, what Christ taught, have great truths in common which leaders of sects and churches have consistently obscured. The great teachers of the future, in my view, will be the men who will reveal those truths in all their simplicity and starkness and, without claiming the archaic authority of the guru, lead men to examine such truths within themselves."
— GEORGE WOODCOCK

Loving Kindness

"Right from the moment of our birth, we are under the care and kindness of our parents and then later on in our life, when we are oppressed by sickness and become old, we are again dependent on the kindness of others. Since at the beginning and end of our lives we are so dependent on other's kindness, how can it be that in the middle we neglect kindness towards others?"

— DALAI LAMA

A Precious Human Life

"Every day, think as you wake up, today I am fortunate to have woken up, I am alive, I have a precious human life, I am not going to waste it, I am going to use all my energies to develop myself, to expand my heart to others, to achieve enlightenment for the benefit of all beings, I am going to have kind thoughts towards others, I am not going to get angry, or think badly about others. I am going to benefit others as much as I can."

— DALAI LAMA

Compassion

"Usually, our concept of compassion or love refers to the feeling of closeness we have with our friends and loved ones. Sometimes compassion also carries a sense of pity. This is wrong. Any love or compassion which entails looking down on the other is not genuine compassion. To be genuine, compassion must be based on respect for the other, and on the realization that others have the right to be happy and overcome suffering, just as much as you. On this basis, since you can see that others are suffering, you develop a genuine sense of concern for them."

— DALAI LAMA